CYNICAL THEORIES

CYNICAL THEORIES

How Activist Scholarship Made Everything
about Race, Gender, and Identity
—and Why This Harms Everybody

HELEN PLUCKROSE
& JAMES LINDSAY

Pitchstone Publishing
Durham, North Carolina

Pitchstone Publishing
Durham, North Carolina
www.pitchstonebooks.com

10 9 8 7 6 5

Library of Congress Cataloging-in-Publication Data

Names: Pluckrose, Helen, author. | Lindsay, James, author.
Title: Cynical theories : how activist scholarship made everything about
    race, gender, and identity-and why this harms everybody / Helen
    Pluckrose and James Lindsay.
Description: First Edition. | Durham : Pitchstone Publishing, 2020. |
    Includes bibliographical references and index. | Summary: "Outlines the
    origin and evolution of postmodern thought over the last half century
    and argues that the unchecked spread and application of postmodern ideas
    — from academia, to activist circles, to the public at large — presents
    an authoritarian ideological threat not only to liberal democracy but
    also to modernity itself"— Provided by publisher.
Identifiers: LCCN 2019054122 (print) | LCCN 2019054123 (ebook) | ISBN
    9781634312028 (hardcover) | ISBN 9781634312035 (ebook)
Subjects: LCSH: Postmodernism. | Philosophy, Modern—20th century. |
    Authoritarianism.
Classification: LCC B831.2 .A36 2020 (print) | LCC B831.2 (ebook) | DDC
    149/.97—dc23
LC record available at https://lccn.loc.gov/2019054122
LC ebook record available at https://lccn.loc.gov/2019054123

To my husband, David, who makes all things possible, and my daughter, Lucy, who never wants to hear about postmodernism again. My work there is done.

And to my wife, Heather, who just wanted a simple life and never to have learned that any of this exists.

CONTENTS

CONTENTS

ACKNOWLEDGMENTS

We owe our gratitude to many people for making this work possible, accessible, and clear, and the list of those deserving extends well beyond those we have space to mention here. Our thanks go especially to Mike Nayna, the long-suffering editor of many early drafts of this book and our chief advisor on accessibility to the layperson. We hope we eventually grew sufficient ovaries for his satisfaction (well, Jim doesn't, but nevertheless). Thanks to Peter Boghossian for his support and editorial advice and for his constant nagging of us to spend less time arguing these points on Twitter and more on writing them in the book. Special appreciation goes to Jonathan Church for the fruitful discussions of DiAngelo's work on white fragility and his identification of the fallacy of reification, which helped us to give shape to the third stage of postmodern thought. We are indebted to Alan Sokal for his close reading of our manuscript and numerous helpful suggestions for clarifications, qualifications, and additions that greatly improved the text. We are particularly grateful to our editor, Iona Italia, for her unsurpassable wordsmithery and to everybody who provided feedback, support, and encouragement, notably including Gauri Hopkins, Dayne and Clyde Rathbone, Heather Heying, and Bret Weinstein.

INTRODUCTION

During the modern period and particularly in the last two centuries in most Western countries there has developed a broad consensus in favor of the political philosophy known as "liberalism." The main tenets of liberalism are political democracy, limitations on the powers of government, the development of universal human rights, legal equality for all adult citizens, freedom of expression, respect for the value of viewpoint diversity and honest debate, respect for evidence and reason, the separation of church and state, and freedom of religion. These liberal values developed as ideals and it has taken centuries of struggle against theocracy, slavery, patriarchy, colonialism, fascism, and many other forms of discrimination to honor them as much as we do, still imperfectly, today. But the struggle for social justice has always been strongest when it has cast itself as the defender of liberal values universally, insisting that they be applied to all individuals, not just to wealthy white males. It must be noted that the general philosophical position that we call "liberalism" is compatible with a wide range of positions on political, economic, and social questions, including both what Americans call "liberal" (and Europeans call "social-democratic") and moderate forms of what people in all countries call "conservative." This philosophical liberalism is opposed to authoritarian movements of all types, be they left-wing or right-wing, secular or theocratic. Liberalism is thus best thought of as a shared common ground, providing a framework for conflict resolution and one within which people with a variety of views on political, economic, and social questions can rationally debate the options for public policy.

However, we have reached a point in history where the liberalism and modernity at the heart of Western civilization are at great risk on the level of the ideas that sustain them. The precise nature of this threat is complicated, as it arises from at least two overwhelming pressures, one revolutionary and the other reactionary, that are waging war with each other over which illiberal direction our societies should be dragged. Far-right populist movements claiming to be making a last desperate stand for liberalism and democracy against a rising tide of progressivism and globalism are on the rise around the world. They are increasingly turning toward leadership in dictators and strongmen who can maintain and preserve "Western" sovereignty and values. Meanwhile, far-left progressive social crusaders portray themselves as the sole and righteous champions of social and moral progress without which democracy is meaningless and hollow. These, on our furthest left, not only advance their cause through revolutionary aims that openly reject liberalism as a form of oppression, but they also do so with increasingly authoritarian means seeking to establish a thoroughly dogmatic fundamentalist ideology regarding how society ought to be ordered. Each side in this fray sees the other as an existential threat, and thus each fuels the other's greatest excesses. This culture war is sufficiently intense that it has come to define political—and increasingly social—life through the beginning of the twenty-first century.

Though the problem to the right is severe and deserves much careful analysis in its own right, we have become experts in the nature of the problem on the left. This is partly because we believe that, while the two sides are driving one another to madness and further radicalization, the problem coming from the left represents a departure from its historical point of reason and strength, which is liberalism. It is that liberalism that is essential to the maintenance of our secular, liberal democracies. As we have written previously, the problem arises from the fact that,

> The progressive left has aligned itself not with Modernity but with
> postmodernism, which rejects objective truth as a fantasy dreamed

up by naive and/or arrogantly bigoted Enlightenment thinkers who underestimated the collateral consequences of Modernity's progress.[1]

It is this problem that we have dedicated ourselves to learning about and hope to explain in this volume: the problem of postmodernism, not just as it initially arose in the 1960s but also how it has evolved over the last half century. Postmodernism has, depending upon your view, either become or given rise to one of the least tolerant and most authoritarian ideologies that the world has had to deal with since the widespread decline of communism and the collapses of white supremacy and colonialism. Postmodernism was developed in relatively obscure corners of academia as an intellectual and cultural reaction to all of these changes, and since the 1960s it has spread to other parts of the academy, into activism, throughout bureaucracies, and to the heart of primary, secondary, and post-secondary education. It has, from there, begun to seep into broader society to the point where it, and backlashes against it—both reasonable and reactionary—have come to dominate our sociopolitical landscape as we grind ever more painfully into the third decade of the new millennium.

This movement nominally pursues and derives its name from a broad goal called "social justice," which is a term dating back almost two hundred years. Under different thinkers at different times, this term has taken on various meanings, all of which are concerned on some level with addressing and redressing social inequalities, particularly where it comes to issues of class, race, gender, sex, and sexuality, particularly when these go beyond the reach of legal justice. Perhaps most famously, the liberal progressive philosopher John Rawls laid out much philosophical theory dedicated to the conditions under which a socially just society might be organized. In this, he set out a universalist thought experiment in which a socially just society would be one in which an individual given a choice would be equally happy to be born into any social milieu or identity group.[2] Another, explicitly anti-liberal, anti-universal, approach to achieving social justice has also been employed, particularly since the middle of the twentieth century, and that is one rooted in *critical theory*. A critical theory is chiefly concerned with revealing hidden biases and underexamined assumptions, usually by pointing out what have been termed "problematics," which are ways in which society and the systems that it operates upon are going wrong.

Postmodernism, in some sense, was an offshoot of this critical approach that went its own theoretical way for a while and was then taken up again by critical social justice activists through the 1980s and 1990s (who, incidentally, very rarely reference John Rawls on the topic). The movement that takes up this charge presumptuously refers to its ideology simply as "Social Justice" as though it alone seeks a just society and the rest of us are all advocating for something entirely different. The movement has thus come to be known as the "Social Justice Movement" and its online critics often refer to it, for brevity, as "SocJus" or, increasingly, "wokeism" (due to its belief that it alone has "awakened" to the nature of societal injustice). Social Justice, as a proper noun with capital S and capital J, refers to a very specific doctrinal interpretation of the meaning of "social justice" and means of achieving it while prescribing a strict, identifiable orthodoxy around that term. Although we are reluctant to seem to concede the essential liberal aim for social justice to this illiberal ideological movement, this is the name by which it is known and so, for the sake of clarity, we will refer to it as capitalized "Social Justice" throughout this book. "Social justice" in the lowercase will be reserved to describe the broader and generic meanings of the term. Let us make clear our own social and political commitments: we find ourselves against capitalized Social Justice because we are generally for lowercase social justice.

It is becoming increasingly difficult to miss the influence of the Social Justice Movement on society—most notably in the form of "identity politics" or "political correctness." Almost every day, a story comes out about somebody who has been fired, "canceled," or subjected to a public shaming on social media, often for having said or done something interpreted as sexist, racist, or homophobic. Sometimes the accusations are warranted, and we can comfort ourselves that a bigot—whom we see as entirely unlike ourselves—is receiving the censure she "deserves" for her hateful views. However, increasingly often, the accusation is highly interpretive and its reasoning tortuous. It sometimes feels as though any well-intended person, even one who values universal liberty and equality, could inadvertently say something that falls foul of the new speech codes, with devastating consequences for her career and reputation. This is confusing and counterintuitive to a culture accustomed to placing human dignity first and thus valuing charitable interpretations and tolerance of a wide range of views. At best, this has a chilling effect on the culture of free expression, which has served liberal democracies well for more than two centuries, as good people self-censor to avoid saying the "wrong" things. At worst, it is a malicious form of bullying and—when institutionalized—a kind of authoritarianism in our midst.

This deserves an explanation. In fact, it *needs* one because these changes, which are happening with astonishing rapidity, are very difficult to understand. This is because they stem from a very peculiar view of the world—one that even speaks its own language, in a way. Within the English-speaking world, they speak English, but they use everyday words differently from the rest of us. When they speak of "racism," for example, they are not referring to prejudice on the grounds of race, but rather to, as they define it, a racialized system that permeates all interactions in society yet is largely invisible except to those who experience it or who have been trained in the proper "critical" methods that train them to see it. (These are the people sometimes referred to as being "woke," meaning awakened, to it.) This very precise technical usage of the word inevitably bewilders people, and, in their confusion, they may go along with things they wouldn't if they had a common frame of reference to help them understand what is actually meant by the word.

Not only do these scholar-activists speak a specialized language—while using everyday words that people assume, incorrectly, that they understand—but they also represent a wholly different *culture*, embedded within our own. People who have adopted this view may be physically close by, but, intellectually, they are a world away, which makes understanding them and communicating with them incredibly difficult. They are obsessed with power, language, knowledge, and the relationships between them. They interpret the world through a lens that detects power dynamics in every interaction, utterance, and cultural artifact—even when they aren't obvious *or real*. This is a worldview that centers social and cultural grievances and aims to make everything into a zero-sum political struggle revolving around identity markers like race, sex, gender, sexuality, and many others. To an outsider, this culture feels as though it originated on another planet, whose inhabitants have no knowledge of sexually reproducing species, and who interpret all our human sociological interactions in the most cynical way possible. But, in fact, these preposterous attitudes are completely human. They bear witness to our repeatedly demonstrated capacity to take up complex spiritual worldviews, ranging from tribal animism to hippie spiritualism to sophisticated global religions, each of which adopts its own interpretive frame through which it sees the entire world. This one just happens to be about a peculiar view of power and its ability to create inequality and oppression.

Interacting with proponents of this view requires learning not just their language—which in itself is challenging enough—but also their customs and even their mythology of "systemic" and "structural" problems inherent in our society, systems, and institutions. As experienced travelers know, there's more to communicating in a completely different culture than learning the language. One must also learn the idioms, implications, cultural references, and etiquette, which define how to communicate appropriately. Often, we need someone who is not just a translator but also an *interpreter* in the widest sense, someone savvy about both sets of customs, to communicate effectively. That is what we set out to provide in this book: a guide to the language and customs that are presently widely promoted under the pleasant-sounding moniker "Social Justice." We are fluent in both the language and culture of Social Justice scholarship and activism, and we plan to guide our readers through this alien world, charting the evolution of these ideas from their origins fifty years ago right up to the present day.

We begin in the late 1960s, when the group of theoretical concepts clustered around the nature of knowledge, power, and language that came to be known as *postmodernism* emerged from within several humanities disciplines at once. At its core, postmodernism rejected what it calls *metanarratives*—broad, cohesive explanations of the world and society. It rejected Christianity and Marxism. It also rejected science, reason, and the pillars of post-Enlightenment Western democracy. Postmodern ideas have shaped what has since mostly been called *Theory*—the entity which is, in some sense, the protagonist of this book. In our view, it is crucial to understand the development of Theory from the 1960s until the present day if we are to come to terms with and correct for the rapid shifts we have been experiencing in society ever since its inception, and especially since 2010. Of note, throughout this book, *Theory* (and related words, such as Theorist and Theoretical) with a capital T will refer to the approach to social philosophy that stems from postmodernism.

Cynical Theories explains how Theory has developed into the driving force of the culture war of the late 2010s—and proposes a philosophically *liberal* way to counter its manifestations in scholarship, activism, and everyday life. The book charts the development of the evolving branches of cynical postmodern Theory over the last fifty years and shows that it has influenced current society in ways the reader will recognize. In chapter 1, we will guide you through the key ideas of the original postmodernists of the 1960s and 1970s, and draw out two principles and four themes that have remained central to all the Theory that followed. Chapter 2 will explain how these ideas mutated, solidified, and were made politically actionable in a set of new Theories that emerged in the late 1980s and 1990s. This we will refer to as *applied postmodernism*. Chapters 3 to 6 will delve into each of the following in more detail: postcolonial Theory, queer Theory, critical race Theory, and intersectional feminism. Chapter 7 will look at the relative newcomers, disability studies and fat studies, which draw on all these Theories.

In chapter 8, we explore the second evolution of these postmodern ideas, beginning around 2010, which asserted the absolute truth of the postmodern principles and themes. This approach we call *reified postmodernism*, as it takes the assumptions of postmodernism to be real, objective truths—The Truth According to Social Justice. This change occurred when scholars and activists combined the existing Theories and Studies into a simple, dogmatic methodology, best known simply as "Social Justice scholarship."

This book aims to tell the story of how postmodernism applied its cynical Theories to deconstruct what we might agree to call "the old religions" of human thought—which include conventional religious faiths like Christianity and secular ideologies like Marxism, as well as cohesive modern systems such as science, philosophical liberalism, and "progress"—and replaced them with a new religion of its own, called

"Social Justice." This book is a story about how despair found new confidence, which then grew into the sort of firm conviction associated with religious adherence. The faith that emerged is thoroughly postmodern, which means that, rather than interpreting the world in terms of subtle spiritual forces like sin and magic, it focuses instead on subtle material forces, such as systemic bigotry, and diffuse but omnipresent systems of power and privilege.

While this new-found conviction has caused significant problems, it is also helpful that Theory has become increasingly confident and clear about its beliefs and goals. It makes it easier for liberals—from the political left, right, or center—to get at those ideas and counter them. On the other hand, this development is alarming because it has made Theory so much more easily grasped and acted upon by believers who want to reshape society. We can see its impact on the world in their attacks on science and reason. It is also evident in their assertions that society is simplistically divided into dominant and marginalized identities and underpinned by invisible systems of white supremacy, patriarchy, heteronormativity, cisnormativity, ableism, and fatphobia. We find ourselves faced with the continuing dismantlement of categories like knowledge and belief, reason and emotion, and men and women, and with increasing pressures to censor our language in accordance with The Truth According to Social Justice. We see radical relativism in the form of double standards, such as assertions that only men can be sexist and only white people can be racist, and in the wholesale rejection of consistent principles of nondiscrimination. In the face of this, it grows increasingly difficult and even dangerous to argue that people should be treated as individuals or to urge recognition of our shared humanity in the face of divisive and constraining identity politics.

Although many of us now recognize these problems and intuitively feel that such ideas are unreasonable and illiberal, it can be difficult to articulate responses to them, since objections to irrationalism and illiberalism are often misunderstood or misrepresented as opposition to genuine social justice—a legitimate philosophy that advocates a fairer society. This dissuades too many well-intentioned people from even trying. In addition to the danger of being labelled an enemy of social justice that comes with criticizing the methods of the Social Justice Movement, there are two other obstacles to effectively addressing them. First, the underlying values of Social Justice are so counterintuitive that they are difficult to understand. Second, few of us have ever had to defend universally liberal ethics, reason and evidence against those claiming to stand for social justice. They have, until quite recently, always been understood as the best way to work *for* social justice. Thus, once we have finished making the underlying principles of Social Justice Theory comprehensible, we move on to discuss how to recognize them and counter them. In chapter 9, we look at the ways in which these ideas have escaped the bounds of academia and are impacting the real world. Finally, chapter 10 will make a case that we should counter these ideas through a clearly articulated mass commitment to the universally liberal principles and rigorous, evidence-based scholarship that define modernity. With luck, our last two chapters will show how we might write the last chapter in the story of Theory—its hopefully quiet and inglorious end.

This book is therefore written for the layperson who has no background in this type of scholarship but sees the influence of it on society and wants to understand how it works. It is for the liberal to whom a just society is very important, but who can't help noticing that the Social Justice movement does not seem to facilitate this and wants to be able to make a liberal response to it with consistency and integrity. *Cynical Theories* is written for anyone from any part of the political spectrum who believes in the marketplace of ideas as a way to examine and challenge ideas and advance society and wants to be able to engage with Social Justice ideas as they really are.

This is not a book that seeks to undermine liberal feminism, activism against racism, or campaigns for LGBT equality. On the contrary, *Cynical Theories* is born of our commitment to gender, racial and LGBT equality and our concern that the validity and importance of these are currently being alarmingly undermined by Social Justice approaches. Nor will this book attack scholarship or the university in general. Quite the contrary, we seek to defend rigorous, evidence-based scholarship and the essential function of the university as a center of knowledge production against anti-empirical, anti-rational, and illiberal currents on the left that threaten to give power to anti-intellectual, anti-equality, and illiberal currents on the right.

This book, then, ultimately seeks to present a philosophically liberal critique of Social Justice scholarship and activism and argues that this scholarship-activism does not further social justice and equality aims. There are some scholars within the fields we critique who will be derisive of this and insist that we are really reactionary right-wingers opposed to studies into societal injustice experienced by marginalized people. This view of our motivations will not be able to survive an honest reading of our book. More scholars within these fields will accept our liberal, empirical, and rational stance on the issues, but reject them as a modernist delusion that centers white, male, Western, and heterosexual constructions of knowledge and maintains an unjust status quo with inadequate attempts to incrementally improve society. "The master's tools will never dismantle the master's house,"[3] they will tell us. To them, we concede that we are far less interested in dismantling liberal societies and empirical and rational concepts of knowledge and much more interested in continuing the remarkable advances for social justice that they have brought. The master's house is a good one and the problem has been limited access to it. Liberalism increases access to a solid structure that can shelter and empower everyone. Equal access to rubble is not a worthy goal. Then there will be a few scholars in these fields who believe our criticisms of Social Justice scholarship have some merits and will engage with us in good faith about them. These are the exchanges we look forward to and the ones that can set us back on the path of having productive and ideologically diverse conversations about social justice.

1 POSTMODERNISM

A Revolution in Knowledge and Power

A fundamental change in human thought took place in the 1960s. This change is associated with several French Theorists who, while not quite household names, float at the edges of the popular imagination, among them Michel Foucault, Jacques Derrida, and Jean-François Lyotard. Taking a radically new conception of the world and our relationship to it, it revolutionized social philosophy and perhaps social *everything*. Over the decades, it has dramatically altered not only what and how we think but also how we think about thinking. Esoteric, academic, and seemingly removed from the realities of daily existence, this revolution has nevertheless had profound implications for how we interact with the world and with one another. At its heart is a radical worldview that came to be known as "postmodernism."

Postmodernism is difficult to define, perhaps by design. It represents a set of ideas and modes of thought that came together in response to specific historical conditions, including the cultural impact of the World Wars and how these ended, widespread disillusionment with Marxism, the waning credibility of religious worldviews in post-industrial settings, and the rapid advance of technology. It is probably most useful to understand postmodernism as a rejection of both modern*ism*—an intellectual movement that predominated through the late nineteenth century and the first half of the twentieth—and modern*ity*—that epoch known as the Modern period, which began after the end of the Middle Ages and in which we (probably) still live. This new kind of radical skepticism to the very possibility of obtaining objective knowledge has since rippled outward from the academy, to challenge our social, cultural, and political thinking in intentionally disruptive ways.

Postmodern thinkers reacted to modern*ism* by denying the foundations of some aspects of Modern thought, while claiming that other aspects of Modern thinking didn't go far enough. In particular, they rejected the underlying modernist desire for authenticity, unifying narratives, universalism, and progress, achieved primarily through scientific knowledge and technology. At the same time, they took the modernists' relatively measured, if pessimistic, skepticism of tradition, religion, and Enlightenment-era certainty—along with their reliance on self-consciousness, nihilism, and ironic forms of critique—to extremes.[1] Postmodernism raised such radical doubts about the structure of thought and society that it is ultimately a form of cynicism.

Postmodernism is also a reaction to and rejection of modern*ity*, meaning "the profound cultural transformation which saw the rise of representative democracy, the age of science, the supersedence of reason over superstition, and the establishment of individual liberties to live according to one's values."[2] Although postmodernism openly rejects the possibility of the foundations that have built modernity, it has nevertheless had a profound impact on the thinking, culture, and politics of those societies that modernity built. As literary theorist Brian McHale points out, postmodernism became "the dominant cultural tendency (it might be safer to say a dominant tendency) during the second half of the twentieth century in the advanced industrial societies of the West, spreading eventually to other regions of the globe."[3]

Since its revolutionary beginnings, postmodernism has evolved into new forms, which have preserved its original principles and themes, while gaining increasing influence over culture, activism, and scholarship, especially in the humanities and social sciences. Understanding postmodernism is therefore a matter of some urgency precisely because it radically rejects the foundations upon which today's advanced civilizations are built and consequently has the potential to undermine them.

Postmodernism isn't just hard to define; it's also notoriously difficult to summarize. It was and is a multifaceted phenomenon, encompassing vast tracts of intellectual, artistic, and cultural terrain. To make matters more difficult, its boundaries, nature, form, purpose, values, and proponents have always been disputed. This seems fitting for a mode of thought that prides itself on plurality, contradiction, and ambiguity, but it isn't very helpful when you're trying to understand it or its philosophical and cultural descendants.

The difficulties of defining postmodernism are not just philosophical; they are spatial and temporal because it has not been one unitary movement. The first manifestations of the cultural phenomenon called "postmodernism" were artistic and appeared around 1940, but, by the late 1960s, it was far more prominent within various fields of the humanities and social sciences, including psychoanalysis, linguistics, philosophy, history, and sociology. Further, postmodernism manifested differently in these different fields and at different times. As a result, nothing in postmodern thought is entirely new, and its original thinkers constantly draw upon their precursors in the realms of surrealist art, antirealist philosophy, and revolutionary politics. Postmodernism also manifested differently from country to country, producing distinct variations on common themes. Italian postmodernists tended to foreground its aesthetic elements and viewed it as a continuation of modernism, while American postmodernists leaned toward more straightforward and pragmatic approaches. The French postmodernists were altogether more focused on the social and on revolutionary and *deconstructive* approaches to modernism.[4] It is the French approach that will be of most interest to us, because it is primarily some of the French ideas, especially about knowledge and power, which have evolved over the course of successive variants of postmodernism's central occupation, that which is often simply called *Theory*. In simpler and more actionable and concrete forms, these ideas have been incorporated into Social Justice activism and scholarship and into the mainstream social conscience—although, interestingly, this has occurred more in the English-speaking world than in France itself.

Since our ultimate focus is on the applied derivatives of postmodern thought that have become socially and culturally influential—even powerful—today, this chapter will not attempt to survey the vast terrain of postmodernism.⁵ Nor will it address the ongoing debate about which thinkers it is acceptable to call "postmodern" and whether "postmodernism" is a meaningful term, or whether it would be better to separate the critics of postmodernity from the poststructuralists and those whose work is centered on the method of *deconstruction*. There are certainly distinctions to be made, but such taxonomies are primarily of interest to academics. Instead, we are going to highlight some consistent underlying themes of postmodernism that have come to drive contemporary activism, shape educational theory and practice, and inform our current national conversations. These include skepticism about objective reality, the perception of language as the constructor of knowledge, the "making" of the individual, and the role played by power in all of these. These factors underlie the "postmodern turn," which is primarily a product of the 1960s and 1970s. Within that broad change, more specifically, we wish to explain how these foundational ideas have gained cultural popularity and legitimacy through the academy, creating a conceptual schism that underlies many of our current social, cultural, and political divisions.

THE ROOTS, PRINCIPLES, AND THEMES OF POSTMODERNISM

Postmodernism arguably emerged between 1950 and 1970—the exact dates depending upon whether one is primarily interested in its artistic or social aspects. The earliest changes began in art—we can trace them as far back as the 1940s, in the work of artists such as Argentine writer Jorge Luis Borges—but, for our purposes, the late 1960s are key, since they witnessed the emergence of French social Theorists such as Michel Foucault, Jacques Derrida, and Jean-François Lyotard, who were the original architects of what later came to be known simply as "Theory."

In Europe, in the middle of the twentieth century, a number of profound social changes happened all at once. The First and Second World Wars had shaken Europe's confidence in the notion of progress and made people anxious about the power of technology. Leftwing intellectuals across Europe thereby became suspicious of liberalism and Western civilization, which had just allowed the rise of fascism, often by the will of aggrieved electorates, with cataclysmic results. Empires collapsed, and colonialism had ceased to be morally tenable for most people. Former imperial subjects began to migrate to the West, prompting the leftist intelligentsia to pay more attention to racial and cultural inequalities and, particularly, to the ways in which structures of power had contributed to them. Activism on behalf of women and the LGBT and, in the United States, the Civil Rights Movement, were gaining broad cultural support, just as disillusionment with Marxism—until then, the main, longstanding leftist social-justice cause—was spreading through the political and cultural left. Given the catastrophic results of communism everywhere it had been put into practice, this disillusionment was well founded and radically altered the worldviews of leftist cultural elites. As a result, confidence in science, which was still ascendant in every meaningful regard, was interrogated for its role in enabling, producing, and justifying the previously impossible horrors of the preceding century. Meanwhile, a vibrant youth culture was beginning to form, producing a powerful popular culture, which vied with "high culture" for dominance. Technology also began to advance rapidly, which, together with the mass production of consumer goods, enabled this "middle culture" to fuel a new postrationing desire for art, music, and entertainment. This, in turn, sparked fears that society was degenerating into an artificial, hedonistic, capitalist, consumerist world of fantasy and play.

This reaction often took the form of the pervasive pessimism that characterizes postmodern thinking, fueling fears about human hubris on one hand and the loss of meaning and authenticity on the other. This despair was so pronounced that postmodernism itself could be characterized as a profound cultural crisis of confidence and authenticity alongside a growing distrust of liberal social orders. Growing fears of the loss of meaning caused by rapid improvements in technology defined the era.

Postmodernism was particularly skeptical of science and other culturally dominant ways of legitimizing claims as "truths" and of the grand, sweeping explanations that supported them. It called them *metanarratives*,[6] which it viewed as a kind of cultural mythology and a significant form of human myopia and arrogance. Postmodernism posited a radical and total skepticism about such narratives. This skepticism was so profound as to be better understood as a type of cynicism about the entire history of human progress, and as such, it was a perversion of a sweeping cultural current of skepticism that long preceded it. Skepticism of sweeping narratives—though not cynicism about them—was prominent in Enlightenment thought and in modernism and had been gaining momentum in Western societies for several centuries by the time postmodernism showed up in the 1960s.

In its earlier forms, broad but reasonable cultural skepticism was crucial to the development of scientific and other forms of Enlightenment thought, which had had to break away from previous dominant metanarratives (mostly of a religious nature). For example, during the sixteenth century, Christianity was reevaluated as a result of the Reformation (during which the religion splintered, forming numerous Protestant sects, all challenging both the preceding orthodoxy and each other). At the end of the sixteenth century, treatises against atheism also began to appear, which clearly suggests that disbelief in God had begun to circulate. During the seventeenth century, medicine and anatomy, which had previously been modeled on the knowledge of the ancient Greeks, underwent a revolution and knowledge of the body advanced rapidly. The Scientific Revolution was the result of widespread questioning of received wisdom and the rapid proliferation of different kinds of knowledge production. The development of the scientific method in the nineteenth century was centered on skepticism and the need for increasingly rigorous testing and falsification.

Beyond cynical "skepticism," the postmodernists had concerns about the deaths of authenticity and meaning in modern society that also carried considerable weight, especially with French Theorists. These concerns were especially acutely expressed by Jean Baudrillard. For Baudrillard, whose nihilistic despair at the loss of the "real" drew heavily on the work of French psychoanalyst Jacques Lacan, all realities had become mere simulations (imitations of real-world phenomena and systems) and simulacra ("copies" of things without an original).[7] Baudrillard described three levels of simulacra: associated with the premodern, modern, and postmodern. In premodern times—those before Enlightenment thought revolutionized our relationship to knowledge—he said, unique realities existed, and people attempted to represent them. In the modern period, this link broke down because items began to be mass-produced and each original could therefore have many identical copies. In the postmodern period, he concluded, there is no original and all is simulacra, which are unsatisfactory imitations and images of the real. This state Baudrillard referred to as the *hyperreal*.[8] This evinces the postmodernists' tendency to seek the roots of meaning in language and to become overly concerned with the ways in which it shapes social reality through its ability to constrain and shape knowledge—that which represents what is true.

These same authenticity-threatening phenomena were central concerns of other postmodern thinkers as well. French philosophers Gilles Deleuze and Félix Guattari, for instance, argued that the self was being constrained by capitalist, consumer society.[9] In a similar vein, the American Marxist scholar Frederic Jameson particularly deplored the shallowness of postmodernity, which he saw as being all surface with no deeper meaning. Like Baudrillard, he regarded the postmodern state as one of *simulation*—everything is artificial and comprised of mere copies, not originals. In a typical expression of the despair at the heart of postmodernism, he diagnosed a *waning of affect*—the idea that there is no longer any heart to anything. For Jameson, surface aesthetics preoccupy our attention and distance and distract people from caring too deeply. In this way, he also openly complained about the cynicism at the heart of postmodernity. "The death of the subject," as he calls it, refers to a loss of individuality and confidence in a stable self. "Pastiche," he said, had replaced parody: there was no purpose or depth to mimicry, only a relentless borrowing and recycling. The satiety provided by cheaply available experiences had evoked a constant *sublime*—a perpetual artificial euphoria. Overall, this aimlessness and loss of purpose and grounding had resulted in *nostalgia*—a constant looking backwards in search of our present.[10] Crucially, all this profound hopelessness at the center of criticisms of postmodernity was largely descriptive rather than prescriptive. Prescriptions would come later.

The reactionary skepticism about modernism and modernity that characterizes postmodern thought found especially sharp expression in dissatisfaction with and anxiety about technology and consumer societies. This produced, at least in academics focused on cultural criticism, what the philosopher, sociologist, and literary critic Jean-François Lyotard would in 1979 summarize as "the postmodern condition." This he characterized as a profound skepticism of the possibility of any broad meaning-making structure underpinning people's lives. The anthropologist and geographer David Harvey refers to this situation as "the condition of postmodernity," which he sees as resulting from "the breakdown of the Enlightenment project."[11] Ultimately, these thinkers are referring to a general feeling that the scientific and ethical certainties that characterized much thought about modernity had become untenable, and the loss of their preferred analytic tools rendered the situation completely hopeless. Their summary of this state took the form of an extremely radical skepticism and profound cynicism, particularly about language, knowledge, power, and the individual.[12]

What, though, is postmodernism? The online *Encyclopedia Britannica* defines postmodernism as

> a late 20th-century movement characterized by broad skepticism, subjectivism, or relativism; a general suspicion of reason; and an acute sensitivity to the role of ideology in asserting and maintaining political and economic power.[13]

Walter Truett Anderson, writing in 1996, describes the four pillars of postmodernism:

1. The social construction of the concept of the self: Identity is constructed by many cultural forces and is not given to a person by tradition;

2. Relativism of moral and ethical discourse: Morality is not found but made. That is, morality is not based on cultural or religious tradition, nor is it the mandate of Heaven, but is constructed by dialogue and choice. This is relativism, not in the sense of being nonjudgmental, but in the sense of believing that all forms of morality are socially constructed cultural worldviews;

3. Deconstruction in art and culture: The focus is on endless playful improvisation and variations on themes and a mixing of "high" and "low" culture; and

4. Globalization: People see borders of all kinds as social constructions that can be crossed and reconstructed and are inclined to take their tribal norms less seriously.[14]

Many agree that postmodernism is centered on a number of primary themes, no matter how much postmodernists might resist such a characterization. (We might describe these themes as the basis of a "postmodern metanarrative.") For Steinar Kvale, professor of psychology and director of the Center of Qualitative Research, the central themes of postmodernism include doubting that any human truth provides an objective representation of reality, focusing on language and the way societies use it to create their own local realities, and denying the universal.[15] These, he explains, resulted in an increased interest in narrative and storytelling, particularly when "truths" are situated within particular cultural constructs, and a relativism that accepts that different descriptions of reality cannot be measured against one another in any final—that is, objective—way.[16]

The key observation, following Kvale,[17] is that the postmodern turn brought about an important shift away from the modernist dichotomy between the objective universal and the subjective individual and toward local narratives (and the lived experiences of their narrators). In other words, the boundary between that which is objectively true and that which is subjectively experienced ceased to be accepted. The perception of society as formed of individuals interacting with universal reality in unique ways—which underlies the liberal principles of individual freedom, shared humanity, and equal opportunities—was replaced by multiple allegedly equally valid knowledges and truths, constructed by groups of people with shared markers of identity related to their positions in society. Knowledge, truth, meaning, and morality are therefore, according to postmodernist thinking, culturally constructed and relative products of individual cultures, none of which possess the necessary tools or terms to evaluate the others.

At the heart of the postmodern turn is a reaction to and rejection of modernism and modernity.[18] According to Enlightenment thinking, objective reality can be known through more or less reliable methods. Knowledge about objective reality produced by the scientific method enabled us to build modernity and permits us to continue doing so. For postmodernism, by contrast, reality is ultimately the product of our socialization and lived experiences, as constructed by systems of language.

The sociologist Steven Seidman, who coined the term "the postmodern turn," recognized the profundity of this change in 1994: "A broad social and cultural shift is taking place in Western societies. The concept of the 'postmodern' captures at least certain aspects of this social change."[19] Walter Truett Anderson, writing in 1996, puts it more strongly: "We are in the midst of a great, confusing, stressful and enormously promising historical transition, and it has to do with a change not so much in *what* we believe but *how* we believe. . . . People all over the world are making such shifts in belief—to be more precise, shifts in belief about belief."[20] What Seidman and Anderson are describing here are changes in *epistemology*—that is, in how we obtain and understand knowledge. The postmodern turn is primarily characterized by a rejection of Enlightenment values, especially its values regarding the production of knowledge, which it associates with power and its unjust application. The postmodern view of the Enlightenment is therefore a very narrow one that is accordingly easy to be cynical about.[21] Ultimately, the Enlightenment that postmodernists rejected is defined by a belief in objective knowledge, universal truth, science (or evidence more broadly) as a method for obtaining objective knowledge, the power of reason, the ability to communicate straightforwardly via language, a universal human nature, and individualism. They also rejected the belief that the West has experienced significant progress due to the Enlightenment and will continue to do so if it upholds these values.[22]

TWO PRINCIPLES AND FOUR THEMES

Postmodern thinkers approached the rejection of modernism and Enlightenment thought, especially with regard to universal truths, objective knowledge, and individuality, in strikingly different ways. But we can spot a few consistent themes. The postmodern turn involves two inextricably linked core principles—one regarding knowledge and one regarding politics—which act as the foundation of four significant themes. These principles are

- **The postmodern knowledge principle**: Radical skepticism about whether objective knowledge or truth is obtainable and a commitment to cultural constructivism.

- **The postmodern political principle**: A belief that society is formed of systems of power and hierarchies, which decide what can be known and how.

The four major themes of postmodernism are

1. The blurring of boundaries
2. The power of language
3. Cultural relativism
4. The loss of the individual and the universal

Together, these six major concepts allow us to identify postmodern thinking and understand how it operates. They are the core principles of Theory, which have remained largely unchanged even as postmodernism and its applications have evolved from their deconstructive and hopeless beginnings to the strident, almost religious activism of today. This is the phenomenon we wish to examine, which arose from various theoretical approaches in the humanities, particularly that going by the term "cultural studies," mainly over the last century, and developed into the postmodernist Social Justice scholarship, activism, and culture we see today.

THE POSTMODERN KNOWLEDGE PRINCIPLE

Radical skepticism as to whether objective knowledge or truth is obtainable and a commitment to cultural constructivism

Postmodernism is defined by a radical skepticism about the accessibility of objective truth. Rather than seeing objective truth as something that exists and that can be provisionally known (or approximated) through processes such as experimentation, falsification, and defeasibility—as Enlightenment, modernist, and scientific thought would have it—postmodern approaches to knowledge inflate a small, almost banal kernel of truth—that we are limited in our ability to know and must express knowledge through language, concepts and categories—to insist that *all* claims to truth are value-laden constructs of culture. This is called *cultural constructivism* or *social constructivism*. The scientific method, in particular, is not seen as a better way of producing and legitimizing knowledge than any other, but as one cultural approach among many, as corrupted by biased reasoning as any other.

Cultural constructivism is not the belief that reality is *literally* created by cultural beliefs—it doesn't argue, for instance, that when we erroneously believed the Sun went around the Earth, our beliefs had any influence over the solar system and its dynamics. Instead, it is the position that humans are so tied into their cultural frameworks that all truth or knowledge claims are merely representations of those frameworks—we have decided that "it is true" or "it is known" that the Earth goes round the Sun *because of the way we establish truth in our current culture*. That is, although reality doesn't change in accordance with our beliefs, what *does* change is what we are able to regard as true (or false—or "crazy") about reality. If we belonged to a culture that produced and legitimated knowledge differently, within that cultural paradigm it might be "true" that, say, the Sun goes round the Earth. Those who would be regarded as "crazy" to disagree would change accordingly.

Although the claim that "we make reality with our cultural norms" is not the same as the claim that "we decide what is true/what is known according to our cultural norms," in practice this is a distinction without a difference. The postmodern approach to knowledge denies that objective truth or knowledge is that which corresponds with reality as determined by evidence—regardless of the time or culture in question and regardless of whether that culture believes that evidence is the best way to determine truth or knowledge. Instead, the postmodern approach might acknowledge that objective reality exists, but it focuses on the barriers to knowing that reality by examining cultural biases and assumptions and theorizing about how they work.[23]

This is what the American postmodern philosopher Richard Rorty refers to when he writes, "We need to make a distinction between the claim that the world is out there and the claim that the truth is out there."[24] In this sense, postmodernism rests upon a broad rejection of the *correspondence theory of truth*: that is, the position that there are objective truths and that they can be established as true by their correspondence with how things actually are in the world.[25] That there are real truths about an objective reality "out there" and that we can come to know them is, of course, at the root of Enlightenment thinking and central to the development of science. Profoundly radical skepticism about this idea is central to postmodern thinking about knowledge.

French philosopher Michel Foucault—a central figure of postmodernism—expresses this same doubt when he argues that, "in any given culture and at any given moment, there is always only one episteme that defines the conditions of possibility of all knowledge, whether expressed in a theory or silently invested in a practice."[26] Foucault was especially interested in the relationship between language, or, more specifically, *discourse* (ways of talking about things), the production of knowledge, and power. He explored these ideas at length throughout the 1960s, in such influential works as *Madness and Civilization* (1961), *The Birth of the Clinic* (1963), *The Order of Things* (1966), and *The Archaeology of Knowledge* (1969).[27] For Foucault, a statement reveals not just information but also the rules and conditions of a discourse. These then determine the construction of truth claims and knowledge. Dominant discourses are extremely powerful because they determine what can be considered true, thus applicable, in a given time and place. Thus, sociopolitical power is the ultimate determiner of what is true in Foucault's analysis, not correspondence with reality. Foucault was so interested in the concept of how power influences what is considered knowledge that in 1981 he coined the term "power-knowledge" to convey the inextricable link between powerful discourses and what is known. Foucault called a dominant set of ideas and values an *episteme* because it shapes how we identify and interact with knowledge.

In *The Order of Things*, Foucault argues against objective notions of truth and suggests we think instead in terms of "regimes of truth," which change according to the specific episteme of each culture and time. As a result, Foucault adopted the position that there are no fundamental principles by which to discover truth and that all knowledge is "local" to the knower[28]—ideas which form the basis of the postmodern knowledge principle. Foucault didn't deny that a reality exists, but he doubted the ability of humans to transcend our cultural biases enough to get at it.

The main takeaway from this is that postmodern skepticism is not garden-variety skepticism, which might also be called "reasonable doubt." The kind of skepticism employed in the sciences and other rigorous means of producing knowledge asks, "How can I be sure this proposition is true?" and will only tentatively accept as a provisional truth that which survives repeated attempts to disprove it. These propositions are put forth in models, which are understood to be provisional conceptual constructs, which are used to explain and predict phenomena and are judged according to their ability to do so. The principle of skepticism common among postmodernists is frequently referred to as "*radical skepticism.*" It says, "All knowledge is constructed: what is interesting is theorizing about why knowledge got constructed this way." Thus, radical skepticism is markedly different from the scientific skepticism that characterized the Enlightenment. The postmodern view wrongly insists that scientific thought is unable to distinguish itself as especially reliable and rigorous in determining what is and isn't true.[29] Scientific reasoning is construed as a *metanarrative*—a sweeping explanation of how things work—and postmodernism is radically skeptical of all such explanations. In postmodern thinking, that which is known is only known within the cultural paradigm that produced the knowledge and is therefore representative of its systems of power. As a result, postmodernism regards knowledge as provincial and intrinsically political.

This view is widely attributed to the French philosopher Jean-François Lyotard, who critiqued science, the Enlightenment, and Marxism.

Each of these projects was, for Lyotard, a prime example of a modernist or Enlightenment metanarrative. Ultimately, Lyotard feared that science and technology were just one "language game"—one way of legitimating truth claims—and that they were taking over all other language games. He mourned the demise of small local "knowledges" passed on in narrative form and viewed the loss of meaning-making intrinsic to scientific detachment as a loss of valuable narratives. Lyotard's famous characterization of postmodernism as a "skepticism towards metanarratives" has been extremely influential on the development of postmodernism as a school of thought, analytical tool, and worldview.[30]

This was the great postmodernist contribution to knowledge and knowledge production. It did not invent the skeptical reevaluation of well-established beliefs. It did, however, fail to appreciate that scientific and other forms of liberal reasoning (such as arguments in favor of democracy and capitalism) are not so much metanarratives (though they can adopt these) as imperfect but self-correcting processes that apply a productive and actionable form of skepticism to everything, including themselves. This mistake led them into their equally misguided political project.

THE POSTMODERN POLITICAL PRINCIPLE

A belief that society is formed of systems of power and hierarchies,
which decide what can be known and how

Postmodernism is characterized politically by its intense focus on power as the guiding and structuring force of society, a focus which is codependent on the denial of objective knowledge. Power and knowledge are seen as inextricably entwined—most explicitly in Foucault's work, which refers to knowledge as "power-knowledge." Lyotard also describes a "strict interlinkage"[31] between the language of science and that of politics and ethics, and Derrida was profoundly interested in the power dynamics embedded in hierarchical binaries of superiority and subordination that he believed exist within language. Similarly, Gilles Deleuze and Félix Guattari saw humans as *coded* within various systems of power and constraint and free to operate only within capitalism and the flow of money. In this sense, for postmodern Theory, power decides not only what is factually correct but also what is morally good—power implies domination, which is bad, whereas subjugation implies oppression, the disruption of which is good. These attitudes were the prevailing mood at the Sorbonne in Paris through the 1960s, where many of the early Theorists were strongly intellectually influenced.

Because of their focus on power dynamics, these thinkers argued that the powerful have, both intentionally and inadvertently, organized society to benefit them and perpetuate their power. They have done so by legitimating certain ways of talking about things as true, which then spread throughout society, creating societal rules that are viewed as common sense and perpetuated on all levels. Power is thus constantly reinforced through discourses legitimized or mandated within society, including expectations of civility and reasoned discourse, appeals to objective evidence, and even rules of grammar and syntax. As a result, the postmodernist view is difficult to fully appreciate from the outside because it looks very much like a conspiracy theory. In fact, the conspiracies it alludes to are subtle and, in a way, not *conspiracies* at all, since there are no coordinated actors pulling the strings; instead, we're all participants. Theory, then, is a conspiracy theory with no conspirators in particular. In postmodern Theory, power is not exercised straightforwardly and visibly from above, as in the Marxist framework, but permeates all levels of society and is enforced by everyone, through routine interactions, expectations, social conditioning, and culturally constructed discourses that express a particular understanding of the world. This controls which hierarchies are preserved—through, say, due process of law or the legitimizing mechanism of scientific publishing—and the systems within which people are positioned or coded. In each of these examples, note that it is the *social system* and its inherent power dynamics that are seen as the causes of oppression, not necessarily willful individual agents. Thus, a society, social system, or institution can be seen as in some way oppressive without any individual involved with it needing to be shown to hold even a single oppressive view.

The postmodernists do not necessarily see the system of oppression as the result of a consciously coordinated, patriarchal, white supremacist, heteronormative conspiracy. Instead, they regard it as the inevitable result of self-perpetuating systems that privilege some groups over others, which constitute an *un*conscious, *un*coordinated conspiracy inherent to systems involving power. They believe, however, that those systems are patriarchal, white supremacist, and heteronormative, and therefore necessarily grant unfair access to straight, white Western men and work to maintain that status quo by excluding the perspectives of women and of racial and sexual minorities.

Put more simply, one central belief in postmodern political thought is that powerful forces in society essentially order society into categories and hierarchies that are organized to serve their own interests. They effect this by dictating how society and its features can be spoken about and what can be accepted as true. For example, a demand that someone provide evidence and reasoning for their claims will be seen through a postmodernist Theoretical lens as a request to participate within a system of discourses and knowledge production that was built by powerful people who valued these approaches and designed them to exclude alternative means of communicating and producing "knowledge." In other words, Theory views science as having been organized in a way that serves the interests of the powerful people who established it—white Western men—while setting up barriers against the participation of others. Thus, the cynicism at the heart of Theory is evident.

Because they focused on self-perpetuating systems of power, few of the original postmodern Theorists advocated any specific political actions, preferring instead to engage in playful disruption or nihilistic despair. Indeed, meaningful change was largely regarded as impossible under the original postmodernism, due to the inherent meaninglessness of everything and the culturally relative nature of morality. Nevertheless, throughout postmodern Theory runs the overtly left-wing idea that oppressive power structures constrain humanity and are to be deplored. This results in an ethical imperative to deconstruct, challenge, problematize (find and exaggerate the problems within), and resist all ways of thinking that support oppressive structures of power, the categories relevant to power structures, and the language that perpetuates them— thus embedding a value system into what might have been a moderately useful descriptive theory.

This impulse generates a parallel drive to prioritize the narratives, systems, and knowledges of marginalized groups. Foucault is the most explicit about the ever-present danger of oppressive systems:

> My point is not that everything is bad, but that everything is dangerous, which is not exactly the same as bad. If everything is dangerous, then we always have something to do. So, my position leads not to apathy but to a hyper- and pessimistic activism. I think that the ethico-political choice we have to make every day is to determine which is the main danger.[32]

Postmodern Theorists often present this perception as innovative, but, again, it is hardly new except in its aims for revolution (in the French style). The gradual formation of liberal, secular democracy over the Enlightenment and the Modern periods was characterized by struggles against oppressive forces and the search for freedom. The battle against the hegemony of the Catholic Church was primarily an ethical and political conflict. The French Revolution opposed both church and monarchy. The American Revolution opposed British colonial rule and nonrepresentative government. Throughout these earlier periods, institutions like, first, monarchical rule and slavery, then patriarchy and class systems, and finally enforced heterosexuality, colonialism, and racial segregation were challenged by *liberalism*—and overcome. Progress occurred fastest of all in the 1960s and 1970s, when racial and gender discrimination became illegal and homosexuality was decriminalized. This all occurred *before* postmodernism became influential. Postmodernism did not invent ethical opposition to oppressive power systems and hierarchies—in fact, much of the most significant social and ethical progress occurred during the preceding periods that it rejects and continues to be brought about by applying the methods of liberalism.

The postmodern approach to ethically driven social critique is intangible and unfalsifiable. As the idea of radical skepticism shows, postmodern thought relies upon Theoretical principles and ways of seeing the world, rather than truth claims. Because of its rejection of objective truth and reason, postmodernism refuses to substantiate itself and cannot, therefore, be argued with. The postmodern perception, Lyotard writes, makes no claim to be true: "Our hypotheses, therefore, should not be accorded predictive value in relation to reality, but strategic value in relation to the question raised."[33] In other words, postmodern Theory seeks not to be factually true but to be strategically useful: in order to bring about its own aims, morally virtuous and politically useful by its own definitions.

This generalized skepticism about the objectivity of truth and knowledge—and commitment to regarding both as culturally construct-ed—leads to a preoccupation with four main themes: the blurring of boundaries, the power of language, cultural relativism, and the loss of the individual and the universal in favor of group identity.

1. The Blurring of Boundaries

Radical skepticism as to the possibility of objective truth and knowl-edge, combined with a belief in cultural constructivism in the service of power, results in a suspicion of all the boundaries and categories that previous thinkers widely accepted as true. These include not only the boundaries between objective and subjective and between truth and be-lief, but also those between science and the arts (especially for Lyotard), the natural and the artificial (particularly for Baudrillard and Jameson), high and low culture (see Jameson), man and other animals, and man and machine (in Deleuze), and between different understandings of sex-uality and gender as well as health and sickness (see, especially, Foucault). Almost every socially significant category has been intentionally compli-cated and problematized by postmodern Theorists in order to deny such categories any objective validity and disrupt the systems of power that might exist across them.

2. The Power of Language

Under postmodernism, many ideas that had previously been regarded as objectively true came to be seen as mere constructions of language. Fou-cault refers to them as "discourses" that construct knowledge; Lyotard, expanding upon Wittgenstein, calls them "language games" that legiti-mize knowledges. In postmodern thought, language is believed to have enormous power to control society and how we think and thus is inherently dangerous. It is also seen as an unreliable way of producing and transmitting knowledge.

The obsession with language is at the heart of postmodern thinking and key to its methods. Few thinkers exhibit the neurotic postmodern fixation upon words more explicitly than Jacques Derrida, who, in 1967, published three texts—*Of Grammatology*, *Writing and Difference*, and *Speech and Phenomena*—in which he introduced a concept that would become very influential in postmodernism: *deconstruction*. In these works, Derrida rejects the commonsense idea that words refer straightforwardly to things in the real world.[34] Instead, he insists that words refer only to other words and to the ways in which they differ from one another, thus forming chains of "signifiers," which can go off in all directions with no anchor—this being the meaning of his famous and often-mistranslated phrase, "there is nothing [read: no meaning] outside of text."[35] For Derrida, meaning is always relational and deferred, and can never be reached and exists only in relation to the discourse in which it is embedded. This unreliability of language, Derrida argues, means that it cannot represent reality or communicate it to others.

In this understanding, language operates hierarchically through binaries, always placing one element above another to make meaning. For example, "man" is defined in opposition to "woman" and taken to be superior. Additionally, for Derrida, the speaker's meaning has no more authority than the hearer's interpretation and thus intention cannot outweigh impact. Thus, if someone says that there are certain features of a culture that can generate problems, and I choose to interpret this statement as a dog whistle about the inferiority of that culture and take offense, there is no space in Derridean analysis to insist that my offense followed from a misunderstanding of what had been said. The author's intentions are irrelevant, when those can be known, due to Derrida's adaptation of Roland Barthes' concept of "the death of the author."[36] Consequently, since discourses are believed to create and maintain oppression, they have to be carefully monitored and deconstructed. This has obvious implications for moral and political action. The most common postmodernist response to this derives from Derrida's proposed solution: to read "deconstructively," by looking for internal inconsistencies (*aporia*) in which a text contradicts and undermines itself and its own purposes when the words are examined closely enough (which is to say, too closely and, especially since the 1990s, with an agenda—Theory's normative agenda). In practice, deconstructive approaches to language therefore look very much like nitpicking at words in order to deliberately miss the point.

3. Cultural Relativism

Because, in postmodern Theory, truth and knowledge are believed to have been constructed by the dominant discourses and language games that operate within a society, and because we cannot step outside our own system and categories and therefore have no vantage point from which to examine them, Theory insists that no one set of cultural norms can be said to be better than any other. For postmodernists, any meaningful critique of a culture's values and ethics from within a different culture is impossible, since each culture operates under different concepts of knowledge and speaks only from its own biases. All such critique is therefore erroneous at best and a moral infraction at worst, since it presupposes one's own culture to be objectively superior. Moreover, Theory insists that, although one can critique one's own culture from within the system, one can only do so using discourses available in that system, which limit its ability to change. Which discourses one can use is largely dependent on one's position within the system, therefore critiques can be accepted or dismissed depending on a political assessment of the status of the critic's position. In particular, criticism from any position deemed powerful tends to be dismissed because it is assumed either to be ignorant (or dismissive) of the realities of oppression, by definition, or a cynical attempt to serve the critic's own interests. The postmodern belief that individuals are vehicles of discourses of power, depending on where they stand in relation to power, makes cultural critique completely hopeless except as a weapon in the hands of those Theorized to be marginalized or oppressed.

4. The Loss of the Individual and the Universal

Consequently, to postmodern Theorists, the notion of the autonomous individual is largely a myth. The individual, like everything else, is a product of powerful discourses and culturally constructed knowledge. Equally, the concept of the universal—whether a biological universal about human nature; or an ethical universal, such as equal rights, freedoms, and opportunities for all individuals regardless of class, race, gender, or sexuality—is, at best, naive. At worst, it is merely another exercise in power-knowledge, an attempt to enforce dominant discourses on everybody. The postmodern view largely rejects both the smallest unit of society—the individual—and the largest—humanity—and instead focuses on small, local groups as the producers of knowledge, values, and discourses. Therefore, postmodernism focuses on sets of people who are understood to be positioned in the same way—by race, sex, or class, for example—and have the same experiences and perceptions due to this positioning.

ISN'T POSTMODERNISM DEAD?

The prevailing view among many thinkers today is that postmodernism has died out. We don't think it has. We think it has merely matured, mutated, and evolved (at least twice since its origins in the 1960s) and that the two characteristic principles and four themes detailed above remain pervasive and culturally influential. Theory is intact, although the ways in which its core principles and themes are presented, used, and interacted with have changed significantly over the last half-century. It is Theory as it is currently being applied that concerns us most and forms the subject of the rest of this book. Before explaining how Theory evolved, however, we should put to rest the common myth that postmodernism died two or three decades ago.

There are many arguments about when exactly postmodernism allegedly died. Some argue that it ended in the 1990s, giving way to postcolonialism; others that it ended with September 11, 2001, when we entered a new era whose character has yet to be determined. It is certainly true that the proliferation of postmodern texts in the second half of the 1960s, 1970s, and much of the 1980s did not continue into the 1990s. The early forms of postmodernism—with their ultimate meaninglessness, lack of direction, and concern only to deconstruct, disrupt, and problematize without providing any resources for rebuilding—could only survive for so long. In that sense, postmodern Theory's *high deconstructive phase* burnt itself out by the mid-1980s. But did postmodernism and Theory end there? They did not. Far from dying out, the ideas set out in this chapter evolved and diversified into distinct strands—the cynical Theories we have to live with today—and became more goal-oriented and actionable. For this reason, we call the next wave of activism-scholarship *applied postmodernism*, and it is to this development we now turn our attention.

2 POSTMODERNISM'S APPLIED TURN

Making Oppression Real

Postmodernism first burst onto the intellectual scene in the late 1960s and quickly became wildly fashionable among leftist and left-leaning academics. As the intellectual fad grew, its proselytes set to work, producing reams of radically skeptical Theory, in which existing knowledge and ways of obtaining knowledge understood as belonging to Western-modernity were indiscriminately criticized and dismantled. The old religions—in the broadest sense of the word—had to be torn down. Thus, the ideas that we can come to know objective reality and that what we call "truth" in some way corresponds to it were placed on the chopping block, together with the assumptions that modernity had been built upon. The postmodernists sought to render absurd our ways of understanding, approaching, and living in the world and in societies. Despite proving simultaneously modish and influential, this approach had its limits. Endless dismantling and disruption—or, as they call it, *deconstruction*—is not only destined to consume itself; it is also fated to consume everything interesting and thus render itself *boring*.[1]

That is, Theory couldn't content itself with nihilistic despair. It needed something to do, something actionable. Because of its own morally and politically charged core, it had to apply itself to the problem it saw at the core of society: unjust access to power. After its first big bang beginning in the late 1960s, the high deconstructive phase of postmodernism burnt itself out by the early 1980s. But postmodernism did not die. From the ashes arose a new set of Theorists whose mission was to make some core tenets of postmodernism applicable and to *reconstruct* a better world.

The common wisdom among academics is that, by the 1990s, postmodernism had died.[2] But, in fact, it simply mutated from its earlier high deconstructive phase into a new form. A diverse set of highly politicized and actionable Theories developed out of postmodernism proper. We will call this more recent development *applied postmodernism*. This change occurred as a new wave of Theorists emerged in the late 1980s and early 1990s. These new applied postmodernists also came from different fields, but, in many respects, their ideas were much more alike than those of their predecessors and provided a more user-friendly approach. During this turn, Theory mutated into a handful of Theories—postcolonial, queer, and critical race—that were put to work in the world to deconstruct social injustice.

We therefore might think of postmodernism as a kind of fast-evolving virus. Its original and purest form was unsustainable: it tore its hosts apart and destroyed itself. It could not spread from the academy to the general population because it was so difficult to grasp and so seemingly removed from social realities. In its evolved form, it spread, leaping the "species" gap from academics to activists to everyday people, as it became increasingly graspable and actionable and therefore more contagious. It mutated around a core of Theory to form several new strains, which are far less playful and far more certain of their own (meta)narratives. These are centered on a practical aim that was absent before: to reconstruct society in the image of an ideology which came to refer to itself as "Social Justice."

THE MUTATION OF THEORY

For postmodernists, Theory refers to a specific set of beliefs, which posit that the world and our ability to gather knowledge about it work in accordance with the postmodern knowledge and political principles. Theory assumes that objective reality cannot be known, "truth" is socially constructed through language and "language games" and is local to a particular culture, and knowledge functions to protect and advance the interests of the privileged. Theory therefore explicitly aims to *critically* examine discourses. This means something specific. It means to examine them closely so as to expose and disrupt the political power dynamics it assumes are baked into them so that people will be convinced to reject them and initiate an ideological revolution.

Theory, in this sense, has not gone away, but neither has it stayed the same. Between the late 1980s and roughly 2010, it developed the applicability of its underlying concepts and came to form the basis of entirely new fields of scholarship, which have since become profoundly influential. These new disciplines, which have come to be known loosely as "Social Justice scholarship," co-opted the notion of social justice from the civil rights movements and other liberal and progressive theories. Not coincidentally, this all began in earnest just as legal equality had largely been achieved and antiracist, feminist, and LGBT activism began to produce diminishing returns. Now that racial and sexual discrimination in the workplace was illegal and homosexuality was decriminalized throughout the West, the main barriers to social equality in the West were lingering prejudices, embodied in attitudes, assumptions, expectations, and language. For those tackling these less tangible problems, Theory, with its focus on systems of power and privilege perpetuated through discourses, might have been an ideal tool—except that, as it was wholly deconstructive, indiscriminately radically skeptical, and unpalatably nihilistic, it was not really fit for any productive purpose.

The new forms of Theory arose within postcolonialism, black feminism (a branch of feminism pioneered by African American scholars who focused as much on race as on gender[3]), intersectional feminism, critical race (legal) Theory, and queer Theory, all of which sought to describe the world critically *in order to change it*. Scholars in these fields increasingly argued that, while postmodernism could help reveal the socially constructed nature of knowledge and the associated "problematics," activism was simply not compatible with fully radical skepticism.

They needed to accept that certain groups of people faced disadvantages and injustices based on who they were, a concept that radically skeptical postmodern thinking readily deconstructed. Some of the new Theorists therefore criticized their predecessors for their privilege, which they claimed was demonstrated by their ability to deconstruct identity and identity-based oppression. Some accused their forebears of being white, male, wealthy, and Western enough to afford to be playful, ironic, and radically skeptical, because society was already set up for their benefit. As a result, while the new Theorists retained much Theory, they did not entirely dispense with stable identity and objective truth. Instead, they laid claim to a limited amount of both, arguing that some identities were privileged over others and that this injustice was objectively true.

While the original postmodern thinkers dismantled our understanding of knowledge, truth, and societal structures, the new Theorists reconstructed these from the ground up, in accordance with their own narratives, many of which derived from the means and values of New Left political activism, which in turn had been the product of the Critical Theory of the Frankfurt School. Thus, while the original (postmodern) Theorists were fairly aimless, using irony and playfulness to reverse hierarchies and disrupt what they saw as unjust power and knowledge (or power-knowledge) structures, the second wave of (*applied*) postmodernists focused on dismantling hierarchies and making truth claims about power, language, and oppression. During its applied turn, Theory underwent a *moral* mutation: it adopted a number of beliefs about the rights and wrongs of power and privilege. The original Theorists were content to observe, bemoan, and play with such phenomena; the new ones wanted to reorder society. If social injustice is caused by legitimizing bad discourses, they reasoned, social justice can be achieved by delegitimizing them and replacing them with better ones. Those social sciences and humanities scholars who took Theoretical approaches began to form a left-wing moral community, rather than a purely academic one: an intellectual organ more interested in advocating a particular *ought* than attempting a detached assessment of *is*—an attitude we usually associate with churches, rather than universities.

A NEW DEFAULT VIEW

New Theories arose, which primarily looked at race, gender, and sexuality, and were explicitly critical, goal-oriented, and moralistic. They retained, however, the core postmodern ideas that knowledge is a construct of power, that the categories into which we organize people and phenomena were falsely contrived in the service of that power, that language is inherently dangerous and unreliable, that the knowledge claims and values of all cultures are equally valid and intelligible only on their own terms, and that collective experience trumps individuality and universality. They focused on cultural power, regarding it as objectively true that power and privilege are insidious, corrupting forces, which work to perpetuate themselves in almost mysterious ways. They explicitly stated that they were doing this with the purpose of remaking society according to their moral vision—all while citing the original postmodern Theorists.[4]

Brian McHale, the American literary theorist whose work centers on postmodernism, observes this change when he writes,

> With the arrival of poststructuralism in North America, "theory" was born, in the freestanding sense of the term that became so familiar in subsequent decades: not theory of this or that—not, for instance, theory of narrative, as structuralist narratology aspired to be—but theory in general, what in other eras might have been called speculation, or even indeed philosophy.[5]

Elsewhere, he notes,

> "[T]heory" itself, in the special sense that the term began to acquire from the mid-sixties on, is a postmodern phenomenon, and the success and proliferation of "theory" is itself a symptom of postmodernism.[6]

That is, by the late 1990s, postmodernism in its purest, original form had fallen out of fashion, but Theory had not. It provided radical activists, including scholar-activists, with an all-encompassing way of thinking about the world and society, which still informs much scholarship in the humanities and has made considerable inroads into the social sciences, especially sociology, anthropology, and psychology.[7] Postmodernism had been reenvisioned and has since become the backbone of dominant forms of scholarship, activism, and professional practice around identity, culture, and Social Justice.

Nevertheless, it is not uncommon for academics who work according to the postmodern knowledge and political principles to be disparaging of postmodernism and insist that they do not use it in their work. Jonathan Gottschall, noted scholar of literature and evolution, offers an explanation of this strange phenomenon. He argues that what he calls the "liberationist paradigm"—an understanding of society that seeks to detach human nature from biology—has become so pervasive among left-wing academics as to be simply the default in many fields. "Buzzing rumors of the demise of Theory," Gottschall therefore tells us, "are clearly premature."[8]

Perhaps, ironically, Theory has been internalized by—and thus rendered invisible to—many academics, even those who consider themselves to have eschewed Theory and claim to work with empirical data.[9] As Brian McHale argues,

> "[T]heory" itself has survived down to the new millennium. If it is less conspicuous now than it was in the peak years of postmodernism in the seventies and eighties, this is only because it has become so pervasive as to pass largely unnoticed. Since the late eighties, "theory" has especially animated the discourses of feminism, gender studies, and sexuality studies, and it underwrites what has come to be called "cultural studies."[10]

Whether we call it "postmodernism," "applied postmodernism," "Theory," or anything else, then, the conception of society based on the postmodern knowledge and political principles—that set of radically skeptical ideas, in which knowledge, power, and language are merely oppressive social constructs to be exploited by the powerful—has not only survived more or less intact but also flourished within many identity- and culture-based "studies" fields, especially in the so-called "Theoretical humanities." These, in turn, influence and often hold sway over the social sciences and professional programs like education, law, psychology, and social work, and have been carried by activists and media into the broader culture. As a result of the general academic acceptance of Theory, postmodernism has become applicable, and therefore accessible to both activists and the general public.

APPLYING THE INAPPLICABLE

In the early seventeenth century, as the Enlightenment began to take hold and revolutionize human thought in Europe, a number of thinkers of the time started to grapple with a new problem: radical doubt—a belief that there is no rational basis to believe *anything*. Most famous among these was the French mathematician, scientist, and philosopher René Descartes, who articulated what was, for him, a bit of philosophical bedrock upon which belief and philosophy could rest. In 1637, he first wrote the phrase, *"Je pense, donc je suis,"* in *Discourse on the Method,*[11] which was later rewritten in the far more famous Latin—*"Cogito, ergo sum"* (I think, therefore I am). This was Descartes' response to the deconstructive power that Enlightenment skepticism introduced to the world.

Something similar occurred some three and a half centuries later, in the 1980s. Faced with the far more intense deconstructive power of postmodern radical skepticism, an emerging band of cultural Theorists found themselves in a similar crisis. Liberal activism had won tremendous successes, the radical New Left activism of previous decades had fallen well out of favor, and the antirealism and nihilistic despair of postmodernism wasn't working and couldn't produce change. The correction to this problem required grasping upon something both radically actionable and real, and Theory and activism therefore started to coalesce on a new idea in parallel to Descartes' most famous meditation. For him, the ability to think implied existence—that *something* must be real. For the activist-scholars of the 1980s, the suffering associated with oppression implied the existence of something that could suffer and a mechanism by which that suffering can occur. "I think, therefore I am" was given new life under the axiomatic acceptance of new existential

bedrock: "I experience oppression, therefore I am… and so are dominance and oppression."

As postmodernism progressed, building itself upon this new philosophical rock, a number of new academic enclaves emerged. These
drew upon Theory, often heavily, focusing on specific aspects of the ways
in which language and power influence society. Each of these fields—
postcolonial, queer, and critical race Theories, along with gender studies, disability studies, and fat studies—will receive detailed treatment in
its own chapter. Among them, queer Theory is the only field that exclusively applies postmodern Theoretical approaches, but all these fields of
study have come to be dominated by applied postmodernist thinking.
The Theorists who took elements of postmodernism and sought to apply them in specific ways were the progenitors of the applied postmodern turn and therefore of Social Justice scholarship.

Postcolonial studies was the first applied postmodern discipline to
emerge. Although other approaches to studying the aftermath of colonialism exist, postmodern Theory formed so much of the basis of this
discipline that postmodernism and postcolonialism are often taught together. Edward Said, the founding father of postcolonial Theory, drew
heavily on Michel Foucault, and his work therefore focused on how discourses construct reality.[12] For Said, it was not enough to simply deconstruct power structures and show how perceptions of the East had been
constructed by the West. It was necessary to revise and rewrite history.
In his ground-breaking book, *Orientalism*, he argues that "history is made
by men and women, just as it can also be unmade and rewritten…so that
'our' East, 'our' Orient becomes 'ours' to possess and direct."[13]

Said's successors, Homi K. Bhabha and Gayatri Chakravorty Spivak, also valued Foucault, but relied more on Derrida. They distrust
the ability of language to convey meaning at all—but they also believe
it conceals within it unjust power dynamics. Because of this focus on
power conveyed through language, postcolonial Theory developed an
explicitly political purpose: to deconstruct Western narratives about the
East in order to uncover and amplify the voices of colonized peoples. As
the postcolonial scholar Linda Hutcheon puts it,

The post-colonial, like the feminist, is a dismantling but also constructive political enterprise insofar as it implies a theory of agency and social change that the postmodern deconstructive impulse lacks. While both "post-"s use irony, the post-colonial cannot stop at irony.[14]

Another new Theory developed within women's studies—and, later, gender studies—which grew out of the overlap between feminist thought and literary theory. Women's studies did not begin as postmodern, however. For the most part, it tracked with other forms of feminist theory, many of which analyzed the status of women through a critical Marxist lens, according to which Western patriarchy is largely an extension of capitalism, through which women are uniquely exploited and marginalized. Foucault famously rejected this top-down understanding of power, in favor of a society-permeating grid, produced by discourses. The Foucauldian Theorists who established queer Theory followed him in this.

By the late 1980s, this distinction had begun to drive a wedge between various types of feminists, who disagreed as to how far to take deconstructive methods,[15] a disagreement which persists today. Mary Poovey, a materialist feminist—a feminist who focuses primarily on how patriarchal and capitalist assumptions force women into socially constructed gender roles—described this clearly. Poovey was attracted to deconstructive techniques for their ability to undermine what she saw as socially constructed gender stereotypes (the belief that such stereotypes reflect intrinsic human nature is often referred to as "essentialism"), but as a materialist she was concerned that deconstruction in its purest form did not allow the category "woman" to exist at all.[16] This was new.

Like the postcolonial Theorists, Poovey wanted to adapt postmodern techniques for the purposes of activism. She therefore advocated a "toolbox" approach to feminism, in which deconstructive techniques could be used to dismantle gender roles, but not sex. She argued that we must accept as true the oppression of one class of people—women— by another—men—in order to combat it. This requires giving a sense of stable and objective reality to the classes of "women" and "men" and the power dynamic between them. She introduced some aspects of Theory into feminism and gender studies.

Judith Butler, a feminist and LGBT scholar and activist who was foundational to the development of queer Theory, epitomizes the opposite approach to this dilemma. In her most influential work, *Gender Trouble,*[17] published in 1990, Butler focuses on the socially constructed nature of both gender *and* sex. For Butler, "woman" is not a class of people but a performance that constructs "gendered" reality. Butler's concept of *gender performativity*—behaviors and speech that make gender real—allowed her to be thoroughly postmodern, deconstruct everything, and reject the notion of stable essences and objective truths about sex, gender, and sexuality, all while remaining politically active. This worked on two levels. Firstly, by referring to "reality-effects" and social or cultural "fictions," Butler is able to address what she sees as the reality of social constructions of gender, sex, and sexuality. For Butler, the specific constructions themselves are not real, but it is true that constructions exist. Secondly, because the "queer" is understood to be that which falls outside of categories, especially those used to define male and female, masculine and feminine, heterosexual and homosexual, disrupting and dismantling those categories is essential to activism. "To queer" can therefore be used as a verb in the Butlerian sense, and the "queering" of something refers to the destabilization of categories and the disruption of norms or accepted truths associated with it. The purpose of this is to liberate the "queer" from the oppression of being categorized.

Despite drawing heavily on both Foucault and Derrida, Butler does not consider herself a postmodernist. In fact, she does not consider "postmodernism" a coherent term. However, this is not a disparagement of postmodernism, since incoherence and indefinability are central to Butler's queer Theory. In her 1995 essay, "Contingent Foundations: Feminism and the Question of 'Postmodernism,'" Butler writes, in her usual semi-incomprehensible prose, that the point of postmodernism is to understand that oppressive power structures form as a result of firm definitions and stable categories and that recognizing this enables queer political activism.[18] Therefore, rather than denying postmodern assumptions or methods, Butler argues that—just as it is better not to define sexes, genders, or sexualities—it is better not to define postmodernism. To do so would allow or even cause it to become yet another powerful oppressive force—a violence of categorization, an idea which she derives from Jacques Derrida.

Butler avoided the aimlessness that handicapped the original postmodernism by making indefinability and ambiguity integral to her own philosophies. She explains that "the task is to interrogate what the theoretical move that establishes foundations authorizes, and what precisely it excludes or forecloses."[19] In Butlerian thought, the endless examination and deconstruction of categories can enable us to liberate those who do not fit neatly into categories.

In a different Theoretical thread, another highly influential feminist, whose work began in the late 1980s and who saw the need to modify postmodern Theory, is bell hooks (the pen name of Gloria Watkins, which she intentionally writes in lower case). hooks is an African American scholar and activist who took issue with postmodernism—especially postmodern Theory and feminism—for its exclusion of black people, women, and the working class, which she felt limited its ability to achieve social and political change. She criticized postmodernism not for its assumptions or thought, but for its association with, development by, and popularity among elite white male thinkers. hooks' 1990 essay, "Postmodern Blackness," criticizes postmodernism for being dominated by white male intellectuals and academic elites, even as it usefully draws attention to difference and otherness. She was particularly critical of its dismissal of stable identity, arguing that postmodernism should apply the politics of identity:

> The postmodern critique of "identity," though relevant for renewed black liberation struggle, is often posed in ways that are problematic. Given a pervasive politic of white supremacy which seeks to prevent the formation of radical black subjectivity, we cannot cavalierly dismiss a concern with identity politics.[20]

She asks,

> Should we not be suspicious of postmodern critiques of the "subject" when they surface at a historical moment when many subjugated people feel themselves coming to voice for the first time?[21]

For hooks, the problem was not that postmodernism was useless; it was that it was tailored to the experiences of white male intellectuals and did not allow for identity politics. hooks claimed that postmodern thought erred in destabilizing the concept of identity, which led it to exclude the unified voices and experiences of black Americans—particularly black women—and their aspirations to disrupt dominant narratives for the purposes of pursuing racial equality. She even suggested that postmodernism had silenced the black voices that had arisen in the 1960s, who had achieved civil rights by adopting a modernist universalizing agenda.[22] To be of value, hooks argued, postmodernism needed to come out of the universities and into the world; question the perspective of the white male, who could afford to doubt the importance of identity because of his privilege; and serve everyday activism being done by the politically radical black layperson. She writes,

> Postmodern culture with its decentered subject can be the space where ties are severed or it can provide the occasion for new and varied forms of bonding. To some extent ruptures, surfaces, contextuality and a host of other happenings create gaps that make space for oppositional practices which no longer require intellectuals to be confined by narrow, separate spheres with no meaningful connection to the world of every day.[23]

hooks' ideas arose in parallel with critical race Theory, which originated with critical legal scholars, most notably Derrick Bell. One of Bell's students was a legal scholar much influenced by black feminists like hooks: Kimberlé Crenshaw. Crenshaw makes a similar critique of postmodernism in her groundbreaking 1991 essay, "Mapping the Margins: Intersectionality, Identity Politics, and Violence Against Women of Color,"[24] which developed the groundwork for the hugely influential concept of *intersectionality*, which she had introduced two years earlier, in a more polemic piece (see chapter 5).

Intersectionality accurately recognizes that it is possible to uniquely discriminate against someone who falls within an "intersection" of oppressed identities—say black and female—and that contemporary discrimination law was insufficiently sensitive to address this. Crenshaw noticed that it would be possible, for example, to legally discriminate against black women in a workplace that hired plenty of black men and white women, but almost no black women. She also rightly recognized that the prejudices that intersecting identity groups face can include not only the ones directed against both identity groups but also unique ones. For example, a black woman might face the usual prejudices that come with being black and with being a woman while also experiencing additional prejudices that apply specifically to black women. Crenshaw makes some important points. Simultaneously, she was generally positive about the deconstructive potential of postmodern Theory and centered it in her new "intersectional" framework for addressing discrimination against women of color. She wrote, "I consider intersectionality to be a provisional concept linking contemporary politics with postmodern theory,"[25] and set out a more politicized form of postmodernism that would be actionable for race activists.[26]

Like Poovey, Butler, and hooks, Crenshaw wanted to both keep the Theoretical understanding of race and gender as social constructs and use deconstructive methods to critique them, *and* assert a stable truth claim: that some people were discriminated against on the grounds of their racial or sexual identities, a discrimination she planned to address legally, using identity politics. She writes,

> While the descriptive project of postmodernism of questioning the ways in which meaning is socially constructed is generally sound, this critique sometimes misreads the meaning of social construction and distorts its political relevance. . . . But to say that a category such as race or gender is socially constructed is not to say that that category has no significance in our world. On the contrary, a large and continuing project for subordinated people—and indeed, one of the projects for which postmodern theories have been very helpful in thinking about—is the way power has clustered around certain categories and is exercised against others.[27]

Crenshaw argues that (identity) categories "have meaning and consequences";[28] that is, they are objectively real. She distinguishes between a "black person" and a "person who happens to be black,"[29] and sides with the former, arguing that this distinction is integral to identity politics and marks its difference from the universal liberal approaches that characterized the civil rights movements. These are common themes within the applied turn in postmodernism.

Once identity and power had been made objectively real and analyzed using postmodern methods, the concept of intersectionality very rapidly broke the bounds of legal theory and became a powerful tool for cultural criticism and social and political activism. Because applied postmodern Theory explicitly applied postmodernism to identity politics, it began to be used by scholars who were interested in myriad aspects of identity, including race, sex, gender, sexuality, class, religion, immigration status, physical or mental ability, and body size. Following Crenshaw's recommendation, these rapidly emerging fields of critical studies of culture all rely heavily on social constructivism to explain why some identities are marginalized, while arguing that those social constructions are themselves objectively real.

For example, fields like disability studies[30] and fat studies[31] have recently become notable presences on the Social Justice scholarship scene. While disability studies and fat feminism already existed and addressed prejudice and discrimination against the disabled and the obese, these movements have taken a radically socially constructivist approach in recent years, explicitly applying postmodern principles and themes, particularly those of queer Theory. They have become part of the intersectional framework and adopted much of the applied postmodern Theoretical approach, in which the disabled and the fat are believed to have their own embodied knowledge of disability and fatness, which is worth more than scientific knowledge. This is not simply about the obvious truth that disabled and fat people know what it is like to be disabled or fat in a way that able-bodied and slim people do not. Scholars and activists in these fields insist instead that the understanding of disability or obesity as a physical problem to be treated and corrected where possible is itself a social construct born of systemic hatred of disabled and fat people.

THE POSTMODERN PRINCIPLES AND THEMES IN APPLICATION

Despite mutating to become actionable for identity politics, applied postmodernism has retained the two postmodern principles at its core.

- **The postmodern knowledge principle**: Radical skepticism about whether objective knowledge or truth is obtainable and a commitment to cultural constructivism.

This denial of objective knowledge or truth and commitment to cultural constructivism, and belief that whatever it is we call truth is nothing more than a construct of the culture calling it that, has been largely retained, with one important proviso: under applied postmodern thought, identity and oppression based on identity are treated as known features of objective reality. That is, the conception of society as comprised of systems of power and privilege that construct knowledge is assumed to be objectively true and intrinsically tied to social constructions of identity.

- **The postmodern political principle**: A belief that society is formed of systems of power and hierarchies, which decide what can be known and how.

This has also been retained. In fact, this is central to the advocacy of identity politics, whose politically actionable imperative is to dismantle this system in the name of Social Justice.

The four key themes of postmodern thought also survived the death of the high deconstructive phase and the subsequent applied postmodern turn.

1. The Blurring of Boundaries

This theme is most evident in postcolonial and queer Theories, which are both explicitly centred on ideas of fluidity, ambiguity, indefinability, and hybridity—all of which blur or even demolish the boundaries between categories. Their common concern with what they call "disrupting binaries" follows from Derrida's work on the hierarchical nature and meaninglessness of linguistic constructions. This theme is less evident in critical race Theory, which can be quite black-and-white (double meaning intended), but, in practice, the intersectional feminist element of critical race Theory encompasses many identity categories simultaneously and tries to be inclusive of "different ways of knowing." This results in a messy mixing of the evidenced with the experiential, in which a personal interpretation of lived experience (often informed—or misinformed—by Theory) is elevated to the status of evidence (usually of Theory).

2. The Power of Language

The power and danger of language are foregrounded in all the newer applied postmodern Theories. "Discourse analysis" plays a central role in all these fields; scholars scrutinize language closely and interpret it according to Theoretical frameworks. For example, many films are watched "closely" for problematic portrayals and then disparaged, even if their themes are broadly consistent with Social Justice.[32] Additionally, the idea that words are powerful and dangerous has now become widespread and underlies much scholarship and activism around discursive (or verbal) violence, safe spaces, microaggressions, and trigger warnings.

3. Cultural Relativism

Cultural relativism is, of course, most pronounced in postcolonial Theory, but the widespread use of intersectionality in Social Justice scholarship and activism and the understanding of the West as the pinnacle of an oppressive power structure have made cultural relativism a norm in all applied postmodern Theories. This applies both in terms of how knowledge is produced, recognized, and transmitted—one cultural artifact—and in terms of moral and ethical principles—another cultural artifact.

4. The Loss of the Individual and the Universal

The intense focus on identity categories and identity politics means that the individual and the universal are largely devalued. While mainstream liberalism focuses on achieving universal human rights and access to opportunities, to allow each individual to fulfill her potential, applied postmodern scholarship and activism is deeply skeptical of these values and even openly hostile to them. Applied postmodern Theory tends to regard mainstream liberalism as complacent, naive, or indifferent about the deeply engrained prejudices, assumptions, and biases that limit and constrain people with marginalized identities. The "individual" in applied postmodernism is something like the sum total of the identity groups to which the person in question simultaneously belongs.

THE EMERGENCE OF SOCIAL JUSTICE SCHOLARSHIP

These changes may seem too slight to consider Theory a serious departure from postmodernism—yet they are significant. By losing the ironic playfulness and despair of meaning characteristic of high-deconstructive postmodernism and by becoming goal-oriented, Theorists of the 1980s and 1990s made postmodernism applicable to institutions and politics. By recovering the idea of identity as something that—although culturally constructed—provided group knowledge and empowerment, they enabled more specific forms of activism-scholarship to develop. Theory therefore turned from being largely descriptive to highly prescriptive—a shift from *is* to *ought*. After the applied postmodern turn, postmodernism was no longer a mode of describing society and undermining confidence in long-established models of reality: it now aspired to be a tool of Social Justice. This ambition would come to fruition in the early 2010s, when a second significant evolutionary mutation in postmodernism occurred.

The new Theories emerging from the applied postmodern turn made it possible for scholars and activists to *do* something with the postmodern conception of society. If knowledge is a construct of power, which functions through ways of talking about things, knowledge can be changed and power structures toppled by changing the way we talk about things. Thus, applied postmodernism focuses on controlling discourses, especially by *problematizing* language and imagery it deems Theoretically harmful. This means that it looks for then highlights ways in which the oppressive problems they assume exist in society manifest themselves, sometimes quite subtly, in order to "make oppression visible." The intense scrutiny of language and development of ever stricter rules for terminology pertaining to identity often known as *political correctness* came to a head in the 1990s and has again become pertinent since the mid-2010s.

This carries politically actionable conclusions. If what we accept as true is only accepted as such because the discourses of straight, white, wealthy, Western men have been privileged, applied Theory indicates this can be challenged by empowering marginalized identity groups and insisting their voices take precedence. This belief increased the aggressiveness of identity politics to such an extent that it even led to concepts like "research justice." This alarming proposal demands that scholars preferentially cite women and minorities—and minimize citations of white Western men—because empirical research that values knowledge production rooted in evidence and reasoned argument is an unfairly privileged cultural construct of white Westerners. It is therefore, in this view, a moral obligation to share the prestige of rigorous research with "other forms of research," including superstition, spiritual beliefs, cultural traditions and beliefs, identity-based experiences, and emotional responses.[33]

As these methods can be applied to virtually anything, a vast body of work drawing on any (or all) identity-based fields has emerged since roughly 2010. It asserts the objective truth of socially constructed knowledge and power hierarchies with absolute certainty. This represents an evolution that began with the applied turn in postmodernism as its new assumptions became known-knowns—that which people take for granted because it is known that they are "known." This work incorporates methodologies known as "feminist epistemology," "critical race epistemology," "postcolonial epistemology," and "queer epistemology," together with the study of broader "epistemic injustice,"[34] "epistemic oppression,"[35] "epistemic exploitation,"[36] and "epistemic violence."[37] ("Epistemology" is the term for the ways in which knowledge is produced and "epistemic" means "related to knowledge.") Frequently, all these approaches are combined to produce what is usually known as "Social Justice scholarship." Though apparently diverse, these approaches to "other knowledges" are all premised on the idea that people with different marginalized identities have different knowledges, stemming from their shared, embodied, and lived experiences as members of those identity groups, especially of systemic oppression. Such people can both be disadvantaged as knowers, when they are forced to operate within a "dominant" system that is not their own, and also enjoy unique advantages, because of their familiarity with multiple epistemic systems. They can alternately be victims of "epistemic violence" when their knowledge is not included or recognized or of "epistemic exploitation" when they are asked to share it.

These changes have been steadily eroding the barrier between scholarship and activism. It used to be considered a failure of teaching or scholarship to work from a particular ideological standpoint. The teacher or scholar was expected to set aside her own biases and beliefs in order to approach her subject as objectively as possible. Academics were incentivized to do so by knowing that other scholars could—and would—point out evidence of bias or motivated reasoning and counter it with evidence and argument. Teachers could consider their attempts at objectivity successful if their students did not know what their political or ideological positions were.

This is not how Social Justice scholarship works or is applied to education. Teaching is now supposed to be a political act, and only one type of politics is acceptable—identity politics, as defined by Social Justice and Theory. In subjects ranging from gender studies to English literature, it is now perfectly acceptable to state a theoretical or ideological position and then use that lens to examine the material, without making any attempt to falsify one's interpretation by including disconfirming evidence or alternative explanations. Now, scholars can openly declare themselves to be activists and teach activism in courses that require students to accept the ideological basis of Social Justice as true and produce work that supports it.[38] One particularly infamous 2016 paper in *Géneros: Multidisciplinary Journal of Gender Studies* even *favorably* likened women's studies to HIV and Ebola, advocating that it spread its version of feminism like an immune-suppressing virus, using students-turned-activists as carriers.[39]

Surprising or worrying as these changes may be, this is not the result of a hidden agenda. The agenda is open and explicit and always has been. For example, in 2013, as activist and scholar Sandra Grey insisted,

Part of being active academic citizens involves challenging our students to do and be more. In early universities it was students who took the ideas of universities to the illiterate, acting as missionaries, teaching new ideas to peasants, thus spreading movements like Lutheranism through the countryside. While not suggesting that our students should be out in society professing Lutheran ideals, I would like to think we provide the tools of critique, debate and research to students to enable active citizenship and even inspire some to take up activist roles. Finally, there is a need for academics as part of their normal working lives to form alliances and connections, and even at times to become members of political and advocacy organisations. Rigorous research carried out "for a cause" must again be accepted as legitimate knowledge generation.[40]

In 2018, activist-scholars published a collection of essays entitled *Taking It to the Streets: The Role of Scholarship in Advocacy and Advocacy in Scholarship*.[41] While scholars can, of course, be activists and activists can be scholars, combining these two roles is liable to create problems and, when a political stance is taught at university, it is apt to become an orthodoxy, which cannot be questioned. Activism and education exist in a fundamental tension—activism presumes to know the truth with enough certainty to act upon it, while education is conscious that it does not know for certain what is true and therefore seeks to learn more.[42]

Applied postmodern ideas have escaped the boundaries of the university in ways that the original postmodern Theory did not, and they did so at least in part because of their ability to be acted upon. Out in the world, these ideas have gained sway. The postmodern knowledge and political principles are now routinely evoked by activists and increasingly also by corporations, media, public figures, and the general public.

We, everyday citizens who are increasingly befuddled about what has happened to society and how it happened so quickly, regularly hear demands to "decolonize" everything from academic curricula to hairstyles to mathematics. We hear laments about cultural appropriation at the same time we hear complaints about the lack of representation of certain identity groups in the arts. We hear that only white people can be racist and that they always are so, by default. Politicians, actors, and artists pride themselves on being intersectional. Companies flaunt their respect for "diversity," while making it clear that they are only interested in a superficial diversity of identity (not of opinions). Organizations and activist groups of all kinds announce that they are inclusive, but only of people who agree with them. American engineers have been fired from corporations like Google for saying that gender differences exist,[43] and British comedians have been sacked by the BBC for repeating jokes that could be construed as racist by Americans.[44]

For most of us, this is both confusing and alarming. Many people are wondering what's happening, how we got here, what it all means, and how (and how soon) we can fix it and restore some common ground, charity, and reason. These are difficult questions. What has happened is that applied postmodernism has come into its own, been *reified*—taken as real, as The Truth according to Social Justice—and widely spread by activists, and (ironically) turned into a dominant metanarrative of its own. It has become an article of faith or an operational mythology for a wide swathe of society, especially on the left. To fail to pay obeisance to it can be literally or—more often figuratively—fatal. One does not merely challenge the dominant orthodoxy.

Fortunately, it is unlikely that the majority of people—let alone corporations, organizations, and public figures—really are radical cultural constructivists, with postmodern conceptions of society and a commitment to intersectional understandings of Social Justice. However, because these ideas offer the appearance of deep explanations to complicated problems and work within the Theory, they have successfully morphed from obscure academic theories—the sorts of things that only intellectuals can believe—to part of the general "wisdom" about how the world works. Because these ideas are so widespread, matters won't improve until we show them for what they are and resist them—ideally by using consistent liberal principles and ethics.

To understand how Social Justice scholarship developed from postmodern Theory via the applied postmodern turn, we have to explore the new Theories in greater depth and specificity. It is these applied Theories—postcolonial, gender, queer, critical race, and so on—not postmodernism itself, that have gone out into the world and manifested themselves in scholarship, activism, and our institutions. Over the next five chapters, we hope to explain how these applied Theories have developed. Then, in chapter 8, we will explain how they came to be taken for granted as capital-T Truth, through the ideology of Social Justice.

3 POSTCOLONIAL THEORY

Deconstructing the West to Save the Other

Postcolonial Theory looks to deconstruct the West, as it sees it, and this ambitious demolition project was undoubtedly the first emanation of applied postmodernism. Unlike race and gender Theories, which had already developed fairly mature lines of thought and scholarship before postmodernism took hold in cultural studies, postcolonial Theory derived directly from postmodern thought. Moreover, postcolonial Theory came about to achieve a specific purpose, *decolonization*: the systematic undoing of colonialism in all its manifestations and impacts.

While postmodernism saw itself as both moving beyond and dismantling the key features of modernity, postcolonialism restricts this project to issues surrounding colonialism. Prominent within postcolonial Theory, more specifically, are both the postmodern knowledge principle, which rejects objective truth in favor of cultural constructivism, and the postmodern political principle, which perceives the world as constructed from systems of power and privilege that determine what can be known. The four primary themes of postmodern thinking—the blurring of boundaries, belief in the overwhelming power of language, cultural relativism, and the loss of the individual and denial of the universal—are found throughout postcolonialism. Though not all postcolonial scholars are postmodern in their outlook, the key figures certainly were and are, and this approach dominates postcolonial Social Justice scholarship and activism today.[1]

Postcolonialism and the related Theory arose in a specific historical context: the moral and political collapse of European colonialism, which had dominated global politics for more than five centuries. European colonialism began in earnest in around the fifteenth century and continued into the middle of the twentieth, and it proceeded upon the assumption that the European powers had a right to expand their territories and exert their political and cultural authority over other peoples and regions. Though this sort of empire-building attitude was a standard one typical to many, if not most, cultures before the twentieth century, European colonialism was equipped with sweeping explanations, stories, and justifications of itself—or metanarratives—that proclaimed and sought to legitimize this right in its own terms. These included *la mission civilisatrice* (the civilizing mission) in French colonialism and Manifest Destiny in North America—concepts central to knowledge production and political organization from before the Enlightenment right through the Modern period.[2]

Then, with surprising rapidity, European colonialism faltered and collapsed in the middle of the twentieth century. Following World War II especially, decolonization efforts proceeded quickly on both the material and political levels, and, by the early 1960s, moral concerns about colonialism were prominent in both the academy and among the general public, especially on the radical left. The collapse of colonialism was therefore at the heart of the social and political milieu in which postmodernism arose, especially in the academies of continental Europe. Eventually postcolonial Theorists established themselves by rejecting colonialist metanarratives by focusing on the discourses (ways of speaking about things) of colonialism. Postcolonialism is therefore mainly a narrowing of postmodernism to focus on one specific element of modernity—colonialism—and the tool it applies is *postcolonial Theory*, which is Theory adapted to that problem. The postcolonial Theorists studied the discourses of colonialism, which sought to protect the interests of the powerful and privileged, not least the so-called right to dominate other cultures that hegemonic "civilized" Western (and Christian) discourses construed as "uncivilized" and "barbaric."

POSTCOLONIALISM AS AN APPLIED POSTMODERN PROJECT

As concerns about colonialism grew through the middle part of the twentieth century, the work of psychiatrist Frantz Fanon rapidly gained influence. Fanon, who was born on Martinique under French colonial rule, is often considered foundational to postcolonial Theory. His 1952 book, *Black Skins, White Masks*,[3] offers a powerful critique of both racism and colonialism. His 1959 work, *A Dying Colonialism*,[4] chronicles the changes in culture and politics during the Algerian War of independence from France. Then, his 1961 book, *The Wretched of the Earth*,[5] set the stage for postcolonialism and postcolonial Theory. Its thesis marked a profound change in thought on the subject. To Fanon, by 1961, colonialism represented, above all else, a systematic denial of the humanity of colonized people: so central is this theme to Fanon's analysis that he speaks throughout of the literal erasure of people's identity and dignity. This, he insists, colonized people must resist violently in order to maintain their mental health and self-respect. Fanon's book was simultaneously deeply critical and openly revolutionary—attitudes that have informed postcolonialism and the more radical aspects of leftist activism ever since.

Writing in 1961, however, Fanon was hardly a postmodernist. His approach is usually understood to be modernist because—while it is profoundly skeptical and clearly both critical and radical—his criticisms draw mainly on Lenin's Marxist critiques of capitalism, his analysis relies heavily on psychoanalytic theory, and his philosophy is essentially humanist. Nevertheless, later thinkers, including Edward Said, the father of postcolonial Theory, took inspiration from Fanon's depiction of the psychological impacts of having one's culture, language, and religion subordinated to another. Fanon argued that the colonialist *mind-set* has to be disrupted and, if possible, reversed within people who have been subjected to colonial rule and the colonialist worldview that justified it.

This focus on attitudes, biases, and discourses fits well with post-modernism. The scholars who look at postcolonialism in a postmodern way—postcolonial Theorists—also see their work as a project geared towards overcoming certain *mind-sets* associated with and putatively legitimizing colonialism (rather than focusing on its practical and material effects). They draw primarily on postmodern ideas of knowledge as a construct of power that is perpetuated by discourses. The key idea in postcolonial Theory is that the West constructs itself in opposition to the East, through the way it talks. "We are rational, and they are superstitious." "We are honest, and they are deceptive." "We are normal, and they are exotic." "We are advanced, and they are primitive." "We are liberal, and they are barbaric." The East is constructed as the foil to which the West can compare itself. The term *the other* or *othering* is used to describe this denigration of other people in order to feel superior. Said called this mind-set "Orientalism"—a move that allowed him to attach a powerful pejorative to Orientalists, meaning contemporary scholars who studied the Far East, South Asia, and especially the Middle East from other perspectives.

Said presented his new ideas in the book *Orientalism*, published in 1978.[6] This book not only laid a foundation for the development of postcolonial Theory, but also brought the concept of applicable post-modern Theory to an American audience. Said, a Palestinian-American Theorist, drew primarily on Fanon and Foucault,[7] especially the latter's notions of "power-knowledge." Although he ultimately had many criticisms of Foucault's approach, he considered power-knowledge instrumental to understanding Orientalism. Of primary significance to Said were Foucault's arguments that how we speak constructs knowledge and that powerful groups in society therefore get to direct the discourse and thus define what constitutes knowledge. For example, Said writes,

> I have found it useful here to employ Michel Foucault's notion of a discourse, as described by him in *The Archaeology of Knowledge* and in *Discipline and Punish*, to identify Orientalism. My contention is that without examining Orientalism as a discourse one cannot possibly understand the enormously systematic discipline by which European culture was able to manage—and even produce—the

Orient politically, sociologically, ideologically, scientifically, and imaginatively during the post-Enlightenment period.[8]

Said argues that at the core of Orientalism lies a Western discourse, and it was this discourse that constructed the East, by imposing upon it a character that both denigrated and exoticized it. The postmodernist influence on Said would be impossible to miss, even if he hadn't insisted that Orientialism "cannot possibly" be understood without Foucault's ideas.

This desire to deconstruct the allegedly hegemonic West has dominated postcolonial Theory ever since: much postcolonial scholarship consists of reading Orientalism into texts. This is in part because Said's project was a thoroughly literary endeavor—he took particular umbrage at Joseph Conrad's 1899 novella, *Heart of Darkness*,[9] an allegory that raises significant questions about both racism and colonialism. Rather than advocating a broad understanding of thematic elements of the text, Said preferred to scrutinize texts through "close reading," in order to uncover the various ways in which Western discourses construct, perpetuate, and enforce the Orientalist binary.

In Said, we see applied postmodern discourse analysis, which reads power imbalances into interactions between dominant and marginalized (regional) cultural groups, and aims to rewrite history from the perspective of the oppressed. Such rewriting often takes the highly productive form of recovering lost voices and perspectives to give a fuller and more accurate picture of history, but it is also frequently used to rewrite history in accordance with local or political narratives or to simultaneously elevate multiple irreconcilable histories and thereby implicitly reject any claim to objective knowledge.

We also see the postmodern idea that knowledge is not found but made in the introduction to *Orientalism*, in which Said writes,

My argument is that history is made by men and women, just as it can also be unmade and rewritten, always with various silences and elisions, always with shapes imposed and disfigurements tolerated, so that "our" East, "our" Orient becomes "ours" to possess and direct.[10]

This, then, is not merely deconstruction, but a call to reconstruction. Postcolonial Theory encompasses a (typically radical) political agenda that the original postmodernism lacked. The prominent postcolonial feminist scholar, Linda Hutcheon, also makes this clear.[11] Speaking of feminist and postcolonial scholarship, she writes, "Both have distinct political agendas and often a theory of agency that allow them to go beyond the postmodern limits of deconstructing existing orthodoxies into the realms of social and political action."[12] Like many of the critical Theorists who followed the postmodernists and sought to apply their ideas, Hutcheon advocates adapting postmodern Theory to support political activism. Explicitly activism-oriented, postcolonial Theory is thus the earliest category to arise within the *applied postmodern* school of thought.

Two other scholars are, with Said, held to be foundational to postcolonial Theory: Gayatri Chakravorty Spivak and Homi K. Bhabha. Like Said's, their work is thoroughly and explicitly postmodern in both derivation and orientation but, due to a greater focus on Jacques Derrida's deconstruction of language, it is linguistically and conceptually difficult to the point of obscurity. Spivak's most significant contribution to postcolonial Theory is probably her 1988 essay, "Can the Subaltern Speak?,"[13] which focuses intensely on language and expresses concern about the role power structures play in constraining it.

Spivak argues that *subalterns*—colonized peoples of subordinate status—have no access to speech, even while seemingly representing themselves. This, she contends, is a direct result of the way power has permeated discourse and created insurmountable barriers to communication for those existing outside of the dominant discourses. Drawing upon Said and Foucault, she developed the concept of *epistemic violence* within "Can the Subaltern Speak?" to describe the injury done to the colonized when their knowledge and status as knowers is marginalized by dominant discourses.

Spivak's postmodernism is especially evident when she adopts from Derrida the deconstructive idea that there is subversive power in maintaining stereotypes within power-laden binaries, while inverting their hierarchy. She calls this "strategic essentialism."[14] *Essentialism*, she tells us, is a linguistic tool of domination. Colonizers justify their oppression of the subordinated group by regarding it as a monolithic "other" that can be stereotyped and disparaged. *Strategic essentialism* applies this same sense of monolithic group identity as an act of resistance, suspending individuality and in-group diversity within the subordinated group for the purpose of promoting common goals through a common identity. In other words, it defines a particular kind of identity politics, built around intentional double standards.

This is typical of Spivak's Theory. Spivak relies more on Derrida than on Said and Foucault—because Foucault is too politically oriented. Because of Derrida's focus on the ambiguity and fluidity of language and his use of deeply incomprehensible prose—which resists saying anything concrete on principle—Spivak's work is deeply ambiguous and obscure. For example, she writes,

> I find [Derrida's] morphology much more painstaking and useful than Foucault's and Deleuze's immediate, substantive involvement with more "political" issues—the latter's invitation to "become woman"—which can make their influence more dangerous for the U.S. academic as enthusiastic radical. Derrida marks radical critique with the danger of appropriating the other by assimilation. He reads catachresis at the origin. He calls for a rewriting of the utopian structural impulse as "rendering delirious that interior voice that is the voice of the other in us."[15]

Impenetrability and impracticality were the Theoretical fashion at the time, especially among postcolonial Theorists. Homi K. Bhabha, another noteworthy postmodern example who held much sway over the field through the 1990s, eclipses Spivak in his ability to produce nearly incomprehensible prose. Bhabha is arguably the most deconstructive of the prominent postcolonial scholars, having been influenced primarily by Lacan and Derrida. He focuses mainly on the role language plays in constructing knowledge.[16]

As befits one who is radically skeptical of the ability of language to convey meaning at all, Bhabha's writing is notoriously difficult to read. In 1998, he won second place in *Philosophy and Literature*'s Bad Writing Contest—beaten only by Judith Butler—for the sentence,

> If, for a while, the ruse of desire is calculable for the uses of discipline, soon the repetition of guilt, justification, pseudo-scientific theories, superstition, spurious authorities, and classifications can be seen as the desperate effort to "normalize" formally the disturbance of a discourse of splitting that violates the rational, enlightened claims of its enunciatory modality.[17]

This bewildering sentence does have a meaning—a thoroughly post-modern one. Broken down, it means that racist, sexual jokes are told by colonizers initially to control a subordinate group, but that, ultimately, they are attempts by colonizers to convince themselves that their own ways of talking about things make sense because they are secretly ter-rified that they don't. This particular mind-reading claim permeates Bhabha's work and underlies his belief that the rejection of stable de-scriptive categories can subvert colonial dominance.[18] This is, of course, entirely unfalsifiable and, when expressed as above, incomprehensible.[19]

Bhabha's work is frequently criticized for being unnecessarily ob-scure and thus difficult to put to use in addressing postcolonial issues. Unlike other postcolonialist scholars, he also explicitly rejects the materi-alist, political approach to postcolonial studies, along with Marxism and nationalism. Bhabha even finds the language of the postmodern Theory he uses potentially problematic, asking, "Is the language of theory mere-ly another power ploy of the culturally privileged Western élite to pro-duce a discourse of the Other that reinforces its own power-knowledge equation?"[20] Here he manages to cite Foucault explicitly and Derrida implicitly, while invalidating them both and, consequently, himself.

Postcolonial Theory's most notable progenitors formed the first branch of the applied postmodern tree, as it grew from its Theoreti-cal trunk. This postmodern focus has consequences. Theirs is not an investigation of the material realities affecting countries and people that were previously under colonial power and the aftermath of that but an analysis of attitudes, beliefs, speech, and mind-sets, which are sacral-ized or problematized. These they construct simplistically from assump-tions that posit white Westerners (and knowledge that is understood as "white" and "Western") as superior to Eastern, black, and brown people (and "knowledges" associated with non-Western cultures) despite that being precisely the stereotype they claim to want to fight.[21]

MIND-SETS COMPARED

Of course, colonialist narratives existed—there is plenty of evidence of them in colonial history (European and otherwise). For example, consider this repulsive passage from 1871:

> The regeneration of the inferior or degenerate races, by the superior races is part of the providential order of things for humanity. . . . Nature has made a race of workers, the Chinese race, who have wonderful manual dexterity, and almost no sense of honour; govern them with justice, levying from them, in return for the blessing of such a government, an ample allowance for the conquering race, and they will be satisfied; a race of tillers of the soil, the Negro; treat him with kindness and humanity, and all will be as it should; a race of masters and soldiers, the European race. . . . Let each do what he is made for, and all will be well.[22]

But this isn't an attitude one encounters much today. It gradually became less and less morally tenable over the twentieth century, with the fall of colonialism and rise of the civil rights movements, and would now rightly be recognized as far-right extremism. Nevertheless, these attitudes are cited in postcolonial Theory as though their past existence produced an indelible imprint upon how people discuss and view issues today. Postcolonial Theory establishes much of its claim to importance by assuming there must be permanent problems that have been handed down to us through language constructed centuries ago.

The real social changes that rendered the attitudes in the above paragraph almost universally objectionable weren't predicated on postmodern analysis, or postmodern in orientation. They preceded those developments and proceeded from and functioned by means of universal and individual liberalism. This form of liberalism holds that science, reason, and human rights are the property of every individual and do not belong exclusively to any set of people—whether they be men or white Westerners or anyone else. Postmodern postcolonial approaches differ radically from this liberal approach and are often criticized for perpetuating Orientalist binaries, rather than seeking to overcome them.

A (Western) colonial mind-set says: *"Westerners are rational and scientific while Asians are irrational and superstitious. Therefore, Europeans must rule Asia for its own good."*

A liberal mind-set says: *"All humans have the capacity to be rational and scientific, but individuals will vary widely. Therefore, all humans must have all opportunities and freedoms."*

A postmodern mind-set says: *"The West has constructed the idea that rationality and science are good in order to perpetuate its own power and marginalize nonrational, nonscientific forms of knowledge production from elsewhere."*

So, while the liberal mind-set rejects the arrogant colonial claim that reason and science belong to white Westerners, the postmodern one accepts it, but regards reason and science themselves as just one way of knowing and as oppressive—an oppression they attempt to redress by applying the core tenets of postmodernism. The applied postmodern mind-set on colonialism is similar to the postmodern mind-set, but adds an activist conclusion.

An applied postmodern mind-set says: "The West has constructed the idea that rationality and science are good in order to perpetuate its own power and marginalize nonrational, nonscientific forms of knowledge production from elsewhere. *Therefore, we must now devalue white, Western ways of knowing for belonging to white Westerners and promote Eastern ones (in order to equalize the power imbalance)."*

This practice is frequently referred to as *decolonizing* and seeking *research justice*.

DECOLONIZE EVERYTHING

While, initially, postcolonial Theory scholarship mostly took the form of literary criticism and the discursive analysis of writing about colonialism—and was frequently couched in highly obscure postmodern Theoretical language—the field gradually expanded and simplified. By the early 2000s, the concept of *decolonizing* everything had begun to dominate scholarship and activism, and new scholars were using and developing the concepts in different ways, with more actionable elements. They retained the postmodern principles and themes and extended the focus beyond ideas and speech about literal colonialism to perceived attitudes of superiority towards people of certain identity statuses. These included displaced indigenous groups and people from racial or ethnic minorities who could be considered in some way subaltern, diasporic, or hybrid, or whose non-Western beliefs, cultures, or customs had been devalued. The aims of postcolonial Theory also became more concrete: focusing less on disrupting discourses they saw as colonialist in the fairly pessimistic way typical of postmodernism and more on taking active steps to decolonize these, using the militant Social Justice approach that has taken hold since 2010. This has mainly occurred via various *decolonize* movements, which can be taken as the product of more recent Theorists having reified the assumptions of postcolonial Theory and put them into action.

What it means to decolonize a thing that is not literally colonized varies considerably. It can refer simply to including scholars of all nationalities and races: this is the primary focus of the United Kingdom's National Union of Students (NUS) campaigns, "Why is My Curriculum White?" (2015) and #LiberateMyDegree (2016).[23] Such campaigns focus on reducing reliance on white scholars from former colonizing powers and replacing them with scholars of color from formerly colonized regions. However, we also see a drive for a diversity of "knowledges" and epistemologies—ways of deciding what is true—under Theory often described as "(other) ways of knowing." This comes with a strong inclination to critique, problematize, and disparage knowledge understood as Western.

This can take the form of reading physical spaces as though they were "texts" in need of deconstruction—an example of how postmodern Theory blurs boundaries and focuses on the power of "language."

The 2015 Rhodes Must Fall movement, which began at the University of Cape Town in 2015 as an effort to remove a statue commemorating Cecil Rhodes and later spread to other universities, including Oxford, provides a good example. As a British businessman and politician in southern Africa, Rhodes had been responsible for much of the legal framework of South African apartheid, and therefore it is perfectly reasonable to object to depictions that paint him in a solely favorable light. However, the rhetoric around this movement went far beyond objecting to the exploitative and illiberal practices of apartheid and colonialism. At Oxford, for instance, demands for symbolic changes, such as the removal of "offensive" colonialist statuary and imagery, were wrapped up with other activist demands.[24] This included yet another push to increase representation of ethnic and racial minorities who agree with Theory on campus and increased focus on *what* was studied in the curriculum and *how* it was being studied.

To elaborate, in the introduction to *Decolonising the University*, volume editors Gurminder K. Bhambra, Dalia Gebrial, and Kerem Nişancıoğlu explain that decolonization can refer to the study of colonialism both in its material manifestations and through discourses, and it can also offer *alternative ways of thinking*.[25] This is a form of *standpoint theory*—the belief that knowledge comes from the lived experience of different identity groups, who are differently positioned in society and thus see different aspects of it.[26] For decolonial scholars, both "Eurocentric forms of knowledge" and "the epistemological authority assigned uniquely to the Western university as the privileged site of knowledge production"[27] are problems, and "the point is not simply to deconstruct such understandings, but to transform them."[28] In other words, by using activism to achieve a symbolic "textual" aim, affecting the statuary on campus, decolonization activists also attempted to bolster their ranks, while "reforming" education to rely more explicitly on their applications of Theory.

Thus, two focal points of postcolonial Theory are evident in the effort to decolonize everything: national origin and race.[29] Bhambra and colleagues, for instance, influenced by Said, see knowledge as situated geographically: "The content of university knowledge remains principally governed by the West for the West."[30] For the Theorist Kehinde Andrews, critical race Theory is more influential, and knowledge is more closely related to skin color: "The neglect of Black knowledge by society is no accident but a direct result of racism." We must, Andrews tells us, "forever leave behind the idea that knowledge can be produced value free. Our politics shape our understanding of the world and the pretence of neutrality ironically makes our endeavours less valid."[31]

Note the assertion that "value free" and "neutral" knowledge is impossible to obtain and must be abandoned forever. Theory holds that objective knowledge—that which is true for everyone, regardless of their identity—is unobtainable, because knowledge is always bound up with cultural values. This is the postmodern knowledge principle. For Theory, the knowledge that is currently most valued is intrinsically white and Western, and it interprets this as an injustice—no matter how reliably that knowledge was produced. This is the postmodern political principle. This common belief is represented by the word "universal" in the "Aims" of the Rhodes Must Fall movement at Oxford, which sought to: "remedy the highly selective narrative of traditional academia—which frames the West as sole producers of universal knowledge—by integrating subjugated and local epistemologies . . . [and creating] a more intellectually rigorous, complete academy."[32]

Throughout even the most recent applications of Theory, then, we see radical skepticism that knowledge can be objectively, universally, or neutrally true. This leads to a belief that rigor and completeness come not from good methodology, skepticism, and evidence, but from identity-based "standpoints" and multiple "ways of knowing."[33] That such an approach doesn't tend to work is considered unimportant because it is deemed to be more *just*. That is, this belief proceeds from an *ought* that is not necessarily concerned about what *is*.

This view is used to advocate and engage in historical revisionism—rewriting history, often in the service of a political agenda—by accusing rigorous methods of being "positivist" and thus biased. As Dalia Gebrial puts it in *Decolonising the University*:

> The public's sense of what history is remains influenced by positivist tendencies, whereby the role of the historian is to simply "reveal" facts about pasts that are worth revealing, in a process removed from power. This epistemological insistence on history as a positivist

endeavour functions as a useful tool of coloniality in the institution, as it effaces the power relations that underpin what the "production of history" has thus far looked like.[34]

The complaint here is, effectively, that history cannot be trusted because it is "written by the winners." While there is some truth beneath that concern, most rigorous, empirical historians attempt to mitigate the tendency of history to be written from the bias of the writer by seeking disconfirming evidence of their claims, to help them get at the truth— which they, unlike Theorists, believe exists. For example, medieval war historians often advise naive readers of accounts of battles to divide the number of soldiers claimed to have been present by ten to get a more realistic figure. This tendency to massively overstate numbers (probably to make the story more exciting) was discovered by empirical historians seeking out records of soldiers' pay. Similarly, empirical feminist scholars have used legal and financial records to reveal that women played a much more active role in society, law, and business than had long been assumed. Our knowledge of history is skewed by the biased records that survive, but the way to mitigate this is to investigate such claims empirically and reveal the falsity of biased narratives, rather than include a greater range of biases and declare some of them immune to criticism.

In addition to criticizing empirical scholarship, decolonial narratives frequently attack rationality, which postcolonial scholars see as a Western way of thinking. For example, the 2018 essay, "Decolonising Philosophy," which appears in the book *Decolonising the University*, begins,

it will be difficult to contest the idea that, generally speaking, philosophy as a field or a discipline in modern Western universities remains a bastion of Eurocentrism, whiteness in general, and white heteronormative male structural privilege and superiority in particular.[35]

They relate the worth of philosophical concepts to their authors' gender, race, sexuality, and geography—in the typical style of standpoint theory. Ironically, the authors do this by introducing Foucault's idea of "power-knowledge," despite the evidence that Foucault was, in fact, a white

Western man, whose influence has been most strongly felt in the West.

Foucault's concept of knowledge and the way in which it is used to deconstruct categories accepted as real is influential on this entire line of Theoretical thought. It appears, for example, in this description of the mission of decolonization:

> Any serious effort to decolonise philosophy cannot be satisfied with simply adding new areas to an existing arrangement of power/ knowledge, leaving the Eurocentric norms that define the field as a whole in place, or reproducing such norms themselves. For example, when engaging in non-European philosophies it is important to avoid reproducing problematic conceptions of time, space and subjectivity that are embedded in the Eurocentric definition of European philosophy and its many avatars.[36]

That is, it is not enough to add other philosophical approaches to the field one wishes to decolonize. Postcolonial Theorists insist European philosophy must be entirely rejected—even to the point of deconstructing *time and space* as Western constructs. (As we shall see, this sort of claim is also found in queer Theory, which operates on very similar postmodern terms, derived from Michel Foucault.)

Within this matured postcolonial Theory, all four of the postmodern themes are evident—the blurring of boundaries, the power of language, cultural relativism, and the loss of the universal and individual in favor of group identity. These themes are explicitly central to the postcolonial Theory mind-set and decolonize movement. We can find them all in this statement of the purpose of decolonizing philosophy:

> Philosophy seems to have a special place among discourses in the liberal arts because it focuses on the roots of the university at large: reason. This includes providing criteria for identifying and demarcating the humanities, the natural sciences and the social sciences, as well as for distinguishing reason from faith, secularism from religion, and the "primitive" and the ancient from the modern. These are central columns in the edifice that sustains modern Western rationality and the modern Western university. The modern

Western research university and liberal arts therefore owe much of their basic conceptual infrastructure to philosophical formulations of rationality, universalism, subjectivity, the relationship between the subject and object, truth and method—all of which become relevant targets of critical analysis in the decolonial turn.[37]

This is a textbook example of applied postmodernism, and it is, of course, actionable. The action it advocates is often referred to as "research justice."

ACHIEVING RESEARCH JUSTICE

Research justice acts upon a belief that science, reason, empiricism, objectivity, universality, and subjectivity have been overvalued as ways of obtaining knowledge while emotion, experience, traditional narratives and customs, and spiritual beliefs have been undervalued. Therefore, a more complete and just system of knowledge production would value the latter at least as much as the former—in fact, more, because of the long reign of science and reason in the West. The 2015 book, *Research Justice: Methodologies for Social Change*, edited by Andrew Jolivette, is a key text here. Jolivette, professor and former department chair of American Indian Studies at San Francisco State University, defines the aims of this method in his introduction:

> "[R]esearch justice" is a strategic framework and methodological intervention that aims to transform structural inequalities in research. . . . It is built around a vision of equal political power and legitimacy for different forms of knowledge, including the cultural, spiritual, and experiential, with the goal of greater equality in public policies and laws that rely on data and research to produce social change.[38]

This is activism. It seeks not only to revolutionize understandings of knowledge and rigor in university curricula—not necessarily to improve them—but also to influence public policies away from evidenced and reasoned work and towards the emotional, religious, cultural, and traditional, with an emphasis on *lived experience*. It seeks to challenge the core understanding of "scholarly research" as the gathering of empirical data for analysis, in order to better understand social issues. This theme comes across most strongly in the 2004 book, *Decolonizing Research in Cross-Cultural Contexts: Critical Personal Narratives*,[39] which focuses on indigenous studies and is edited by Kagendo Mutua, professor of special education at the University of Alabama, and Beth Blue Swadener, Professor of Culture, Society and Education / Justice and Social Inquiry at the University of Arizona. Citing Homi Bhabha, the editors introduce the essays by claiming,

> These works stand at the center of the "beginning of the presencing" of a disharmonious, restive, unharnessable (hence unessentializable) knowledge that is produced at the ex-centric site of neo/post/colonial resistance, "which can never allow the national (*read: colonial/western*) history to look itself narcissistically in the eye."[40] (emphasis in original)

This means that the authors of the essays within this volume are not obliged to make sense, produce reasoned arguments, avoid logical contradiction, or provide any evidence for their claims. The normal expectations of scholarly "research" do not apply when pursuing research justice. This is alarming, and it is justified Theoretically. In the words of professor of indigenous education at the University of Waikato in New Zealand, Linda Tuhiwai Smith,

> [F]rom the vantage point of the colonised, a position from which I write and choose to privilege, the term "research" is inextricably linked to European imperialism and colonialism. The word itself "research" is probably one of the dirtiest words in the indigenous world's vocabulary.[41]

It is unclear how this attitude is likely to help people in the "indigenous world," which, barring the decolonization of time, also happens to have entered the twenty-first century.

Ultimately, "research justice" amounts to judging scholarly productions not by their rigor or quality but by the identity of their producer and privileging those understood by postcolonial theory as marginalized as long as they are advocating knowledge production methods and conclusions that conform to those of postcolonial theory. This is an understandable move for postmodernists, who deny that there can be any objective criteria of rigor or quality, only those that have been privileged and those that have been marginalized. But in science (including social science) there is an objective criterion of quality, namely, correspondence to reality. Some scientific theories work and others don't. It is hard to see how scientific theories that don't correspond with reality and consequently don't work can benefit marginalized people, or anyone.

MAINTAINING THE PROBLEM, BACKWARDS

The attitude that rigorous, evidence-based research and reasoned, non-contradictory arguments belong to the West while experiential, irrational, and contradictory "knowledge" belongs to colonized or displaced indigenous people is of course not universally accepted by colonized and indigenous scholars. Many of them continue to produce empirical and materialist analyses of economic, political, and legal issues in various settings. These scholars criticize the postmodern approach to postcolonialism. Perhaps the most outstanding critic is the Indian postcolonial scholar Meera Nanda. She argues that, by assigning science and reason to the West and traditional, spiritual, experiential beliefs to India, postmodern scholars perpetuate Orientalism and make it very difficult to address the many real issues that can best be tackled using science and reason. In these critics' view, she observes, "modern science is as much a local tradition of the West, as the indigenous knowledge of the non-Western subaltern is a local knowledge of his culture."[42] Thus, criticizing traditional knowledge using science is understood from within postcolonial Theory to be, as Nanda puts it,

> the stuff of "Orientalist" Enlightenment, a colonial modernity which privileges a Western conception of reason and modernity over

non-Western ways of knowing and being. We postcolonial hybrids are supposed to have seen through the claims of "universality" and "progress" of science (the scare quotes are obligatory). We no longer believe in the "binaries" between science and non-science, or truth and customary beliefs, but see them both as a little bit of each. This condition of permanent hybridity thus does not put any pressure to resolve any contradiction . . . : Let a thousand contradictions bloom![43]

Nanda recognizes that the Theoretical approach to postcolonialism maintains the problem of Orientalism by attempting to erect the same categories and simply reverse the power structures (the same very Derridean trick intentionally employed by Spivak). While colonialism constructs the East as a foil to the West, postcolonial Theory intentionally constructs the East in nobly oppressed opposition to the West (while liberalism says that people are people, wherever they live). For Nanda, this postmodern approach, with its focus on nonclass identities, hinders the technological and social progress that would benefit the poorer people of India and thus is much more in keeping with conservative attitudes than progressive ones.[44] Furthermore, Nanda maintains that it is demeaning to Indian people to assign irrational and superstitious knowledge to them and to assume that science is a tradition that belongs to the West, rather than a uniquely human development that is difficult to achieve, but extremely beneficial to all societies.[45]

Indeed. The postmodern position that Western society is dominated by discourses of science and reason is not supported by the evidence that most of us still value our group narratives, cultures, and beliefs and know little of science. Attacks on science from the religious right and the postmodern left are strong influences on society that always have to be struggled against.

A DANGEROUS, PATRONIZING THEORY

As an applied postmodern Theory, postcolonial Theory is of considerable real-world concern and poses threats to society that the original postmodernism did not. The drives to decolonize everything from hair[46] to English literature curricula,[47] to tear down paintings and smash statues, and to erase history while opening up revisionist discussions of it, are particularly alarming. When Winston Churchill, Joseph Conrad, and Rudyard Kipling become nothing more than symbols of racist imperialism and their achievements and writings are too tainted to be acknowledged, we lose not only the potential for any nuanced discussion of history and progress but also the positive contributions of the men themselves.

More egregiously still, postcolonial Theory, with its disparagement of science and reason as provincial Western ways of knowing, not only threatens the foundations of advanced contemporary societies but also impedes the progress of developing ones. Since many developing countries would benefit from technological infrastructure, which could ameliorate some of the world's most significant causes of human suffering—malaria, water shortages, poor sanitation in remote rural areas, and the like—this claim is not only factually wrong, morally vacant, and patronizing; it is also negligent and dangerous.

Great practical harm is also done by postcolonialism's cultural relativism, which is found in both its scholarship and activism. It believes that the West, having trampled other cultures and enforced alien moral frameworks on them, must now cease to criticize, or in some cases help more directly, any aspect of those cultures. This results in great ethical inconsistency in human rights activism, with serious real-world consequences. For example, when feminists from Saudi Arabia, secular liberals from Pakistan, and LGBT rights activists from Uganda have attempted to raise the support of the English-speaking world by using hashtags in English on social media to draw attention to human rights abuses, they have received little response from the applied postmodern scholars and activists who might otherwise be assumed to be in their corners. This may seem baffling or hypocritical, but it makes sense within a theoretical framework that does not operate according to universal principles of human rights but believes in binary systems of power, which allow only for the Western oppressor and Eastern (or globally Southern) oppressed. This results in two common claims:

First, postcolonial Theory insists that getting a non-Western culture to accept that there are human rights abuses taking place locally requires colonizing that culture with Western notions of human rights and their violation. This is verboten, because it reinforces the power dynamic that postcolonial Theory exists to dismantle.

Second, postcolonial Theory frequently claims that any human rights abuses occurring in previously colonized countries are the legacy of colonialism and its analysis stops there. This obviously makes such abuses difficult to address in their own contexts and with their own stated motivations, which are often connected to non-Western religious and cultural beliefs. For instance, the widespread abuse of women, secularists, and LGBT in strict Islamist cultures is not taken as a feature of authoritarian interpretations of Islam—as the Islamists themselves claim—but interpreted as a result of Western colonialism and imperialism, which perverted that culture and caused it to become abusive. This is a direct hindrance to the very secularization campaigns that could help ameliorate those problems.

This arises from first assuming the cause of a phenomenon and then looking for evidence of that cause. Since they look at oppression only in terms of colonialism, colonialism is all these scholars and activists are equipped to find. As a result, not only do they hamstring their ability to understand—and therefore ameliorate—the problems they are seeking to solve, but they also tend to make them worse. This commonly results in a marked tendency to neglect the rights of women and of sexual and religious minorities, unless they are threatened by white Westerners. This goes against achieving social justice—but it's integral to the ideology called Social Justice.

Because they view knowledge and ethics as cultural constructs perpetuated in language, postcolonial Theorists can be extremely difficult to discuss disagreements with. Evidenced and reasoned arguments are understood Theoretically as Western constructs and are therefore considered invalid or even oppressive. Those who disagree with postcolonial Theory are seen as confirming the Theory and as defending racist, colonialist, or imperialist attitudes for their own benefit and to shut out the viewpoints of others.

Furthermore, this scholarship, which proceeds on the assumption that there are power imbalances to be discovered if language and interactions are deconstructed, cannot help but "find" increasing examples of "othering," "Orientalism," and "appropriation" in ever more tendentious ways. This is not a bug, but a feature. It is what the *critical* approach in Theory *means*. There is always more to interpret and more to deconstruct, and, with enough motivation and creativity, anything can be problematized. Intense sensitivity to language and the reading of power imbalances into all interactions that involve an individual with a marginalized identity and a white Westerner are common to all forms of applied postmodern Social Justice scholarship.

This problem should not be underestimated. We can only learn from the realities of colonialism and its aftermath by studying them rigorously. Those postcolonial scholars and activists who deny the attainability of objective reality and seek to revise history along Theoretical lines are not doing this. Neither are those who reject logical reasoning, evidence-based research, science, and medicine, nor those who argue that space and time themselves are Western constructs, nor those who write incomprehensible, obfuscatory prose and deny that language can have meaning anyway.

These scholars, whose influence far outweighs their numbers, generally trained or work in elite Western academia and operate according to a densely theoretical framework that originated in France and proliferated in the United States and the United Kingdom. Their work is of very little practical relevance to people living in previously colonized countries, who are trying to deal with the political and economic aftermath. There is little reason to believe that previously colonized people have any use for a postcolonial Theory or decoloniality that argues that math is a tool of Western imperialism,[48] that sees alphabetical literacy as colonial technology and postcolonial appropriation,[49] that views research as the production of totalizing meta-texts of colonial knowledge,[50] or that confronts France and the United States about their understanding of big black butts.[51]

4 QUEER THEORY

Freedom from the Normal

Queer Theory is about liberation from the normal, especially where it comes to norms of gender and sexuality. This is because it regards the very existence of categories of sex, gender, and sexuality to be oppressive. Because queer Theory derives directly from postmodernism, it is radically skeptical that these categories are based in any biological reality. Instead, it sees them quite artificially—wholly as a product of how we talk about those issues. It thus ignores biology nearly completely (or places it downstream of socialization) and focuses upon them as social constructions perpetuated in language. This does little to encourage its accessibility with most people, who rightly see it as being quite mad.

Queer Theory presumes that oppression follows from categorization, which arises every time language constructs a sense of what is "normal" by producing and maintaining rigid categories of sex (male and female), gender (masculine and feminine), and sexuality (straight, gay, lesbian, bisexual, and so on) and "scripting" people into them. These seemingly straightforward concepts are seen as oppressive, if not violent, and so the main objective of queer Theory is to examine, question, and subvert them, in order to break them down.

This is all done in ways that explicitly rely on the postmodern knowledge principle—which rejects the possibility that an objective reality is attainable—and the postmodern political principle—which understands society to be structured in unjust systems of power that reinforce and perpetuate themselves. Queer Theory makes use of these to satisfy its ultimate purpose, which is to identify and make visible the ways in which the linguistic existence of these categories create oppression, and to disrupt them. In doing so, it exhibits an almost unmodified manifestation of the postmodern themes of the power of language—language creates the categories, enforces them, and scripts people into them—and the blurring of boundaries—the boundaries are arbitrary, oppressive, and can be erased by blurring them into apparent absurdity. Together with its goal of subverting or rejecting anything considered normal and innate in favor of the "queer," this can make queer Theory frustratingly difficult to understand, since it values incoherence, illogic, and unintelligibility. This in turn makes it obscure by design and largely irrelevant, except to itself. Nevertheless, it has been profoundly influential on the development of postmodern Theory into its more recent applied forms, particularly in domains like gender studies, trans activism, disability studies, and fat studies.

A BRIEF HISTORY OF QUEER THEORY

Like postcolonial Theory, queer Theory developed in response to a particular historical context. It grew out of the radical groups that had been revolutionizing feminist, gay, and lesbian studies, and related activism since the 1960s. The civil rights movements also helped spark a new interest in the study of homosexuality, and the ways in which it had been categorized and stigmatized, both historically and in the present. Queer Theory was deeply influenced by the AIDS crisis of the 1980s, which made gay rights issues an urgent central social and political concern.

Like postcolonial Theory, queer Theory has a solid underlying point. We *have* changed the way we see sexuality quite profoundly. Throughout Christian history, male homosexuality has been considered a heinous sin. This is in stark contrast to ancient Greek culture, where it was acceptable for men to have sex with adolescent boys until they were ready to marry—at which point it was expected that they would switch to having sex with women. In both cases, however, homosexuality was *something that people did* rather than *who they were*. The idea that one could *be* a homosexual only began to gain recognition in the nineteenth century, appearing first in medical texts and within homosexual subcultures. Contemporary medical texts described homosexuality as a perversion. Public perception of homosexuals then gradually started to shift, due to the rise of sexology at the end of the nineteenth century, and, by the middle of the twentieth, homosexuals were regarded less as corrupt degenerates who required punishment and more as shamefully disordered individuals who required psychiatric treatment.

Over the second half of the twentieth century, this attitude shifted again until a dominant liberal discourse around homosexuality—which still holds the moral high ground today—evolved. This attitude is best summed up as "Some people are gay. Get over it." Since queer Theory is an applied postmodernist Theory, however, this universal liberal idea, which stresses our common humanity over a specific demographic identity, is considered problematic. It is Theorized as a problem both because it presents LGBT (lesbian, gay, bisexual, and trans) identities as stable categories and because it does not foreground LGBT statuses as social constructs, built by the powerful in the service of dominance and oppression.

While there have been dramatic changes in how we regard homosexuality over the last century and a half, our understanding of sex and gender has changed much less. We have generally always understood our species as overwhelmingly consisting of two sexes, and gender as mostly correlated with sex. Gender *roles*, however, have changed considerably. Throughout most of Christian history, men had been associated with the public sphere and the mind (*sapientia*) and women with the private sphere and the body (*scientia*), which has led to analogies like "men are to women as culture is to nature."[1] Women were therefore considered suited to subservient, domestic, and nurturing roles and men to leadership, public engagement, and assertive managerial roles. These attitudes, which are referred to as *biological essentialism*, represent a largely cultural requirement, which dominated society until roughly the end of the nineteenth century, when feminist thought and activism began to erode them.

As biological essentialism faltered, a need to distinguish with greater clarity between sex and gender arose. Although the word "gender" was not used to describe humans until the twentieth century—some languages still have no comparable word—the *idea* of gender seems to have always been with us. Sex is to gender as man is to manly or woman to womanly. Thus, gender has seemingly always been understood as correlated with but distinct from sex. If the sentence, "She is a very masculine woman," makes sense to you, you already distinguish sex—a biological category—from gender—behaviors and traits commonly manifesting more in one sex. History is full of examples of people referring to "manly" and "womanly," or masculine and feminine, traits and behaviors and applying these adjectives both approvingly and disapprovingly to both men and women.

However, a profound change took place during Western second-wave feminism in the latter half of the twentieth century, when women gained control over their reproductive function and the rights to access all jobs and be paid the same as men for the same work. Now women are to be found in every profession and experience few legal or cultural barriers to entry throughout the West, although they still do not make the same choices in the same numbers as men do. Similar changes resulted from the gay rights and eventually Pride and trans rights movements, which have succeeded at removing many legal and cultural barriers for LGBT people. Even though most of these changes were the result of recognizing the biological roots of sex, gender, and sexuality and the attitudes involved were broadly liberal and individualist—"she's a person who is trans; okay, fine"—they are taken as evidence of the social constructedness of gender and sexuality by queer Theorists, especially those with a feminist perspective. For example, the gap between sex and gender has been taken as evidence that gender—and even sex—are social constructions.[2]

Since queer Theorists believe that sex, gender, and sexuality are social constructions, chiefly dependent on the prevailing culture, they are less concerned about material progress than about how dominant discourses erect and enforce categories like "male," "feminine," and "gay." In all fairness, these scholars and activists are rightly concerned about the cultural power dynamics that naturally come along for the ride when such categories are considered real, meaningful, and *normative*. It was in this context that queer Theory arose,[3] and its founders, including Gayle Rubin, Judith Butler, and Eve Kosofsky Sedgwick, drew significantly upon the work of Michel Foucault and his concept of *biopower*— the power of scientific (biological) discourses. Unfortunately, they seem to have missed the point that biologically legitimizing sex, gender, and sexuality statuses tends to lead people to become more accepting, rather than less,[4] and that such discourses are no longer misused to exclude and oppress. Liberalism generated the type of progress postmodern Theories tend to claim credit for—without using postmodern Theories.

TO QUEER, V.; THE QUEER, N.

Queer Theory is dominated by the problematizing of discourses—how things are spoken about—the deconstruction of categories, and a profound skepticism of science. Following Foucault, it frequently examines history and points out that categories and discourses that were accepted as obviously sensible or true in their own time are not accepted as such now. This is used to argue that the categories that seem so obvious to us now—male/female, masculine/feminine, heterosexual/homosexual— are also socially constructed by dominant discourses. This, to the queer Theorist, is reason to believe not only that we will be able to think and speak about and categorize sex, gender, and sexuality differently in the future, but also that we may consider such categories largely arbitrary and nearly infinitely malleable.

This is where the word *queer* comes in. "Queer" refers to anything that falls outside binaries (such as male/female, masculine/feminine, and heterosexual/homosexual) and to a way of challenging the links between sex, gender, and sexuality. For example, it questions expectations that women will be feminine and sexually attracted to men, and it also disputes that one must fall into a category of male or female, masculine or feminine, or any particular sexuality, or that any of these categories should be considered stable. To be queer allows someone to be simultaneously male, female, or neither, to present as masculine, feminine,

neuter, or any mixture of the three, and to adopt any sexuality—and
to change any of these identities at any time or to deny that they mean
anything in the first place. This is not merely a means to individual expression but also a political statement about the socially constructed "realities" of sex, gender, and sexuality.

Like the other postmodern Theories, queer Theory is a political
project, and its aim is to disrupt any expectations that people should fit
into a binary position with regard to sex or gender, and to undermine
any assumptions that sex or gender are related to or dictate sexuality.
Instead, they should defy simple categorization. In general, then, queer
Theory's political agenda is to challenge what is called *normativity*—that
some things are more common or regular to the human condition, thus
more normative from a social (thus moral) perspective, than others. The
main industry of queer Theorists is to intentionally conflate two meanings of "normative," and deliberately make strategic use of the moral
understanding of the term to contrive problems with its descriptive
meaning. Normativity is considered pejoratively by queer Theorists and
is often preceded by a prefix like *hetero-* (straight), *cis-* (gender and sex
match), or *thin-* (not obese). By challenging normativity in all its manifestations, queer Theory therefore seeks to unite the minority groups who
fall outside of normative categories under a single banner: "queer." This
project is understood to be liberating for people who do not fall neatly
into sex, gender, and sexuality categories, along with those who wouldn't
if they hadn't been socialized into them and weren't constrained by social enforcement. It produces a *de facto* coalition of minority gender and
sexual identities under the appropriately unstable set of acronyms that
tend to begin with LGBTQ.[5]

Because this is a political project for queer activists, in recent years it
has become common to hear "queer" used as a verb. *To queer* something
is to cast doubt upon its stability, to disrupt seemingly fixed categories,
and to problematize any "binaries" within it. When scholars speak of
queering something, they mean they intend to remove it from the categories within which we understand it now and look at it in new and
counterintuitive ways. Queering is about unmaking any sense of the
normal, in order to liberate people from the expectations that norms
carry. According to queer Theory, these expectations—whether explicit

or implicit—generate a cultural and political power ("the personal is political"), which is referred to as normativity, and which constrains and oppresses people who fail to identify with it. This phenomenon may not have anything to do with gender or sexuality, and has even expanded to include time and space[6] and queer Theory itself.[7] Queer Theory, then, is essentially about the belief that to categorize gender and sexuality (or anything else) is to legitimize one discourse—the normative one—as knowledge and use it to constrain individuals. It addresses this problem in postmodern ways, which draw especially upon the Theorizing of Michel Foucault and Jacques Derrida.

This makes queer Theory notoriously difficult to define, perhaps partly because being comprehensible would be inconsistent with queer Theory's radical distrust of language and would violate its ambition to avoid all categorization, including of itself. Nevertheless, David Halperin attempts to define "queer" in his 1997 book, *Saint Foucault: Towards a Gay Hagiography*, in which he argues that Foucault's idea that sexuality is a product of discourse revolutionized gay and lesbian political activism. He describes "queer" as "*whatever* is at odds with the normal, the legitimate, the dominant. *There is nothing in particular to which it necessarily refers.* It is an identity without an essence."[8] (emphasis in original)

Because the central feature of queer Theory is that it resists categorization and distrusts language, it is generally difficult to work with. Queer Theory is not only resistant to definition in the usual sense, but also to functional definitions based on what it does. Papers that use queer Theory usually begin by examining an idea, problematizing it in queer (or "queering" or "genderfucking"[9]) ways, and eventually concluding that there can be no conclusions. As Annamarie Jagose, the author of *Queer Theory: An Introduction*, puts it, "It is not simply that queer has yet to solidify and take on a more consistent profile, but rather that its definitional indeterminacy, its elasticity, is one of its constituent characteristics."[10] The incoherence of queer Theory is an intentional feature, not a bug.

THE QUEER LEGACY OF THE HISTORY OF SEXUALITY

Despite the deliberate weirdness—which Jagose lists among its "charms"—queer Theory is *mostly, but not entirely*, unreasonable in its social constructivist views. As most people now acknowledge, many of our ideas about sex, gender, and sexuality—and particularly about their associated roles—are social constructions that are somewhat malleable, since culture changes over time. Very few people are strict biological essentialists anymore—and, those who are, are shown to be wrong by scientists.[11] Nearly everyone accepts that some combination of human biology and culture comes together to create expressions of sex, gender, and sexuality. As evolutionary biologist E. O. Wilson states, "No serious scholar would think that human behavior is controlled the way animal instinct is, without the intervention of culture."[12]

This is not the prevailing view of queer Theorists, however. Because queer Theory is thoroughly postmodern, it is *radically* socially constructivist. There can be absolutely no quarter given to any discourse—even matters of scientific fact—that could be interpreted as promoting or legitimizing biological essentialism. As a result, if biology makes an appearance in queer Theoretical scholarship it is usually for one of two purposes: to problematize it as merely one way of knowing—a chauvinist one that has encoded the biases of powerful groups, such as straight men who identify as men; or to demonstrate something that no one denies—that intersex people exist. The existence of intersex people is pointed out only to obfuscate the facts that an overwhelming proportion of *Homo sapiens* are either male- or female-sexed and that gender expression in humans is overwhelmingly bimodal in nature and strongly correlated with sex. These undeniable facts are summarily problematized as supporting normativity and are therefore suppressed by queer Theory.

This radical neglect of biology limits the ability not just of queer Theory but of *all scholarship on these topics* to rigorously investigate socialized aspects of gender presentation and expectations—while rendering potentially valuable insights from queer Theory nearly completely irrelevant to those serious about such questions. There are biologists and psychologists advancing knowledge of how the sexes differ (or do not differ) biologically and psychologically on average, how sexuality works, and why some people are gay, lesbian, bisexual, or transgender—but their work is not welcome in queer Theory. On the contrary, such knowledge is generally regarded with the utmost suspicion, as an inherently dangerous or even "violent" way to categorize and constrain those who do not fit neatly into one of the following two categories: "masculine man attracted to women" and "feminine woman attracted to men."[13]

This understanding of the oppressive role of science can be largely traced back to Michel Foucault. Foucault studied the production of "power-knowledge"—how knowledge is socially constructed by discourses, in the service of power—and was particularly concerned with "biopower"—how the biological sciences legitimize the knowledge that the powerful use to maintain their dominance. In his four-volume study, *The History of Sexuality*,[14] Foucault argues that, since the late seventeenth century, far from suppressing speech about sex (as neo-Marxist thinkers like Marcuse had argued), there has been an explosion of talk about sex—both the act and the biological concept. As scientists began to study and categorize sexuality, Foucault claims, they simultaneously constructed it and created the sexual identities and categories that accompany these constructions.

> The society that emerged in the nineteenth century—bourgeois, capitalist, or industrial society, call it what you will—did not confront sex with a fundamental refusal of recognition. On the contrary, it put into operation an entire machinery for producing true discourses concerning it.[15]

Foucault's view was that the discourses produced by this "machinery" gained social legitimacy as "truth" and then permeated all levels of society. This is a process of power but not, as the Marxist philosophers had claimed, one in which religious or secular authorities enforce an ideology on the common people. In Marxist thought, power is like a weight, pressing down on the proletariat. For Foucault, power operated more like a grid, running through all layers of society and determining what people held to be true and, consequently, how they spoke about it. The view from Foucault, thus Theory, is that power is a system we're all constantly participating in by how we talk about things and what ideas we're willing to consider legitimate, a system into which we are socialized. The prime culprit for legitimizing knowledge—and thus power—in Foucault's view was science, which held prestige in society for exactly that purpose. This is what Foucault referred to as "biopower," claiming that scientific discourse "set itself up as the supreme authority in matters of hygienic necessity," and "in the name of biological and historical urgency, it justified the racisms of the state" because "[i]t grounded them in 'truth.'"[16] Foucault argues that power runs through the whole system of society, perpetuating itself through powerful discourses. He called this the "omnipresence of power."

· "Power is everywhere," Foucault writes, "not because it embraced everything, but because it comes from everywhere."[17] For Foucault, power is present on all levels of society because certain knowledges have been legitimized and accepted as true. This leads people to learn to speak in these discourses, which further reinforces them. Power works like this, for Foucault, "not because it has the privilege of consolidating everything under its invincible unity, but because it is produced from one moment to the next, at every point, or rather in every relation from one point to another."[18] This view has gone on to become one of the core beliefs of applied postmodernism and Social Justice activism today: unjust power is everywhere, always, and it manifests in biases that are largely invisible because they have been internalized as "normal."[19] Consequently, speech is to be closely scrutinized to discover which discourses it is perpetuating, under the presumption that racism, sexism, homophobia, transphobia, or other latent prejudices must be present in the discourses and thus endemic to the society that produces them. (This is circular reasoning.) These "problematics" need to be identified and exposed, whether they manifest in a president's address or in the decade-old adolescent tweet history of a relative nobody. The widespread slang term "woke" describes having become aware of and more able to see these problematics.

From these basic premises, first spelled out in the 1970s, Foucault provided the philosophical foundations for the queer Theory of the 1990s, which included a deep suspicion of science as an oppressive exercise of power rather than a knowledge producer, a skepticism of all categories that describe gender and sexuality, a commitment to social constructivism, and an intense focus on language, as the means by which power disguised as knowledge infiltrates all levels of society and establishes what is accepted as normal.

THE FAIRY GODMOTHERS OF QUEER THEORY

Queer Theory evolved out of a postmodernist consideration of sex, gender, and sexuality. Its three founding figures are Gayle Rubin, Judith Butler, and Eve Kosofsky Sedgwick, all of whom drew heavily upon Foucault. Each also vigorously resisted normativity in the three main domains to which queer Theory devotes the bulk of its attention. These three Theorists laid the cornerstones of the core projects of queer Theory, which emerged in the mid-1980s.

In her 1984 essay, "Thinking Sex," Gayle Rubin argues that what we consider "good sex" and "bad sex" (in moral terms, all quality assurances aside) are socially constructed by various groups and their discourses about sexuality.[20] Drawing on Foucault's concept of the social construction of sexuality beginning in the nineteenth century, she became deeply skeptical of any biological studies of sex and sexuality. Her essay made a foundational contribution to queer Theory by rejecting what she saw as "sexual essentialism"—"the idea that sex is a natural force that exists prior to social life and shapes institutions."[21] For Rubin,

> It is impossible to think with any clarity about the politics of race or gender as long as these are thought of as biological entities rather than as social constructs. Similarly, sexuality is impervious to political analysis as long as it is primarily conceived as a biological phenomenon or an aspect of individual psychology.[22]

This is a highly pragmatic, even agenda-driven, argument. Rubin asserts that we should believe sex, gender, and sexuality to be social constructs, *not* because it's necessarily true, but because it is *easier to politicize them and demand change* if they are social constructs than if they are biological. Where one might at least see Foucault's cynical reading of the history of sexuality as descriptive of what has been and is, Rubin's was plainly one that was ready to take up an *ought* and put it ahead of what *is*. This is a feature of *applied* postmodernism that distinguishes it somewhat from the postmodernism that came before—and it has consequences. It undermines public trust in the academy, which is generally considered a guardian of what *is*, by making it more like a church, which conveys that which people *ought* to think and believe.

This agenda-driven view, which lies at the heart of queer Theory, goes against both the rigor of scientific inquiry and the ethics of universal liberal activism for gender and LGBT equality: liberalism does not require one to believe that gender and sexuality are socially constructed in order to argue that there is no justification for discriminating against anyone. Rubin states her position on this in "Thinking Sex":

> Concepts of sexual oppression have been lodged within that more biological understanding of sexuality. It is often easier to fall back on the notion of a natural libido subjected to inhumane repression than to reformulate concepts of sexual injustice within a more constructivist framework. But it is essential that we do so.[23]

Rubin insists that it is crucial to reject biology and fully embrace the idea that sex and sexuality have been constructed in an unjust hierarchy,[24] even though she recognizes that it would be easier to accept what is far more likely to be true—that different sexualities exist naturally and some of them have been unfairly discriminated against.

Rubin's "Thinking Sex" provides both an early indication of the coming development of intersectionality and a rejection of contemporary forms of radical feminism. Describing the hierarchy of sexuality, Rubin notes, "This kind of sexual morality has more in common with ideologies of racism than with true ethics. It grants virtue to the dominant groups, and relegates vice to the underprivileged."[25] She also recognizes that "sex is a vector of oppression . . . cut[ting] across other modes of social inequality, sorting out individuals and groups according to its own intrinsic dynamics."[26] Rubin therefore took aim at the dominant form of (radical) feminism at the time—which was very negative about sex and sexuality and focused on the material harms of sexual objectification—and (not wholly wrongly) likened its approach to socially conservative, right-wing views.

For Rubin, radical constructivism and a focus on the discourses around sex were essential to the liberation of those whose sexuality or gender identity was not typically cisgendered, gender-conforming, and heterosexual. The dismissal of biology and any explanation of variations in sexuality or gender identity it might offer was considered a political necessity, justified through a profound moral relativism about sexuality (including a defense of pedophilia). Thus, we see in queer Theory a rejection of science when it returns results that deviate from Theory, of liberalism when it puts universal humanity first, and of feminism when it regards women as a class of people oppressed by another class of people—men—and, instead, the prioritization of "queerness."

The most influential queer Theorist who theorized this issue of queerness is Judith Butler, and it is her work that has most successfully broken the bounds of queer Theory and become influential on many forms of scholarship and even in wider society. Butler is an American philosopher, influenced by French feminist thought, who draws heavily upon postmodernism, especially the work of Foucault and Derrida. Butler's chief contribution to queer Theory was to question the links between sex—the biological categories of male and female—gender—the behaviors and traits commonly associated with one sex or the other—and sexuality—the nature of sexual desire.

In the 1990s, Butler was phobic about any whiff of biological essentialism. She argued extensively that gender and sex are distinct and that there is no necessary correlation between the two. For Butler, gender is *wholly* socially constructed—a claim so ridiculous that it required much Theorizing to establish it as believable. Butler did so primarily by employing her most well-known concept: *gender performativity*. This is a remarkably complicated idea defined in her 1993 book, *Bodies That Matter: On the Discursive Limits of "Sex,"* as "that reiterative power of discourse to produce the phenomena that it regulates and constrains"[27]—that is, how something is brought into being, placed into meaningful categories, and made "real" by behaviors and expectations encoded in speech. Among other features, one immediately notices the postmodern political principle, as derived from Foucault, and the related theme of the power of language.

Although the term evokes the idea of a stage performance, the concept of gender performativity is derived from a branch of linguistics and doesn't refer to acting. A male actor could, for example, perform a female stage role, while still retaining his belief in himself as a man. This is not what Butler means when she describes gender as "performative,"

as that would require some "preexisting identity by which an act or attri-
bute might be measured,"[28] which she insists does not exist where gender
is concerned. Instead, in her groundbreaking book, *Gender Trouble: Feminism and the Subversion of Identity* (1990), Butler claims that gender roles are
taught and learned—often unwittingly, through socialization—as sets
of actions, behaviors, manners, and expectations, and people perform
those roles accordingly. Gender, for Butler, is a set of things a person *does*,
not something to do with who they *are*. Society enforces these actions and
associates them with linguistic cues like "male" and "manly," so these
roles become "real" through gender performativity. For Butler, because
of the immense socializing pressures and normativity of gender roles,
people are unable to help learning to perform their gender "correctly,"
as though playing out a rehearsed script, and thereby end up perpetuating the social reality called "gender."

Butler's view is that people are not born knowing themselves to be
male, female, straight, or gay, and thus do not act in accordance with
any such innate factors. Instead, they are socialized into these roles from
birth by their near ubiquity and the attendant social expectations and
instructions (normativity). In themselves, roles like heterosexuality or homosexuality do not represent stable or fixed categories, but are merely
things people do. It is, for her, only by taking up these roles and "performing" them according to those social expectations (performativity),
that people create the (oppressive) illusion that the roles themselves are
real, stable, and inherently meaningful. The notion of *discursive construction*—the idea that the way a particular society talks about things legiti-
mizes them, making them seem self-evidently true—is therefore key to
understanding queer Theory because it is through discursive construction that these roles and expectations are created and perpetuated.

Butler's ironically detached view of gender therefore follows Foucault closely and describes a vast social conspiracy, which plays out both
intentionally and unwittingly—a common theme in applied postmodern
Theory. She describes "a true gender identity" as "a regulatory fiction"
that needs to be "revealed."[29] The "regulatory fictions" of sex, gender,
and sexuality are, she argues, maintained through the ubiquity of gender performativity, which contains "the strategy that conceals gender's
performative character."[30] For her, the mission of queer Theory and ac-

tivism is therefore to liberate "the performative possibilities for prolifer-ating gender configurations outside the restricting frames of masculinist domination and compulsory heterosexuality."[31] That is, if we recognize gender as performative, we can also see that it can be performed in ways that do not privilege the masculine and heterosexual.

Butler Theorizes this by using the Derridean notion of *phallogocen-trism*—the idea that social reality is constructed by language that privileg-es the masculine—and by expanding upon Adrienne Rich's concept of *compulsory heterosexuality*[32]—wherein heterosexuality is taken as the natural state of being, and homosexuality is therefore scripted as a perversion, to enforce compliance with "doing straightness." Butler, however, was not optimistic about our ability to disrupt these allegedly hegemonic discourses (ways of speaking about things that hold almost unassailable power, a concept adapted into Theory from the views of Marxist phi-losopher Antonio Gramsci). Instead, she believed that it is impossible to step outside of social constructions created by discourses: we can only trouble and disrupt them, to make space for those who do not fit.

Butler's proposed solution to this intractable problem had a pro-found influence upon the activists who followed in her wake: she ad-vocated *the politics of parody*, a "subversive and parodic redeployment of power."[33] This approach attempts to subvert the patterns of gender per-formativity—particularly phallogocentrism and compulsory heterosexu-ality—which "seek to augment themselves through a constant repetition of their logic, their metaphysic, and their naturalized ontologies"[34] by rendering them absurd. To achieve this, Butler advocated deliberately "subversive repetition" that "might call into question the regulatory practice of identity itself."[35] This is often achieved by "genderfucking," which *Wiktionary* defines as "the conscious effort to subvert traditional notions of gender identity and gender roles," through the employment of drag, say, or the "queer-camp" aesthetic.

The purpose of Butlerian parody is to cause people to question the assumptions upon which performativity is based and thus be able to see it as a socially constructed illusion that is, ultimately, both arbitrary and oppressive in its current forms. The point of this is to achieve liberation from these categories and the expectations that come with them. Judith Butler advocates a move towards incoherence. If an activist can make the

incoherence of rigid categories of sex, gender, and sexuality obvious—
if not ridiculous—then those categories and the oppression they create
cease to be as meaningful. Butler asserts this so tenaciously that she has
even called into question whether biological sex can be considered anything other than a cultural construct. In *Gender Trouble*, she writes,

> If the immutable character of sex is contested, perhaps this
> construct called "sex" is as culturally constructed as gender; indeed,
> perhaps it was always already gender, with the consequence that the
> distinction between sex and gender turns out to be no distinction
> at all.[36]

Butler directly challenged the prevailing forms of feminism by asking,
rather incomprehensibly, "Is the construction of the category of women
as a coherent and stable subject an unwitting regulation and reification
of gender relations?"[37] That is, might the ways that we consider "woman" to be a real biological category have the unintended consequence
of creating a "coherent and stable" notion of what it is to be a woman?

For Butler, then, the very existence of coherent and stable categories
like "woman" leads to totalitarian and oppressive discourses. Though
most people would find such a conclusion properly ridiculous, her queer
Theory rests on resisting and subverting these categories. Underscoring
her seriousness, she describes as a kind of violence of categorization
the scripting of people into a category, such as a gender, that they feel
does not adequately or accurately describe them. For Butler, activism
and scholarship must disrupt these discourses to minimize the apparent
harms of this "violence."

The focus on breaking down categories by rendering them apparently incoherent is also central to Eve Kosofsky Sedgwick, whose work
lies at the foundations of queer Theory. Her contributions to Theory are
ultimately about resisting the temptation to resolve contradictions and
finding value in *plurality*—accepting many perspectives all at once, even
when they are mutually contradictory—and in *incoherence*—not attempting to make rational sense of anything. Consistent with the ought-over-is
mind-set that characterizes applied postmodernism in general, she regards these values as useful for activism. She writes,

In consonance with my emphasis on the performative relations of double and conflicted definition, the theorized prescription for a practical politics implicit in these readings is for a multi-pronged movement whose idealist and materialist impulses, whose minority-model and universalist-model strategies, and for that matter whose gender-separatist and gender-integrative analyses would likewise proceed in parallel without any high premium placed on ideological rationalization between them.[38]

Here Sedgwick is saying that a productive movement could incorporate all the ideas to be found in LGBT scholarship and activism—even mutually contradictory approaches—without needing to resolve ideological differences. She argues that the contradictions themselves would be politically valuable, not least because they would make the thinking behind the activism very difficult to understand and thus to criticize. This is, of course, very queer.

These ideas are most prominent in Sedgwick's 1990 book, *The Epistemology of the Closet*, which developed Foucault's idea that sexuality is a social construct brought into being by scientific discourses—especially those legitimized by medical authorities, who classified homosexuality as a psychopathology. She, nevertheless, diverges from Foucault fairly radically, in favor of Derrida. Sedgwick reversed Foucault's belief that dominant discourses created homosexuality and heterosexuality, arguing instead that it is the binary of homosexuality and heterosexuality that gave us binary thinking—people are either gay *or* straight, male *or* female, masculine *or* feminine. For Sedgwick, sexual binaries underlie all social binaries. *The Epistemology of the Closet* spells this out from the beginning:

> The book will argue that an understanding of virtually any aspect of modern Western culture must be, not merely incomplete, but damaged in its central substance to the degree that it does not incorporate a critical analysis of modern homo/heterosexual definition.[39]

For Sedgwick, then, a binary understanding of sexuality forms the basis on which all binary thinking rests. Furthermore, all such thinking is false. Therefore, understanding the fluid complexities of sexuality is key to undoing many forms of black-and-white thinking in society. Sedgwick is therefore a significant player in establishing the queer Theoretical tendency to "interrogate" and resist perpetuating any kind of binaries, lest they become sites of oppression.

Sedgwick's symbolism of the closet is especially predicated on this idea of false binaries. One is never fully in or out of the closet. Some people will know one's sexuality, and others will not. Some things will be said, and others will not, and there is knowledge to be gained both from what has been said and what hasn't. The closet, to Sedgwick, therefore symbolizes occupying contradictory realities at the same time. Embracing this and making it visible are core to her approach to queer Theory, and in this we see the beginnings of the expansion of the queer to matters outside of sexuality, along with its use as a verb.

Because she took a postmodernist approach, Sedgwick identified language—specifically, "speech acts"—as the way in which these unjust binaries and "the closet" were constructed and maintained. She therefore saw her Theoretical approach as potentially revelatory and therefore freeing. She remarks,

> An assumption underlying the book is that the relations of the closet—the relations of the known and the unknown, the explicit and the inexplicit around homo/heterosexual definition—have the potential for being peculiarly revealing, in fact, about speech acts more generally.[40]

These relations Sedgwick views as in need of deconstruction, following Derrida. She emphasizes, for example, analysis that recognizes that homosexuality is considered inferior to heterosexuality, but that the term "heterosexuality" would not exist if homosexuality were not a category of difference. This observation is meant to deconstruct the power relationship in the binary, by highlighting that—because the concept of heterosexuality is dependent on the existence and subordinated status of homosexuality—it cannot be said to have priority status. In this way, she seeks to deconstruct heteronormativity, the widespread expectation that heterosexuality is normal and the default.

Sedgwick finds it useful to generalize from this understanding of binaries that apply to sexuality to other binaries in society, as a way to destabilize hierarchies of superiority and inferiority. In this, she is thoroughly Derridean. Like other Derridean thinkers, this leads her to highlight and exploit what she sees as the tension that arises from holding two seemingly contradictory views at the same time. In sexuality, for Sedgwick, these views are the "minoritizing view" and the "universalizing view." In the *minoritizing view*, homosexual is seen as something that a minority of people are, while the majority are heterosexual. Meanwhile, in the *universalizing view*, sexuality is considered a spectrum in which everybody has a place. That is, everybody is a little bit (or a lot) gay. These two ideas seem contradictory, yet Sedgwick believes that the contradiction itself is productive. As she puts it,

> The book will not suggest (nor do I believe there currently exists) any standpoint of thought from which the rival claims of these minoritizing and universalizing understandings of sexual definition could be decisively arbitrated as to their "truth." Instead, the performative effects of the self-contradictory discursive field of force created by their overlap will be my subject.[41]

For Sedgwick, productive political work can be achieved by forcing the maintenance of a clear contradiction because doing so undermines a stable sense of meaning for the relevant concepts. The incoherence of endorsing two contradictory models of sexuality at once can help us accept the complexity and mutability of sexuality. Thus, we see here, yet again, the commitment to rejecting objective truth and concrete categories and the idea that incoherence and fluidity are liberating and politically necessary. Queer Theorists can expand this thinking to encompass almost anything and they think of this as "queering" the topic. Theorists have, for instance, queered categories of time and history[42] and life and death.[43]

THE POSTMODERN PRINCIPLES AND THEMES IN QUEER THEORY

Queer Theory is one of the most explicitly postmodern forms of Theory within identity studies today, and it owes much of its foundational concept of the social construction of sexuality by discourse to Foucault. The postmodern knowledge principle, in which objective reality is denied or simply ignored, and the postmodern political principle, which insists that society is structured of systems of power and privilege that determine what is understood as knowledge, are front and center in queer Theory. They are most evident in its foundational concept that science is a form of oppressive discipline, which enforces gender conformity and heterosexuality by establishing categories and attempting to assert truths about them with rigorous authority and social legitimacy.

Of the four major postmodern themes, the blurring of boundaries and the intense focus on language (discourses) are absolutely central to queer Theory. These are the two themes most hostile to the concept of a stable reality that we can discuss straightforwardly and therefore the most self-destructive. Queer Theory avoids the self-destructiveness of the original postmodernism, however, by making the blurring of boundaries into its preferred form of political activism and calling it "queering." That is, its destructiveness, which is occasionally self-directed, is meant to have a political purpose. Much of this activity is applied to discourses, leading to an almost pathological obsession with the ways sex, gender, and sexuality are spoken about, which has led to a proliferation of terms demarcating subtle differences in gender identity and sexuality, which simultaneously inhabit a fluid and changeable space and yet demand impossibly extreme sensitivity of language.

The other two of the four themes also appear within queer Theory, but less overtly. The theme of cultural relativism is implicit in that queer Theory assumes that understandings of gender and sexuality are always cultural constructs. This is a trait it shares with postcolonial Theory: hence queer Theorists often use postcolonial Theory and vice versa. Although there are significant differences between the two groups and their goals, these two Theories draw upon one another because their methods are fully compatible, since they are both heavily influenced by Foucault and Derrida. Meanwhile, the loss of the individual and the universal is also implicit in that individuals' gendered and sexual selves are considered to be constructed by discourses of power that they cannot help but learn and can only subvert in minor ways. Universality is therefore queer-impossible, as this would require a common human nature—a concept that queer Theory utterly rejects.

With its focus on deconstructive techniques and its conception of knowledge as a construct of power, queer Theory is, arguably, the purest form of applied postmodernism. It underlies much trans activism and makes an appearance in multiple forms of Social Justice scholarship. The conceptual framework of *intersectionality* formed part of the foundational texts of queer Theory, and although the name "intersectionality" is more associated with critical race Theorist Kimberlé Crenshaw, Butler also spoke of "intersections" with other forms of marginalized identity at the same time as Crenshaw and, seemingly, independently. For her, "gender intersects with racial, class, ethnic, sexual, and regional modalities of discursively constituted identities."[44] Thus, Butlerian queer Theory is easily integrated as a key dimension of intersectional thought. Consequently, intersectional feminists are very likely to include queer Theory in their work.

Perhaps most significantly, queer Theory differs fundamentally from the liberal feminism and LGBT activism that preceded it. Claims that queer Theory is the only way to liberate those who are not heterosexual or gender-conforming are belied by the success of universal liberal approaches both before and since. Pre-Theory liberal activism and thought focused on changing prejudiced attitudes towards people of a certain sex, gender, or sexuality by appealing to our many commonalities and shared humanity, and to universal liberal principles. This is probably something that trans activism could also focus on, as the science around trans issues develops—if queer Theory weren't actively attempting to subvert anything universal or normative.

Queer Theory aims, instead—very unhelpfully—to modify or unmake the concepts of sex, gender, and sexuality themselves and so tends to render itself baffling and irrelevant, if not positively alienating to most members of the society it wishes to change. Queer activists reliant on queer Theory tend to act with surprising entitlement and aggression— attitudes which most people find objectionable—not least by ridiculing normative sexualities and genders and depicting those who recognize them as backwards and boorish. People generally do not appreciate being told that their sex, gender, and sexuality are not real, or are wrong, or bad—something one would think queer Theorists might appreciate better than anyone.

Further, the idea that heterosexuality is a social construct completely neglects the reality that humans are a sexually reproducing species. The idea that homosexuality is a social construct neglects the plentiful evidence that it is also a biological reality. Despite any "liberation" this may achieve, it threatens to undo the considerable progress made by lesbian and gay activists in countering the belief that their romantic and sexual attractions are a mere "lifestyle choice" that could, in two manifestations of the same principle, be Theorized into existence or prayed away. While homosexuality would be a perfectly acceptable lifestyle choice, all the evidence—and the overwhelming testimony of gay men and lesbians—indicates that it is much more than that.[45]

It does not tend to make for productive activism to be dismissive, ironic, antiscientific, and largely incomprehensible by design. It also doesn't help people who wish to have their sex, gender, or sexuality accepted as normal to be continually rescued from any sense of normalcy by arguing that considering things normal is problematic. Therefore, although queer Theory purports to advocate for lesbian, gay, bisexual, and transgender people, the majority of LGBT people are neither familiar with it, nor support it. As it continues to assert itself as the only legitimate way to study or discuss topics of gender, sex, and sexuality, then, it also continues to do harm to the causes it seeks most interestedly to support.

5 CRITICAL RACE THEORY AND INTERSECTIONALITY

Ending Racism by Seeing It Everywhere

Critical race Theory is, at root, an American phenomenon. So thoroughly is this the case that although its ideas have been used outside the United States for some time, they are often highly flavored by U.S. racial history. Critical race Theory holds that race is a social construct that was created to maintain white privilege and white supremacy. This idea originated long before postmodernism with W. E. B. Du Bois, who argued that the idea of race was being used to assert biological explanations of differences that are social and cultural, in order to perpetuate the unjust treatment of racial minorities, especially African Americans.

There are good reasons to accept this claim. Although some average differences in human populations—such as skin color, hair texture, eye shape, and relative susceptibility to certain diseases—are observably real, and an individual's geographical heritage can be discovered via DNA tests, it is not clear why this has been regarded as so significant as to divide people into groups called "races." For one thing, biologists don't. Biologists talk of populations, which can be identified through genetic markers as having had slightly different evolutionary heritages, but reducing this to what we usually call "race" is so often wrong as to be nearly useless in practice. For example, in medicine, "race" is not very useful because socially constructed racial categories do not reliably map meaningfully onto more biologically relevant genetic lineages. For another thing, the contemporary idea of "race" doesn't stand up histori- cally. There is compelling reason to believe that it was not considered sig- nificant in earlier periods. The Bible, for example, written over two thou- sand years ago in the Mediterranean, where black, brown, and white people were to be found, is filled with moralistic tribalism, but makes almost no mention of skin color. In late medieval England, references to "black" people often simply described the hair color of Europeans now regarded as "white."

While other factors may have contributed, race and racism as we understand them today probably arose as social constructions, made by Europeans to morally justify European colonialism and the Atlan- tic slave trade. European historians have tracked the rise of color-based prejudice over the early modern period, from roughly 1500 to 1800, and argued that prejudice on the grounds of religious difference gave way to racism—a belief in the superiority of some races over others—over the course of the seventeenth century.[1] In order to justify the abuses of colonialism and the kidnapping, exploitation, and abuse of slaves, their victims had to be regarded as inferior or subhuman (even if they had converted to Christianity). This raises a common point of confusion, because it is also undeniable that other peoples at other times practiced slavery, colonialism, and even genocidal imperialism, and they justi- fied these atrocities similarly—by characterizing those they enslaved or conquered as inferior, often using characteristics like skin, hair, and eye color, which we might identify with race today. This sort of discrimina- tion and even dehumanization was already widespread, but, in Europe and its colonies, a few key differences led to a unique analysis.

Firstly, the concept of race was not consistently connected to *herit- ability* in Europe until the sixteenth century. Before then, it was generally assumed that traits like skin color were determined largely environmen- tally, rather than genetically, although the related concepts in ancient Greek (*genos*) and Latin (*genus*) along with records from the Chinese and elsewhere indicate that descent wasn't wholly neglected.[2] Secondly, the constructed ideas of race were specifically used to justify the atrocities of European colonialism and the Atlantic slave trade. Third—and perhaps most importantly—this was done by emerging forms of scholarship in what we would now call the social sciences and natural sciences although they had neither separated clearly into the disciplines we would now call "anthropology," "sociology," and "biology" nor formed what we would now consider rigorous methods.

This is important because naturalism and science were rapidly becoming a knowledge-production, thus idea-legitimizing, methodology the likes of which the world had never seen. It is the legitimatizing authority of science that, ultimately, postmodernism rails against most vigorously. The rise of the sciences—and of an intellectual and political culture that accepted science as legitimate—together with the horrors of colonialism and the Atlantic slave trade, led to new social constructions of race. This, we hear from Theorists today, is the "scientific origin" of racism, which can be taken to mean that these discourses that misapplied very preliminary results from science allowed the first *socially constructivist racists* to come into existence. In other words, with this oversimplified, overreaching, and self-serving scientific categorization came social constructions associated with extremely low-resolution categories: being black ("blackness") and being white ("whiteness"), to which value judgments were soon attached. Enter racism as we understand it today.

The earliest contributors to the effort to challenge the assumptions underlying racism were former American slaves, including Sojourner Truth[3] and Frederick Douglass,[4] in the nineteenth century. Later, in the twentieth century, influential race critics like W. E. B. Du Bois[5] and Winthrop Jordan[6] set out the history of color-based racism in the United States. The work of these scholars and reformers should have been sufficient to expose racism for the ugly and unfounded ideology that it is, but belief in the racial supremacy of whites survived nevertheless. This was especially extreme and long-lived in the American South, where slavery remained an essential part of the economy until Abraham Lincoln's emancipation of the slaves in 1863. Jim Crow laws, racial redlining, and legal segregation survived the longest, persisting into the mid-

1960s and, in some ways, beyond. Even after the victories of the Civil Rights Movement under Martin Luther King, Jr., when discrimination on the grounds of race became illegal and attitudes about race changed remarkably fast in historical terms, these longstanding narratives didn't disappear. Critical race Theory was designed to pick at, highlight, and address them.

TAKING A CRITICAL APPROACH

Critical race Theory formally arose in the 1970s, through the critical study of law as it pertains to issues of race. The word *critical* here means that its intention and methods are specifically geared toward identifying and exposing problems in order to facilitate revolutionary political change. This was especially pertinent because, despite a series of profound but imperfect legal changes aimed at preventing racial discrimination, many activists felt a need to continue work on the racism that remained, which was less clearly demonstrable. To accomplish this, they turned to the tools of cultural criticism that were ascendant at the time. This meant adopting critical approaches and, eventually, Theory.

As a result, the critical race approach, like other methods of cultural criticism, has always been somewhat divided into at least two parts—one "materialist" and the other "postmodern"—which both set themselves apart from the liberal approach. As their designation implies, materialist race critics theorize about how material systems—economic, legal, political—affect racial minorities. Postmodern Theorists, by contrast, were more concerned with linguistic and social systems and therefore aimed to deconstruct discourses, detect implicit biases, and counter underlying racial assumptions and attitudes. Because of this fundamental difference in focus, some materialists have criticized postmodernists for conducting intangible and subjective discourse analyses, which usually take place in wealthy and academic milieus, while neglecting salient, widespread material issues, particularly poverty. Postmodernists have countered that, while material reality is of practical importance, it cannot be meaningfully improved while discourses continue to prioritize white people.

Critical race theory in both incarnations, materialist and postmodern, reacted against liberalism and stresses a form of radicalism. As described by critical race Theorists Richard Delgado and Jean Stefancic,

> Unlike traditional civil rights discourse, which stresses incrementalism and step-by-step progress, critical race theory questions the very foundations of the liberal order, including equality theory, legal reasoning, Enlightenment rationalism, and neutral principles of constitutional law.[7]

As Delgado and Stefancic further note,

> [C]ritical race scholars are discontented with liberalism as a framework for addressing America's racial problems. Many liberals believe in color blindness and neutral principles of constitutional law. They believe in equality, especially equal treatment for all persons, regardless of their different histories or current situations.[8]

This is true—and the illiberal nature of critical race Theory is among the strongest and most enduring criticisms against it.

The late Derrick Bell, the first tenured African American professor at Harvard Law School, is often regarded as the progenitor of what we generally call critical race Theory, having derived the name by inserting race into his area of specialty: critical legal theory. Bell was a materialist, who is perhaps best known for having brought critical methods to bear on understanding civil rights and the discourses surrounding them. Bell was an open advocate of historical revisionism and is best known for his "interest convergence" thesis, described in his 1970 book, *Race, Racism, and American Law*.[9] This thesis holds that whites have allowed rights to blacks only when it was in their interest to do so—a dismal view that denies the possibility that any moral progress had been made since the Jim Crow era. This is no exaggeration of his intent; Bell states this explicitly in his 1987 book, *And We Are Not Saved: The Elusive Quest for Racial Justice*[10]: "progress in American race relations is largely a mirage obscuring the fact that whites continue, consciously or unconsciously, to do all in their power to ensure their dominion and maintain their control."[11] This cynical pessimism pervades Bell's analysis. For instance, he also considered that white people had introduced desegregation, not as a solution to black people's problems, but to further their own interests while suppressing black radicalism during the Cold War (and at other times).[12] Because of his beliefs in a pervasive and irreparable system of white dominance in U.S. society,[13] he argued that such changes lead to a whole new raft of problems through which white superiority would continually assert itself over the interests of black people, for instance through white retaliation and white flight.[14] This was typical of the critical-race mood at the time. His contemporary, Alan Freeman, was similarly cynical and pessimistic, and wrote a number of legal papers arguing that antiracist legislation actually supported racism.[15]

Of course, simple legal equality between races is not sufficient to resolve all social inequalities. There is valuable work in addressing measurable imbalances in the political, legal, and economic realms, by comparing funding for schools in majority white and black areas, differences in sentencing of black and white offenders, disparities in housing and lending in black and white communities, differences in representations of black and white people in high-prestige jobs, with a view to learning why these disparities have come about. Nevertheless, there are plenty of general and liberal criticisms to be made of the materialist critical race theorists, in addition to their pessimism. The materialist critical race theorists frequently advocate Black Nationalism and segregation[16] over universal human rights and cooperation. Also, their supposedly empirical analyses of material reality, which usually find that racism and discrimination are not decreasing at all, can look a great deal like cherry-picking and generalizing from the worst examples.

Though the materialists' pessimism persisted, their approach did not. Materialists dominated the critical race movement from the 1970s to the 1980s; but, from the 1990s, postmodernists were increasingly in the ascendant. Over time, the postmodernists came to focus on microaggressions, hate speech, safe spaces, cultural appropriation, implicit association tests, media representation, "whiteness," and all the now familiar trappings of current racial discourse.[17] This change owes much to the influence of a number of female critical Theorists who gained prominence in the late 1980s and 1990s and promoted radical black feminist thought, including bell hooks, Audre Lorde, and Patricia Hill Collins. These scholars were happy to blur the boundaries of scholarly disciplines, while arguing passionately about both patriarchy and white supremacy in ways that mixed the legal with the sociological, literary, and autobiographical in specifically gendered ways. Significantly, they complained at length about the "whiteness" of feminism. They thereby set the stage for another wave of influential Theorists: scholars like Patricia Williams, Angela Harris, and Kimberlé Crenshaw—a student of Bell who helped him create the term "Critical Race Theory." These scholars drew on critical race Theory, which included class analysis, and on feminism, which incorporated ideas about gender and sexuality. This produced a highly layered, "sophisticated" analysis of identity and experience, which included social, legal, and economic factors. By looking at multiple systems of power and privilege and situating experience as a source of knowledge within them, they moved away from materialist analysis and towards the postmodern.

This change implied new commitments. Gone was the central focus on the material realities relevant to systemic and structural understandings of racism, especially poverty. This was replaced by analysis of discourse and power. At the same time, critical race Theory invested heavily in identity politics and its supposed intellectual justification, standpoint theory—roughly, the idea that one's identity and position in society influence how one comes to knowledge. These developments, together with the blurring of boundaries and dissolution of the individual in favor of group identity, reveal the dominance of postmodern thought in critical race Theory by the early 1990s.

This shift is evident throughout writings from the time. For example, Patricia Williams, a professor of commercial law, is best known for her book-length autobiographical essay, *The Alchemy of Race and Rights* (1991).[18] Its publisher, Harvard University Press, describes it as operating at "the intersection of race, gender, and class" and evokes the blurring of boundaries so common to postmodern approaches, writing, "Williams casts the law as a mythological text in which the powers of commerce and the Constitution, wealth and poverty, sanity and insanity, wage war across complex and overlapping boundaries of discourse. In deliberately transgressing such boundaries, she pursues a path toward racial justice that is, ultimately, transformative."[19] In the critical race Theory that emerged, we also see the focus on language and discourses and the need to disrupt them. There is, of course, validity to the applied postmodernist argument that it is much harder to rectify societal imbalances without first addressing prejudiced attitudes and assumptions, which, the Theorists rightly observe, often manifest in ways of speaking about things—discourses.

The best practical use of this recognition would be rigorous (rather than purely theoretical and interpretive) scholarship into social attitudes around race. For the applied postmodernists, however, the focus on discourses is primarily concerned with *positionality*—the idea that one's position within society, as determined by group identity, dictates how one understands the world and will be understood in it. This idea is central to critical race Theory, as is evident from the very first lines of *The Alchemy*: "[S]ubject position is everything in my analysis of the law," Williams writes. Then she articulates the importance of language and discourses and the need to disrupt them, by blurring the boundaries between meanings, legal and otherwise:

> I am interested in the way in which legal language flattens and confines in absolutes the complexity of meaning inherent in any given problem; I am trying to challenge the usual limits of commercial discourse by using an intentionally double-voiced and relational, rather than a traditionally legal black-letter, vocabulary.[20]

The postmodern concept of a "positional" self—a socially constructed identity that occupies a particular location within the privilege/oppression landscape—is evident. Legal scholar Angela Harris develops this idea further by advocating a multiple-consciousness (standpoint) theory: "It is a premise of this article that we are not born with a 'self,' but rather are composed of a welter of partial, sometimes contradictory, or even antithetical 'selves.'"[21] This idea of a multiple consciousness, rooted in identity and positionality, recurs repeatedly in postmodern scholarship on the blending of differing layers of marginalized identity, and has had a huge impact on how knowledge is studied and understood within feminist scholarship and critical race Theory.

Despite the apparent complexity of constantly having to consider the impact of one's social position on being both a speaker and a knower and relating it to the social positions of those around you, critical race Theory is usually exceptionally clear in its exposition. Indeed, the frustratingly obscure and ambiguous postmodern language of postcolonial and queer Theories is conspicuously absent from critical race Theory, probably because of its genesis in legal studies. Critical race Theory maintains a commitment to the role of discourse in constructing social reality and addresses issues of apparently infinite complexity, but it does not usually despair of conveying meaning through clear language. It has a political purpose, which is not limited to deconstructing or disrupting metanarratives. It is therefore much easier to see what the tenets of critical race Theory are—not least because its scholars have a tendency to list them.

For example, the highly influential reader, *Critical Race Theory*, by Richard Delgado and Jean Stefancic, sets out the core tenets thus:

"Racism is ordinary, not aberrational." That is, it is the everyday experience of people of color in the United States.

"[A] system of white-over-color ascendancy serves important purposes, both psychic and material, for the dominant group." That is, white supremacy is systemic and benefits white people. Therefore, "color-blind" policies can tackle only the most egregious and demonstrable forms of discrimination.

"[T]he 'social construction' thesis holds that race and races are products of social thought and relations." Intersectionality and antiessentialism—opposition to the idea of racial difference as innate—are needed to address this.

A "unique voice of color" exists and "minority status . . . brings with it a presumed competence to speak about race and racism." This is not understood as essentialism but as the product of common experiences of oppression. In other words, this is standpoint theory.[22]

These core tenets unambiguously assert what is going on in critical race Theory—racism is present everywhere and always, and persistently works against people of color, who are aware of this, and for the benefit of white people, who tend not to be, as is their privilege.[23] Other Theorists and educators include a fundamental distrust of liberalism, a rejection of meritocracy,[24] and a commitment to working towards Social Justice.[25]

THE SPREAD OF CRITICAL RACE THEORY

Critical race Theory has expanded out of legal studies and into many disciplines concerned with Social Justice. The theory of education (pedagogy) has been particularly strongly affected. As Delgado and Stefancic observe,

> Although CRT [critical race Theory] began as a movement in the law, it has rapidly spread beyond that discipline. Today, many scholars in the field of education consider themselves critical race theorists who use CRT's ideas to understand issues of school discipline and hierarchy, tracking, affirmative action, high-stakes testing, controversies over curriculum and history, bilingual and multicultural education, and alternative and charter schools.[26]

They list critical race Theory's strongest footholds, indicating how effectively it can embed itself in other disciplines:

> Political scientists ponder voting strategies coined by critical race theorists, while women's studies professors teach about intersectionality—the predicament of women of color and others who sit at the intersection of two or more categories. Ethnic studies courses often include a unit on critical race theory, and American studies departments teach material on critical white studies developed by CRT writers. Sociologists, theologians, and health care specialists use critical theory and its ideas. Philosophers

incorporate critical race ideas in analyzing issues such as viewpoint discrimination and whether Western philosophy is inherently white in its orientation, values, and method of reasoning.[27]

Indeed. As we will discuss in chapter 8, critical race and feminist Theoretical approaches hold that reason is a Western philosophical tradition, which unfairly disadvantages women and racial minorities. Consequently, critical race Theory takes an unapologetically activist stance:

> Unlike some academic disciplines, critical race theory contains an activist dimension. It tries not only to understand our social situation but to change it, setting out not only to ascertain how society organizes itself along racial lines and hierarchies but to transform it for the better.[28]

As a result, we hear the language of critical race Theory from activists in all walks of life, and one could be easily forgiven—if critical race Theory didn't consider it racist to forgive this—for thinking that critical race Theory sounds rather racist itself, in ascribing profound failures of morals and character to white people (as consequences of being white in a white-dominant society). We are told that racism is embedded in culture and that we cannot escape it. We hear that white people are inherently racist. We are told that racism is "prejudice plus power," therefore, only white people can be racist. We are informed that only people of color can talk about racism, that white people need to just listen, and that they don't have the "racial stamina" to engage it. We hear that not seeing people in terms of their race (being color-blind) is, in fact, racist and an attempt to ignore the pervasive racism that dominates society and perpetuates white privilege. We can hear these mantras in many spheres of life, but they are particularly prevalent on college campuses. Delgado and Stefancic regard this as positive:

> As this book went to press, students on several dozen campuses were demonstrating for "safe spaces" and protection from racially hostile climates with daily insults, epithets, slurs, and displays of Confederate symbols and flags. These "campus climate" issues are

prompting serious reconsideration among university administrators, and for good reason. With affirmative action under sharp attack, universities need to assure that their campuses are as welcoming as possible. At the same time, a new generation of millennials seems to be demonstrating a renewed willingness to confront illegitimate authority.[29]

Critical race Theory has become very much a part of campus culture in many universities and, interestingly, is most evident at the most elite institutions. Intersectionality is central to this culture and has also taken on a life of its own outside it.

CRITICAL RACE THEORY AS APPLIED POSTMODERNISM

Despite its increasingly postmodern focus on discourses, attitudes, and bias, some scholars have doubted whether this branch of critical race Theory is truly postmodern. One common objection is that postmodernism typically rejected shared meaning and stable identity (or subjecthood). Therefore, identity politics should make little sense from an orthodox postmodern perspective.

Critics making this argument have a point, and are within their rights to insist on only recognizing the first postmodernists as "true" postmodernists, but it is nevertheless true that, in the late 1980s and early 1990s, critical race Theorists took some core postmodern ideas from the radically deconstructive first phase and adapted them to a new, intentionally politically applicable project. The new critical race Theorists explicitly rejected the endless, aimless deconstruction of original postmodernism, often seeing it as a product of the naturally privileged status of white male philosophers like Foucault and Derrida, who failed to account for their privileged positions as white men. The black feminist scholar and activist bell hooks, for example, wrote in the 1980s that the people who wanted to get rid of subjecthood and coherent voices (the original postmodernists) were wealthy, white men, whose voices had been heard and whose identity was dominant in society.[30] In her influential 1990 essay, "Race and Essentialism in Feminist Legal Theory," Angela Harris likewise argues that feminism failed black women by treating their experience as simply a variation on white women's experience. These ideas developed into a core line of thought in critical race Theory that was instrumental to the development of *intersectionality*.

INTERSECTIONALITY

The critical race scholar who references postmodernism most explicitly in her work and who most clearly advocates for a more politicized and actionable use of it is Kimberlé Crenshaw, a founder of critical race Theory and the progenitor of the concept of *intersectionality*. Intersectionality began as a heuristic—a tool that lets someone discover something for themselves—but has long been treated as a theory and is now described by Crenshaw as a "practice." Crenshaw first introduced the idea of intersectionality in a polemical 1989 scholarly law paper called "Demarginalizing the Intersection of Race and Sex: A Black Feminist Critique of Antidiscrimination Doctrine, Feminist Theory and Antiracist Politics."[31] There, she examines three legal discrimination cases and uses the metaphor of a roadway intersection to examine the ways in which different forms of prejudice can "hit" an individual with two or more marginalized identities. She argues that—just as someone standing in the intersection of two streets could get hit by a car coming from any direction or even by more than one at a time—so a marginalized person could be unable to tell which of their identities is being discriminated against in any given instance. Crenshaw argues persuasively that legislation to prevent discrimination on the grounds of race *or* gender is insufficient to deal with this problem or with the fact that a black woman, for instance, might experience unique forms of discrimination that neither white women nor black men face.

This poignant, though seemingly relatively uncontroversial, idea was about to change the world. It was more fully articulated two years later, in Crenshaw's highly influential 1991 essay, "Mapping the Margins: Intersectionality, Identity Politics, and Violence against Women of Color," in which she defines intersectionality as a "provisional concept linking contemporary politics with postmodern theory."[32] For Crenshaw, a postmodern approach to intersectionality allowed both critical race Theory and feminism to incorporate political activism while retaining their understandings of race and gender as cultural constructs. Furthermore, this Theoretical approach allowed for ever more categories of marginalized identity to be incorporated into intersectional analyses, adding layer upon layer of apparent sophistication and complexity to the concept, and the scholarship and activism that utilizes it. This Theoretical complexity, which Patricia Hill Collins dubbed the "matrix of domination" in her 1990 book *Black Feminist Thought*,[33] spurred two decades of fresh activity by scholars and activists. "Mapping the Margins" provided the means: openly advocating identity politics over liberal universalism, which had sought to remove the social significance of identity categories and treat people equally regardless of identity. Identity politics restores the social significance of identity categories in order to valorize them as sources of empowerment and community. Crenshaw writes:

> We all can recognize the distinction between the claims "I am Black" and the claim "I am a person who happens to be Black." "I am Black" takes the socially imposed identity and empowers it as an anchor of subjectivity. "I am Black" becomes not simply a statement of resistance but also a positive discourse of self-identification, intimately linked to celebratory statements like the Black nationalist "Black is beautiful." "I am a person who happens to be Black," on the other hand, achieves self-identification by straining for a certain universality (in effect, "I am first a person") and for a concomitant dismissal of the imposed category ("Black") as contingent, circumstantial, nondeterminant.[34]

In its return to the social significance of race and gender and the empowerment of black and female identity politics, "Mapping the Margins" can be considered central and foundational to Social Justice as it is practiced and studied today. It also revitalized the conditions under which socially constructivist racism takes hold—the reification of socially constructed racial categories—after decades of chipping away by liberal approaches. It thereby laid the groundwork for the "strategic racism" that has come to characterize the racial dimension of Social Justice scholarship in recent years, which will be discussed further in chapter 8. Because intersectionality has become such an important framework within Social Justice scholarship and within the recent explicit rejection of liberal universalism in favor of identity-based politics, it is worth looking at its foundational tenets in more depth. By drawing on postmodern cultural constructivism, while considering oppression objectively real and advocating actionable political goals, it also provides the clearest example of the emergence, imperative, method, and ethos of applied postmodernism, and is paradigmatic of the applied postmodern turn of the late 1980s and early 1990s.

INTERSECTIONALITY AND THE APPLIED POSTMODERN TURN

In "Mapping the Margins," Crenshaw critiques two ways of understanding society: (universal) liberalism and (high-deconstructive) postmodernism. Mainstream liberal discourse around discrimination, Crenshaw felt, was inadequate to understand the ways in which structures of power perpetuated discrimination against people with more than one category of marginalized identity. Because liberalism sought to remove social expectations from identity categories—black people being expected to do menial jobs, women being expected to prioritize domestic and parenting roles, and so on—and make all rights, freedoms, and opportunities available to all people *regardless* of their identity, there was a strong focus on the individual and the universal and a deprioritization of identity categories. This was, to Crenshaw, unacceptable. She writes,

> [For] African Americans, other people of color, and gays and lesbians, among others . . . identity-based politics has been a source of strength, community, and intellectual development. The embrace of identity politics, however, has been in tension with dominant conceptions of social justice. Race, gender, and other identity categories are most often treated in mainstream liberal discourse as vestiges of bias or domination—that is, as intrinsically negative frameworks in which social power works to exclude or marginalize those who are different. According to this

understanding, our liberatory objective should be to empty such categories of any social significance. Yet implicit in certain strands of feminist and racial liberation movements, for example is the view that the social power in delineating difference need not be the power of domination; it can instead be the source of social empowerment and reconstruction.[35]

Crenshaw is initiating a major change here. At the height of its deconstructive phase, postmodernism enabled the analysis of power structures and usefully (in Crenshaw's view) understood race and gender as social constructs. However, because of its radical skepticism, it did not allow for the reality of those social structures and categories that it is essential to acknowledge if one wishes to address discrimination on those grounds. She therefore criticizes that aspect of radically deconstructive postmodernism, while insisting that the postmodern political principle is otherwise cogent:

> While the descriptive project of postmodernism of questioning the ways in which meaning is socially constructed is generally sound, this critique sometimes misreads the meaning of social construction and distorts its political relevance. . . . But to say that a category such as race or gender is socially constructed is not to say that that category has no significance in our world. On the contrary, a large and continuing project for subordinated people—and indeed, one of the projects for which postmodern theories have been very helpful—is thinking about the way power has clustered around certain categories and is exercised against others.[36]

Thus, in the early 1990s, Crenshaw proposed that an entirely new way of thinking was required, one that accepted that complex layers of discrimination objectively exist and so do categories of people and systems of power—even if they have been socially constructed. This is intersectionality. It explicitly embraces the postmodern political principle and accepts a variant on the postmodern knowledge principle—one that sees knowledge as positional. Crenshaw's intersectionality explicitly rejected universality in favor of group identity, at least in the political context in which she wrote, and intersectional feminists and critical race Theorists have largely continued to do so ever since.[37]

Within this framework, far from being irrelevant socially—as in liberalism—gender and race have become sites of renewed political activism, and identity politics is in the ascendant. Intersectionality is the axis upon which the applied postmodern turn rotated and the seed that would germinate as Social Justice scholarship some twenty years later. It is therefore important to understand intersectionality and the ways in which it preserved the postmodern principles and themes, while making actionable use of them.

COMPLEX, YET SO VERY SIMPLE

Since its conception, the meaning and purpose of intersectionality have expanded hugely. For intersectional sociologists Patricia Hill Collins and Sirma Bilge,

> Intersectionality is a way of understanding and analyzing the complexity in the world, in people, and in human experiences. The events and conditions of social and political life and the self can seldom be understood as shaped by one factor. They are generally shaped by many factors in diverse and mutually influencing ways. When it comes to social inequality, people's lives and the organization of power in a given society are better understood as being shaped not by a single axis of social division, be it race or gender or class, but by many axes that work together and influence each other. Intersectionality as an analytic tool gives people better access to the complexity of the world and of themselves.[38]

The number of axes of social division under intersectionality can be almost infinite—but they cannot be reduced to the *individual*. (People often joke that the individual is the logical endpoint of an intersectional approach that divides people into smaller and smaller groups—but this misunderstands the fundamental reliance on *group identity*. Even if a person were a unique mix of marginalized identities, thus intersectionally a unique individual, she would be understood through each and all of those group identities, with the details to be filled in by Theory. She would not be understood as an individual.) Consequently, the categories in which intersectionality is interested are numerous. In addition to those of race, sex, class, sexuality, gender identity, religion, immigration status, physical ability, mental health, and body size, there are subcategories, such as exact skin tone, body shape, and abstruse gender identities and sexualities, which number in the hundreds. These all have to be understood in relation to one another so that the positionality each intersection of them confers can be identified and engaged. Moreover, this doesn't just make intersectionality incredibly internally complex. It is also messy because it is so highly interpretive and operates on so many elements of identity simultaneously, each of which has different claims to a relative degree of marginalization, not all of which are directly comparable.

However, there is nothing complex about the overarching idea of intersectionality, or the Theories upon which it is built. Nothing could be simpler. It does the same thing over and over again: look for the power imbalances, bigotry, and biases that it assumes must be present and pick at them. It reduces *everything* to one single variable, one single topic of conversation, one single focus and interpretation: prejudice, as understood under the power dynamics asserted by Theory. Thus, for example, disparate outcomes can have one, and only one, explanation, and it is prejudicial bigotry. The question is just identifying how it manifests in the given situation. Thus, it always assumes that, in every situation, some form of Theoretical prejudice exists and we must find a way to show evidence of it. In that sense, it is a tool—a "practice"—designed to flatten all complexity and nuance so that it can promote identity politics, in accordance with its vision.

THE CASTE SYSTEM OF SOCIAL JUSTICE

Because of its internal complexity and single-minded focus on oppression, intersectionality is riddled with divisions and subcategories, which exist in competition with—or even in unrepentant contradiction to—each other. Some people in the United States therefore argue that gay white men[39] and nonblack people of color—generally assessed as marginalized groups—need to recognize their privilege and antiblackness.[40] This can lead to the insistence that lighter-skinned black people recognize their privilege over darker-skinned black people.[41] Straight black men have been described as the "white people of black people."[42] It is also not uncommon to hear arguments that trans men, while still oppressed by attitudes towards their trans status, need to recognize that they have ascended to male privilege[43] and amplify the voices of trans women, who are seen as doubly oppressed, by being both trans and women. Gay men and lesbians might well find themselves not considered oppressed at all, particularly if they are not attracted to trans men or trans women, respectively, which is considered a form of transphobia and misgendering.[44] Asians and Jews may find themselves stripped of marginalized status due to the comparative economic success of their demographics, their participation in "whiteness," or other factors.[45] Queerness needs to be decolonized—meaning made more racially diverse—and its conceptual origins in white figures like Judith Butler need to be interrogated.[46]

In the real world, attempting to "respect" all marginalized identities at once, as unique voices with the inherent, unquestionable wisdom connected to their cultural groups, can produce conflict and contradiction. We saw examples of this when the lifelong human rights campaigner Peter Tatchell was accused of racism for criticizing black rap musicians who sang about murdering gay people.[47] It appeared again in the confusion and conflict about whom to support when ethnic minority beauticians essentially misgendered a person claiming to be a trans woman by declining to wax around her testicles on the grounds that their religion and customs prohibited contact with male genitalia.[48]

All this "sophistication" keeps intersectionalists busy, internally argumentative, and divided, but it is all done in the service of uniting the various Theoretically oppressed groups into a single meta-group, "oppressed" or "other," under an overarching metanarrative of *Social Justice*, which seeks to establish a caste system based on Theorized states of oppression. Social Justice in the contemporary sense is therefore markedly different from the activism for universal human rights that characterized the civil rights movements.[49] These liberal, egalitarian approaches sought and seek to equalize opportunities by criminalizing discrimination, remedying disenfranchisement, and defeating bigotry by making prejudice on the grounds of immutable characteristics socially unacceptable. They thus provide an achievable goal for the well-meaning liberal individual: treat people equally regardless of their identity. The Social Justice approach regards this as, at best, naivety about the reality of a deeply prejudiced society, and, at worst, a willful refusal to acknowledge that we live in that kind of society. Consequently, the only way to be a virtuous person under Social Justice is to assume that these power imbalances and prejudices exist everywhere at all times, masked by the egalitarian false-promises of liberalism, and assiduously seek them out, using the right kind of Theoretical analysis. For Collins and Bilge,

> Social justice may be intersectionality's most contentious core idea, but it is one that expands the circle of intersectionality to include people who use intersectionality as an analytic tool for social justice. Working for social justice is not a requirement for intersectionality. Yet people who are engaged in using intersectionality as an analytic tool and people who see social justice as central rather than as peripheral to their lives are often one and the same. These people are typically critical of, rather than accepting of, the status quo.[50]

This is echoed by Rebecca Lind, who defines intersectionality as "a multifaceted perspective acknowledging the richness of the multiple, socially-constructed identities that combine to create each of us as a unique individual."[51] However, by this method, the "unique individual" is not really understood as an individual at all. As noted, the number of axes of social division under intersectionality can be almost infinite—but they cannot be reduced to the *individual*. Theory insists that only by understanding the various groups and the social constructions around those groups can one truly understand society, people, and their experiences. This conceptual shift facilitates group identity and thus identity politics, which are often radical.

Because of intersectionality's sheer versatility as a tool, it appeals to those involved in many different forms of engagement, ranging from legal activism and academic analysis to affirmative action and educational theory.[52] Mainstream activism has also eagerly embraced intersectionality—especially its concept of *privilege*, an idea that is vigorously insisted upon, often to the point of bullying and browbeating.

THE MEME OF SOCIAL JUSTICE

The expansion of intersectionality's sphere of influence has been considerable and perhaps unavoidable. Ange-Marie Hancock, in her book about the intellectual history of intersectionality, remarks on its growing popularity in both the intellectual and academic realms and as a kind of meme, noting that there are many different definitions and conceptualizations of intersectionality available online.[53] Hancock writes, "As a result, intersectionality as an analytical framework is in the process of reaching maximal salience across academe, the nonprofit sector (including global philanthropy), and politics."[54] In popular culture, Hancock notes, intersectionality is often evoked to *cancel* people, and public figures as diverse as Michelle Obama and the feminist group Code Pink have been criticized for failing "to understand and act from a place deeply cognizant of the multicategory dynamics of power at play."[55] Applying critical race Theory, Hancock argues that the mainstreaming of intersectionality is itself problematic because it whitens and "memeifies" intersectionality. For Hancock, the danger of "whitening" intersectionality and taking it away from the experiences of black women[56] happens at all levels, whether by tracing the concept back to (white male) Foucault or expanding it to encompass myriad forms of simplified cultural critique, which she belittles as "memeifying."[57]

As Hancock notes, intersectionality has gone viral and has rapidly taken on new and unexpected applications—especially in activism—many of which are justified by the academic literature on the subject. In 2017, Crenshaw herself observed that intersectionality had both expanded beyond her intended scope and also become a way of talking about complicated intersections of marginalized identity, rather than doing anything to alleviate oppression.[58] Thus, in addition to the confusion that stems from its highly interpretive Theoretical approach, which is rooted in the postmodern principles and themes we've outlined, critical race Theory and intersectionality are characterized by a great deal of divisiveness, pessimism, and cynicism. The beliefs that the decline in racist attitudes has largely been a mirage and that white people only allow people of color rights and opportunities when it is in their interest to do so can produce profound paranoia and hostility, especially among activists, on college campuses, and within competitive workplace environments. These feelings occasionally erupt, fracturing institutions from within, especially when well-meaning people, who don't want to incessantly defend themselves against accusations of racism and white supremacy, either submit to, retreat from, or avoid these situations.[59]

Critical race Theory's hallmark paranoid mind-set, which assumes racism is everywhere, always, just waiting to be found, is extremely unlikely to be helpful or healthy for those who adopt it. Always believing that one will be or is being discriminated against, and trying to find out how, is unlikely to improve the outcome of any situation. It can also be self-defeating. In *The Coddling of the American Mind*, attorney Greg Lukianoff and social psychologist Jonathan Haidt describe this process as a kind of reverse cognitive behavioral therapy (CBT), which makes its participants *less* mentally and emotionally healthy than before.[60] The main purpose of CBT is to train oneself *not* to catastrophize and interpret every situation in the most negative light, and the goal is to develop a more positive and resilient attitude towards the world, so that one can engage with it as fully as possible. If we train young people to read insult, hostility, and prejudice into every interaction, they may increasingly see the world as hostile to them and fail to thrive in it.

NOBLE ENDS, TERRIBLE MEANS

Critical race Theory and intersectionality are centrally concerned with ending racism, through the unlikely means of making everyone more aware of race at all times and places. They proceed upon an assumption that racism is normal and permanent, and the problem is primarily that people—particularly white people—are failing to see, acknowledge, and address it. As scholar-activists Heather Bruce, Robin DiAngelo, Gyda Swaney (Salish), and Amie Thurber put it at the influential National Race and Pedagogy Conference at Puget Sound University in 2015,[61]

"The question is not 'Did racism take place?'" for that is to be assumed, "but rather 'How did racism manifest in that situation?'" That is, we are to assume that racism is always taking place and our job is to examine situations for evidence of it. This follows from the beliefs that "all members of society are socialized to participate in the system of racism, albeit in varied social locations," and that "all white people benefit from racism regardless of intentions."[62] These quintessentially critical-race claims prompt some familiar Theoretical imperatives: "Racism must be continually identified, analysed, and challenged. No one is ever done," and "The racial status quo is comfortable for most whites. Therefore, anything that maintains white comfort is suspect." Moreover, "Resistance is a predictable reaction to anti-racist education and must be explicitly and strategically addressed."[63]

The core problems with critical race Theory are that it puts social significance back into racial categories and inflames racism, tends to be purely Theoretical, uses the postmodern knowledge and political principles, is profoundly aggressive, asserts its relevance to all aspects of Social Justice, and—not least—begins from the assumption that racism is both ordinary and permanent, everywhere and always. Consequently, every interaction between a person with a dominant racial identity and one with a marginalized one must be characterized by a power imbalance (the postmodern political principle). The job of the Theorist or activist is to draw attention to this imbalance—often described as racism or white supremacy—in order to begin dismantling it. It also sees racism as omnipresent and eternal, which grants it a mythological status, like sin or depravity.[64] Because the member of the marginalized racial group is said to have a unique voice and a counternarrative that, under Theory, *must* be regarded as authoritative to the degree that it is Theoretically "authentic" (the postmodern knowledge principle), there is no real way to dispute her reading of the situation. Therefore, everything the marginalized individual interprets as racism is considered racism by default—an episteme that encourages confirmation bias and leaves wide open the door to the unscrupulous. In scholarship, this leads to theories built only upon theories (and upon Theory), and no real means of testing or falsifying them. Meanwhile, adherents actively search for hidden and overt racial offenses until they find them, and they allow of no alternative or mitigating explanations—racism is not only permanently everywhere and latent in systems; it is also utterly unforgivable. This can lead to mob outrage and public shamings, and it tends to focus all our attention on racial politics, which inevitably become increasingly sensitive and fraught.

In addition, interpreting everything as racist and saying so almost constantly is unlikely to produce the desired results in white people (or for minorities). It could even undermine antiracist activism by creating skepticism and indignation and thus producing a reluctance to cooperate with worthwhile initiatives to overcome racism. Some studies have already shown that diversity courses, in which members of dominant groups are told that racism is everywhere and that they themselves perpetuate it, have resulted in increased hostility towards marginalized groups.[65] It is bad psychology to tell people who do not believe that they are racist—who may even actively despise racism—that there is nothing they can do to stop themselves from being racist—and then ask them to help you. It is even less helpful to tell them that even their own good intentions are proof of their latent racism. Worst of all is to set up double-binds, like telling them that if they notice race it is because they are racist, but if they don't notice race it's because their privilege affords them the luxury of not noticing race, which is racist. Finally, by focusing so intently on race and by objecting to "color blindness"—the refusal to attach social significance to race—critical race Theory threatens to undo the social taboo against evaluating people by their race. Such an obsessive focus on race, combined with a critique of liberal universalism and individuality (which Theory sees as largely a myth that benefits white people and perpetuates the status quo), is not likely to end well—neither for minority groups nor for social cohesion more broadly. Such attitudes tear at the fabric that holds contemporary societies together.

6 FEMINISMS AND GENDER STUDIES

Simplification as Sophistication

Seeking to improve the lives of just over half the population of Earth, feminism has been, for well over a century, one of the most significant social movements in human history. It has always been controversial and hugely unpopular with many—perhaps not least for its successes. Something, however, changed in feminism around the turn of the millennium. These changes reoriented most feminist scholarship and activism, as a surprising number of activists took up a new, "increasingly sophisticated" approach called "intersectionality," which combined many forms of identity Theory. The liberal, materialist, and radical approaches that had characterized feminism for much of the previous century were almost wholly displaced by the new intersectional approach. Multiple axes of marginalized identity were Theorized into existence right under the noses of the earlier feminists and, with them, a new need to read everything through a lens that magnifies potential oppression, bigotry, injustice, and grievance—and one's own complicity in systems of power and privilege. This change was so quick and thorough that, by the early 2000s, a spate of academic papers had appeared insisting, in a kind of scholarly death rattle, that materialist and radical approaches to feminist theory were still needed.[1] Not long afterwards, these gave way to papers explaining the dramatic shift and why it represented the right direction for the high culture of feminist thought in our academies.

From the outside, the intersectional approach seems grating, fractious, and incomprehensible. It appears to operate like a kind of circular firing squad, continually undermining itself over petty differences and grievances. It does this through calls for the various oppressed tribes to support each other: under the banner of first "allyship" and later "solidarity"—both of which go on to be Theorized as problematic in "centering" the needs of more privileged allies at the expense of oppressed minority groups of ever-increasing specificity. It is hard to escape the impression, which is accurate, that it isn't possible to do anything right, perhaps by design.

FEMINISMS, THEN AND NOW

In all fairness, feminism has never presented a unified front. This may be because *feminism*, in its most basic definition, means "belief in gender equality," and, in these terms, the majority of the population is now feminist.[2] Feminist scholarship and activism, however, have always been much more ideological and theoretical, and the dominant ideologies and theories have changed dramatically over time—accompanied by much factional infighting. Feminism, in the political and philosophical sense, has therefore come to include a dizzying array of camps: radical cultural feminists, radical lesbian feminists, radical libertarian feminists, separatists, French psychoanalytical feminists, womanists, liberal feminists, neoliberal feminists, Marxist feminists, socialist/materialist feminists, Islamic feminists, Christian feminists, Jewish feminists, choice feminists, equity feminists, postfeminists, and intersectional feminists.[3] All these groups are interested in women's rights, roles, and experiences in society, but they differ widely on how they understand these.

Clearly, there are far too many branches of feminism to investigate individually in any depth, so we will restrict ourselves to four (highly simplified) genuses of feminist thought here: liberal feminism, radical feminism, materialist feminism, and intersectional feminism. Liberal feminism was the most broad-based activist form during the "second wave," from the late 1960s through the mid-1980s. Radical and materialist feminisms are somewhat overlapping, somewhat competing scholarly branches of feminism, dominant during the same period. Intersectional feminism is the new variant, which replaced the others in scholarly and activist arenas from the mid-1990s onwards. Intersectional approaches to feminism are decisively dominant in our new millennium—and it is the intersectional perspective that is the source of the profound change described above.

From the outset of second-wave feminist activism in the 1960s, the three main branches of feminism were liberal, materialist, and radical. Liberal feminism worked incrementally to extend all the rights and freedoms of a liberal society to women. It was popular with broader liberal society "on the ground" and successfully reshaped the landscape of society, particularly in the workplace. The other two feminisms were also present in activism and dominant in feminist scholarship. Materialist feminists were concerned with how patriarchy and capitalism act together to constrain women, especially within environments like the workplace and the home. Thus, their theories drew on to varying degrees Marxism and socialism more broadly. Radical feminists foregrounded patriarchy and viewed women and men as oppressed and oppressor classes. They were revolutionaries who aimed to remake society, dismantle the concept of gender (but *not* sex), and overthrow patriarchy and capitalism. These three main branches (which incorporated many smaller branches too numerous to detail here) developed differently in different places. Most important to understand is that the liberal feminist approach enjoyed the most support from society, but radical and materialist (effectively socialist) feminism dominated the academy, especially from the 1970s onwards.

This began to change in the late 1980s and 1990s, when a new crop of Theorists successfully packaged a more "sophisticated" approach—postmodern Theory—for a new generation of activists. This approach was applied postmodernism, which accepted identity oppression as "real" and thus made postmodernism relevant to feminist activism. It incorporated aspects of queer Theory, postcolonial Theory, and, particularly, critical race Theory through the concept of intersectionality. These new developments fundamentally changed the character of feminism both in the popular consciousness and in the academy. The resulting "third-wave" approach to feminism tended to neglect class issues and focus on identity in the form of race, gender, and sexuality.[4] Rather than rallying around the shared identity of women, understood as a "sister-hood," intersectional and queer feminisms denied that women had common experiences and complicated what it even meant to be a woman. While liberal feminists had wanted the freedom to reject gender roles and access the same opportunities as men, and radical feminists had wanted to dismantle gender entirely as an oppressive social construct, intersectional feminists saw gender as both culturally constructed and as something that people could experience as real and expect to have acknowledged as such.

AN "INCREASINGLY SOPHISTICATED" THEORY

By the early 2000s, the intersectional shift in feminism had become undeniable. Previous feminist scholarship and activism treated women as a class and sought to create positive change for that class. As the influence of applied postmodernism crept into feminism, however, the focus switched from material disadvantages within social structures like law, economics, and politics to the oppressive nature of discourses. In 2006, Judith Lorber, professor (now emerita) of sociology and gender studies, summarized the four main tendencies of this "paradigm shift":

1. Making gender—not biological sex—central;

2. Treating gender and sexuality as social constructs;

3. Reading power into those constructions—power that acts in the Foucauldian sense of a permeating grid; and

4. Focusing upon one's *standpoint*—that is, one's identity.[5]

These changes were billed, in Lorber's words, as an "increasingly sophisticated" model for feminist thought. They are, in truth, the direct result of the influence of applied postmodern Theory. Each of the four characteristics embodies the postmodern knowledge principle and the postmodern political principle, as they came to be expressed through queer Theory (hence the focus on gender and its status as a social construction), critical race Theory (intersectionality), and postcolonial Theory (extending intersectionality to include postcolonial themes). In this new feminist paradigm, knowledge is "situated," which means that it comes from one's "standpoint" in society, by which they mean one's membership in intersecting identity groups. This, in turn, renders objective truth unobtainable and ties knowledge to power and both knowledge and power to the discourses that are believed to create, maintain, and legitimize dominance and oppression within society.

These applied derivatives of Theory possess a number of features that probably led to their adoption. Most importantly, intersectionality offered activists a renewed sense of purpose, as it provided them with new problems to interrogate and new accusations to make—especially against each other. For example, much of the black feminist thought and critical race Theory that informed this shift accused feminism of being "white" and of ignoring problems relevant to race, due to the corrupting influences of white privilege. Meanwhile, queer feminist thought accused feminism of being exclusionary of first lesbian, then LGB, then LGBT, and later LGBTQ issues, because of various assumptions of normativity and their associated privileges. This led care-oriented scholars to become increasingly "woke" not only to the ways in which others are oppressed but also to the guilt-inducing ways in which feminism itself could be Theorized to have participated in or been complicit with oppression. Ultimately, this last concern was subsumed into *gender studies*, which draws upon and informs feminist thinking, but is technically distinct from it.

This must be understood in terms of the development of gender studies, which has its own story. The academic study of gender emerged in the 1950s and 1960s, mainly from literary theory. At first, it was simply called "women's studies," because it looked at women's issues and advocated the political empowerment of women. Key texts included Simone de Beauvoir's *The Second Sex* (1949),[6] a groundbreaking book that argued that women are constructed by cultural understandings of their inferiority to men, and Betty Friedan's *The Feminine Mystique* (1963),[7] which criticized the idea that women were fulfilled by domesticity and motherhood. Kate Millet's *Sexual Politics* (1970)[8] provided a close reading of negative representations of women in literary texts by men, and Germaine Greer's *The Female Eunuch* (1970)[9] argued that women were sexually repressed and alienated from their own bodies and unaware of how much men hated them. These texts all fall within radical feminism, argue that womanhood is culturally constructed and imposed by men (in a top-down power dynamic), and advocate the revolutionary overthrow of patriarchy.

In the 1970s and much of the 1980s, feminist scholars looked closely at women's roles in the family and workforce and at social expectations that women be feminine, submissive, and beautiful, if not sexually available and pornographic. Marxist ideas of women as a subordinated class that exists to support men (who, in turn, support capitalism) abounded, and feminists met for "consciousness-raising" sessions. There, they attempted to fully comprehend their own oppression and its culturally constructed nature along the lines of the Marxist concept of "false consciousness"—which means ways of thinking that prevent someone from being able to ascertain the realities of her situation. This is akin to the concept of "internalized misogyny," which describes women who accept the social enforcement of women's inferiority as normal and natural. However, in the late 1980s and early 1990s, the landscape began to change, as the applied postmodern influence of queer Theory, postcolonial Theory, and intersectionality began to make itself felt.

Judith Lorber's 2006 essay "Shifting Paradigms and Challenging Categories" describes the way in which Marxist feminism saw women as a *class*.[10] She argues that, having addressed inequalities in the workplace through the 1970s and early 1980s, "Marxist feminists expanded their analysis to show that the exploitation of housewives was an integral part of the capitalist economy."[11] This materialist feminist view presents a metanarrative about men, women, and society, based on a simple oppressive male/oppressed female binary. Such a binary was unacceptable to the postmodern Theorists, who would read it through a Derridean lens that assumes a similar dynamic of dominance and subordination is present in any such "language game." In response, the new Theorists, who gained much influence over feminist thought in the late 1980s, drew on queer Theory to challenge the categories of "women" and "men" at their linguistic foundations.

This conceptual change was summarized in Jane Pilcher and Imelda Whelehan's account of the development of gender studies.[12] These changes are important, they point out, because, in the postmodern view, "The individual status and position of those we group together and call 'women' and of those we call 'men' are argued to vary so greatly over time, space and culture that there is little justification for the use of these collective nouns."[13] By the early 2000s, then, a dominant view within feminism was that—because gender has been constructed differently by dominant discourses at different times and places—to speak of "women" and "men" at all is incoherent. They argued that, under Theory, "'women' and 'men' are regarded as constructions or representations—achieved through discourse, performance, and repetition—rather than 'real' entities."[14] This new view makes sex an inherently unstable basis for study—and one which risks neglecting the experiences of people working within different cultural frameworks. This necessitated a shift from *feminism* to a broader and looser study of gender and gender identity. To try to study "women" or "men" under Theory is to miss the point. For the applied postmodernists, the topic of interest is "gender"—which they define as the behaviors and expectations that people considered men and women are taught to perform, which—though they cannot be entirely done away with—can be disrupted, confused, and complicated.

Theory not only dramatically changed feminism, by shifting the understanding of social constructions of gender from a simplistic oppressive binary to a fluid and unstable phenomenon with liberatory potential; it also made feminism focus on intersectionality.[15] This, Pilcher and Whelehan tell us, marks the conceptual shift from feminism to gender studies: "As understandings of gender have developed as a complex, multi-faceted and multi-disciplinary area, involving the study of relationships within as well as between genders, 'gender studies' has become a term with increasing currency, albeit not uncontested."[16] In other words, throughout the applied postmodernism phase, uniting various minority-status groups under the single flag of *oppression* came to be seen as the only "right" way to do feminism. Meanwhile, feminism gave way to gender studies under the auspices of queer Theory and adopted intersectionality as a kind of Grand Unifying Theory of Social Power and Societal Injustice.

Lorber describes this new plurality and indeterminacy, in which a focus on how women as a class are oppressed by men as a class is simply not tenable:

> Feminist research now looks at men and women of many different social groups, not just white women. It is sensitive to multicultural perspectives and tries not to impose Western comparisons in data analysis. It is exploring the intricate and reciprocal interplay of gender, sex, and sexuality. By recognizing the multiplicity of genders, sexes, and sexualities, feminist research is able to go beyond the conventional binaries. The problem they have begun to solve is how to generate categories for comparison, even while critically deconstructing them.[17]

Meanwhile, gender studies was by then doing its postmodern thing. It had come to regard knowledge as a cultural construct (postmodern knowledge principle), worked within many vectors of power and privilege (postmodern political principle), and was deconstructing categories, blurring boundaries, focusing on discourses, practicing cultural relativism, and honoring identity-group wisdom (four postmodern themes).

Lorber breaks the change down into four aspects. First, there is the centrality of gender as an overarching organizing principle for all of society:

> The paradigm shift in feminist social science starts with the concept of gender as an organizing principle of the overall social order in modern societies and all social institutions, including the economy, politics, religion, the military, education, and medicine, not just the family. In this conceptualization, gender is not just part of personality structures and identity, but is a formal, bureaucratic status, as well as a status in multidimensional stratification systems, political economies, and hierarchies of power.[18]

By the time Lorber documented this shift, in 2006, feminism had organized itself around a belief that gender is central to the systems of power and privilege. Moreover, it had taken on the postmodern conception of the world—that is, it had reorganized itself around Theory. Feminist thought could no longer understand "patriarchy" as the literal "rule of the fathers" (and husbands), but instead as, in Foucauldian terms, vague notions of male dominance permeating every discourse. The new paradigm saw power and privilege as an "organizing principle," awarding "a status in multidimensional stratification systems"—that is, people are categorized hierarchically, which informs the way they think and speak.

Lorber goes on,

> The second aspect of this paradigm shift is that gender and sexuality are socially constructed. This principle provides the content of gender as an organizational process, a framework for face-to-face interaction, and the behavioral aspects of personal identity.[19]

Gender, in the new, applied postmodernist conception, became something that is done by and to people and that we all do to each other. Like "to queer," which emerged as a verb in queer Theory because of the perceived importance of "speech acts"—creating reality with one's speech—"to gender" became a verb. As a result, Theorists turned their attention to the ways in which structures of society are "gendered." For example, while, previously, an advertisement showing a woman using dishwashing detergent might have been seen as reinforcing patriarchal expectations and exploiting women in a material sense, after the applied postmodern turn it would be seen as a way of "gendering" domestic tasks—using discourses to legitimize the idea that washing dishes is part of what it means to be a woman. This "gendering" occurs when the ad presents that idea as a part of a set of socially legitimized discourses that define female gender roles for women to be socialized into. This view emphasizes social constructivism.

Lorber explains the role of power in creating and maintaining these social constructions:

The third focus is the analysis of the power and social control imbricated in the social construction of gender and sexuality, which lays bare the hegemony of dominant men, their version of masculinity, and heterosexuality.[20]

Thus, despite the shift toward postmodernism that occurred in the 1980s and 1990s, the influence of Simone de Beauvoir, who saw women as subordinated to second-class status, was still very much felt. So too was that of many radical feminist ideas, especially about the ways in which feminine roles are subordinated to masculine ones. Nevertheless, there was a strong move away from materialist concerns about law, politics, and economics and toward postmodern discourse analysis (although it was still understood that the construction of gender makes men the default sex and heterosexuality the default sexuality, with women and homosexuality constructed in a position of otherness to these). These earlier feminist ideas were retained, but the focus and understanding of them changed. What had previously been seen as legally mandated roles and restrictions and overtly sexist expectations of adherence to gender roles imposed by men, was, after the applied postmodern shift, attributed to more subtle, interactional, learned, performed, and internalized expectations, perpetuated by everybody. This is in keeping with the postmodern view of power promoted by Michel Foucault.

Lorber addresses the construction of knowledge after the paradigm shift, advocating the importance of standpoint (meaning, which groups you belong to and their social positions relative to power) and intersectionality:

Fourth, feminist social science has devised research designs and methodologies that have allowed the standpoints of oppressed and repressed women throughout the world to come to the forefront, and which reflect increasingly sophisticated intersectional analyses of class, racial ethnicity, religion, and sexuality.[21]

Lorber views standpoint theory and intersectionality as now central to knowledge production within gender studies. By 2006, then, "women's studies"—which was primarily radical or materialist and used a relatively simple form of standpoint theory that focused on biological sex categories and the construction of gender in the service of capitalism—had become "gender studies"—which are strongly postmodern and use an "increasingly sophisticated," as Lorber put it, intersectional model.

This alleged increase in sophistication is, in all likelihood, the reason intersectional thought and the postmodern Theory it is based on caught on so quickly, widely, and decisively.[22] The (mostly liberal feminist) activists had made tremendous progress toward the legal, professional, and social equality of the sexes, but, in their success, they had made themselves redundant because it left relatively little to do. The top-down patriarchal-capitalist models promoted by the radical and materialist feminists—especially the scholars—had also begun to seem less tenable. Intersectional thought introduced entirely new lines of work, not only within society but also *within feminism itself*. The intersectional turn was pushed by scholars and activists, who used elements of queer Theory, postcolonial Theory, and especially critical race Theory *to problematize feminism and feminists*, in addition to commenting on what they painted as an intractably complicated and oppressive society. Intersectional Theory provided an entirely new, "increasingly sophisticated" way to understand power dynamics in society, allowing them to repurpose their failing theoretical models into something more diffuse and less falsifiable.[23]

We often observe this kind of shift to a more "sophisticated" and nebulous model when people are highly personally and ideologically committed to a theoretical approach that is clearly failing. This phenomenon was first described by Leon Festinger, in his study of UFO cults, and led to the development of the concept of *cognitive dissonance*.[24] Festinger observed that highly committed cultists did not abandon their beliefs when the predictions of the cult failed to manifest—when the UFO never came. Instead, cultists resolved this undeniable contradiction by claiming the event had occurred, but in some unfalsifiable way (specifically, they claimed God decided to spare the planet as a result of the faith of the cultists).

Before the postmodern turn, Marxist, socialist, and other radical feminist theories saw power as an intentional, top-down strategy by powerful men in patriarchal and capitalist societies, but the advances of second-wave feminism made this conception somewhat redundant. While boorish men with patriarchal assumptions continued to exist, it became increasingly untenable to view Western society as genuinely patriarchal or to see most men as actively colluding against the success of women. Postmodern Theory offered an opportunity to retain the same beliefs and predictions—male domination exists and serves itself at the expense of women—while redefining them in terms diffuse enough to be a matter of faith, requiring no evidence: social constructions, discourses, and socialization. The Foucauldian idea of a diffuse grid of power dynamics that constantly operates through everyone through their unwitting uses of language fit the bill perfectly.[25]

DOING GENDER STUDIES

What, then, is being studied in gender studies through its increasingly sophisticated model, which incorporates race, class, gender, and sexuality? Everything. Gender studies is so interdisciplinary, its scholars feel justified to study everything that humans typically engage in. The one point of consistency is that they study it in a specific way. They apply lenses of gendered analysis that draw on intersectionality, queer Theory, and postcolonial Theory and thus, ultimately, on postmodern conceptions of knowledge, power, and discourses.

Take the concept of "gendering" as an oppressive action. It's not usually something powerful individuals do knowingly. Instead, it is created by social interactions on all levels, interactions that become ever more complex as further layers of identity are added to the analytical mix. In their massively influential 1987 paper, "Doing Gender"[26]—the most cited work in gender studies, which has contributed to over thirteen thousand other academic papers, articles, and books since its first publication—Candace West and Don H. Zimmerman aimed "to advance a new understanding of gender as a routine accomplishment embedded in everyday interaction." They write,

> We contend that the "doing" of gender is undertaken by women
> and men whose competence as members of society is hostage

to its production. Doing gender involves a complex of socially guided perceptual, interactional, and micropolitical activities that cast particular pursuits as expressions of masculine and feminine "natures."[27]

Consistent with the shift away from sex and toward gender, understood as a social construction, West and Zimmerman explicitly reject biology as a source of differences in male and female behaviors, preferences, or traits, noting,

> Doing gender means creating differences between girls and boys and women and men, differences that are not natural, essential, or biological. Once the differences have been constructed, they are used to reinforce the "essentialness" of gender.[28]

This process, they argue, is achieved by socialization and is well underway by the age of five.

> Being a "girl" or a "boy" then, is not only being more competent than a "baby," but also being competently female or male, that is, learning to produce behavioral displays of one's "essential" female or male identity.[29]

In Judith Butler's iconic work *Gender Trouble*, which emerged at around the same time as "Doing Gender" and drew strongly on Foucault's ideas about the construction of sexuality, gender is made real by being learned and reproduced, like language. West and Zimmerman understand gender in roughly the same way.[30]

In 1995, the concept of gender as something that is "done" was given a more intersectional slant by Candace West and Sarah Fenstermaker. In a follow-up essay to "Doing Gender," called "Doing Difference," West and Fenstermaker look at the intersections of gender with race and class. This is part of the increasing focus on standpoint that Lorber would point out a decade later. Since then, gender studies has attempted to take an increasing number of diverse identities into account—growing ever more complicated in the process—particularly as trans studies has increased in relevance. In 2010, Catherine Connell problematized and expanded this line of analysis to encompass the concept of "redoing gender," which, she argued, had not been adequately addressed by the ideas in "Doing Gender," although she retained the idea that "routine interactions" between people were central to policing gender displays.[31] Plainly, gender studies is no longer about gender expectations of women as determined by reproductive function, but a sprawling field of study tackling a much more complex and unruly collection of identities—all essentially in the same way, by looking for "problematics" to complain about until they find them.

THE DEATH OF LIBERAL FEMINISM

It is not only radical and materialist feminists who have been largely displaced by postmodern intersectionalists. Liberal feminists—who have always been more prominent in everyday activism than in scholarship—were also overwhelmed by the postmodern feminists. Because liberal feminism works in accordance with *modernist* ideals of secular, liberal democracy, individual agency within a framework of universal human rights, and an Enlightenment focus on reason and science, it has been the explicit, central target of *postmodernists*. Pilcher and Whelehan explain why in their 2004 account of the emerging field of gender studies:

> Liberal feminism draws on the diversity of liberal thought dominant in Western society since the Enlightenment, which affirms that women's subordinate social position can be addressed by existing political processes under democracy. For liberals the key battle is access to education; following Mary Wollstonecraft, it is argued that if men and women are educated equally then it follows that they will get equal access to society. Liberal feminists would be loath to use the language of "revolution" or "liberation" favoured by radicals and socialists, in their belief that democracy itself is naturally adaptable to equality for both sexes. This liberal position is broadly held to be the dominant, "commonsense" stance

on feminism, applicable to the majority of women who identify as "feminist," and remains highly visible in popular discourse.[32]

Liberal feminists generally believe society already provides almost all the opportunities required for women to succeed in life. They simply want the same access to those opportunities as men and advocate measures that allow and protect that access—educational opportunities, affordable childcare, flexible working hours, and so on. Liberal feminism does not automatically assume that differences in outcomes imply discrimination, however, and thus it eschews the equity-based approaches of intersectional feminism. The liberal focus on removing the social significance of identity categories—that is, the legal and social requirements to comply with gender, class, or race expectations—seeks to refine the legacies of the Enlightenment project and the civil rights movements, rather than overthrow them for socialist or postmodern ends. Consequently, many liberal feminists believed their work would be largely done once women gained legal equality with men and had control over their own reproductive choices and when societal expectations had changed so much that it was no longer surprising to see women in all fields of work.

This liberal approach to feminism is angrily refuted and problematized by applied postmodernists, who desperately want to return social significance to certain identity categories, so they can apply identity politics and provide a meaning-making structure for (especially racial) minorities. Hence Kimberlé Crenshaw's emphasis on the importance of saying "I am Black" instead of "I am a person who happens to be Black"[33] and the queer-Theoretical project to make LGBTQ identities more visible. In every branch of applied postmodern Theory, objections to liberalism are a central tenet. Recall, for example, critical race Theory's claim that liberalism primarily benefits the dominant, postcolonial Theory's view of liberalism as a form of imperialist universalizing, and queer Theory's objection to the liberal (and Enlightenment) science that seeks to understand variations in sexuality and gendered traits, rather than condemning them as sinful or criminal. The Enlightenment-inspired liberal confidence in the existence of objective truths that can be ascertained by science and reason is seen, by the postmodernists, as mainly a way of trying to make everyone conform to white, Western, male, heterosexual discourses of knowledge. The Theoretical view is that the opportunities to which liberal feminists sought equal access are never equally accessible on principle and the promise of equality through liberalism is yet another lie by the powerful used to obscure the irreparable injustices inherent in the system. Theory posits that opportunities are more accessible to some (white, cisgender, heterosexual, etc.) women than others, and those same women are *complicit* in the systems of injustice that Theory seeks to criticize.

Consequently, while radical feminists seek to overthrow capitalist and patriarchal systems they see as oppressing women, and postmodern feminists seek to problematize existing structures and analyze and deconstruct the categories that uphold them, liberal feminists (and liberals generally) want to preserve the structures and institutions of secular, liberal democracy and refine them. Pilcher and Whelehan distinguish between three different goals within feminism: equality, difference, and diversity (or equity). The equality approach is favored by liberal (and to an extent by radical) feminists. This approach seeks to "extend to women the same rights and privileges that men have, through identifying areas of unequal treatment and eliminating them via legal reforms."[34] Intersectional feminists frequently critique this approach for what they perceive as the expectation that marginalized groups must conform to white, masculinist ways of knowing and being in the world.

THE TRIALS AND TRIBULATIONS OF THE DIVERSITY THEORISTS

The diversity Theorists—intersectionalists—advocate a different approach altogether. They want a shift toward "mutual respect" and "affirmation of difference," that is, a sense of solidarity and allyship among marginalized groups.[35] Note that this is a respect for differences between social and cultural groups—not for individuals with different viewpoints. They do not defend the right to express different ideas, but affirm the value of those ideas that are marked out as belonging to certain groups. This requires cultural relativism and standpoint theory—the view that belonging to a marginalized group provides special access to truth, by allowing members insight into both dominance and their own oppression. Diversity Theorists therefore do not usually permit any approach to feminism that is individualistic or centers the personal choices made by women ("choice feminism"), which some Theorists have called a form of betrayal.[36] As a result, the intersectional approach is contradictory and messy. It has been used to assign specific values and beliefs to certain groups, mark them as authoritative or problematic, and ignore the ideological and intellectual diversity within groups. It uses this Theoretical construction to attempt to achieve—not equality—but *social equity*, the readjustment of social and economic shares, so that citizens (or groups of citizens) are "made equal."

The understanding that different groups have different experiences, beliefs, and values was largely influenced by some black feminists, who criticized second-wave feminism for not recognizing that black women faced different prejudices and stereotypes than white women. bell hooks' 1982 book, *Ain't I a Woman?*, which carries a title that seeks to place her in the same mold as Sojourner Truth, was especially influential. hooks argues,

> When the woman's movement began in the late 60s, it was evident that the white women who dominated the movement felt it was "their" movement, that is the medium through which a white woman would voice her grievance to society. Not only did white women act as if feminist ideology existed solely to serve their own interests because they were able to draw public attention to feminist concerns. They were unwilling to acknowledge that non-white women were part of the collective group women in American society.[37]

Similarly, in her 1990 book, *Black Feminist Thought*,[38] Patricia Hill Collins describes the stereotypes that affect African American women uniquely. She traces several stereotypes she saw as excluded from (white) feminism—including The Mammy, a servile sexless figure; The Matriarch, an assertive (and therefore unfeminine) ruler of her family; The Welfare Mother, a passive baby-making machine; and The Jezebel, a sexually aggressive and sexually available black woman—back to tropes used to justify slavery. However, attempts by (white) feminists to include these racialized sexist tropes did not go down well with Collins either. She writes in a 1993 essay:

> The longstanding effort to "colorize" feminist theory by inserting the experiences of women of color represents at best genuine efforts to reduce bias in Women's Studies. But at its worst, colorization also contains elements of both voyeurism and academic colonialism.[39]

The "increasingly sophisticated" new Theory is actually overly simplistic—*everything* is problematic *somehow*, because of power dynamics based on identity. It is also functionally impossible, a characteristic that is misinterpreted as extreme complexity. The needle Collins expects (white) feminists to thread involves including—but not appropriating—the experiences of women of color, providing space for them to be heard, and amplifying their voices—without exploiting them or becoming voyeuristic consumers of their oppression. These kinds of impossible, contradictory, double-binding demands are a persistent feature of applied postmodern Theory and continue to plague gender studies and other forms of Social Justice scholarship. And that's just the issue of race. Similar problems arise from the application of queer Theory, and, as a result, attempts to include more lesbian, gay, bisexual, and transgender voices in gender studies have often met with frustration.

A CLASSLESS THEORY

One casualty of this "increasingly sophisticated" intersectional model, which focuses primarily on the power of discourses, is the neglect of the most materially relevant variable in many of the problems faced by women (and by many racial and sexual minorities): economic class. This conspicuous neglect has been a matter of grave concern to left-leaning liberal feminists, socialist feminists, and socialists more broadly.[40]

Not altogether unironically, the axis that has replaced class in social theory is *privilege*. As we have noted, privilege is a concept most closely associated with the Theorist Peggy McIntosh, a well-off white woman, and the author of a 1989 essay called "White Privilege: Unpacking the Invisible Knapsack."[41] Influenced by critical race Theory, McIntosh focuses on *white* privilege, but the concept of social privilege, unconnected to economic class, was soon extended to other identity categories—male, straight, cisgender, thin, able-bodied, and so on—to describe the relative statistical absence of discrimination against and disenfranchisement of such groups, by comparison with that experienced by various marginalized identity categories. Privilege-consciousness has since nearly completely replaced class-consciousness as the primary concern of those on the academic, activist, and political left, and one's status as privileged is assessed intersectionally, using the appropriate applied postmodern Theories. This attempt to flip the script by strategically redefining the *absence* of discrimination and disenfranchisement as unjust and problematic has arguably been a catastrophe for left-leaning politics throughout the developed world.

This shift away from class and towards gender identity, race, and sexuality troubles traditional economic leftists, who fear that the left is being taken away from the working class and hijacked by the bourgeoisie within the academy. More worryingly still, it could drive working-class voters into the arms of the populist right.[42] If the group it has traditionally supported—the working class—believe that the political left has abandoned them, the left may lose many of the voters it requires to attain political power. As it divests itself of universalism, this resentment is likely to grow. New York University historian Linda Gordon has summarized working-class resentment of intersectionality:

> Some criticism is ill-informed but understandable nevertheless. A poor white man associates intersectionality with being told that he has white privilege: "So when that feminist told me I had 'white privilege,' I told her that my white skin didn't do shit." He explains: "Have you ever spent a frigid northern-Illinois winter without heat or running water? I have. At 12 years old were you making ramen noodles in a coffee maker with water you fetched from a public bathroom? I was."[43]

As intersectionality developed and became dominant in both main-stream political activism and scholarship, it became increasingly common to hear that "straight, white, cisgendered men" were the problem. For example, Suzanna Danuta Walters, editor-in-chief of the prestigious feminist journal *Signs: Journal of Women in Culture and Society*, penned a 2018 op-ed for the *Washington Post* that asks, with startling frankness, "Why can't we hate men?"[44] This is unlikely to endear intersectionalists to heterosexual white men—especially if they have experienced poverty, homelessness, or other major hardships.

OF MASCULINITIES AND MEN

The development of (critical) "studies" of "men and masculinities" within gender studies does not seem likely to alleviate this situation. Although the scholars of men's and masculinities studies are mostly men, they study masculinity within a feminist framework. The journal *Men and Masculinities*, founded by Michael Kimmel, author of *The Politics of Manhood: Profeminist Men Respond to the Mythopoetic Men's Movement*, provides ample evidence of this.[45] Nowhere in gender studies can one find men or masculinities being studied through any lens but feminism. This is not particularly surprising because it is completely consistent with Theory. Men speaking for themselves would be speaking from power into powerful discourses, and women speaking for men would be speaking into those already-powerful discourses, neither of which can be allowed.

Men's and masculinities studies often rely heavily on the concept of "hegemonic masculinity," developed by Australian gender Theorist Raewyn Connell (who has also published under "Robert" or "Bob").[46] Hegemonic masculinity refers to dominant forms of masculinity, which are understood to maintain men's superiority over women and perpetuate aggressive and competitive expressions of maleness, which are socially enforced by hegemonic—dominant and powerful—discourses around what it means to be a "real man." Hegemonic masculinity is connected to the concept of "toxic masculinity," developed by Terry Kupers in his research on the discourses about masculinity that emerge in prisons, and defined by him as "the constellation of socially regressive male traits that serve to foster domination, the devaluation of women, homophobia, and wanton violence."[47] This controversial concept has proven instrumental in applying Theory to the supposedly urgent questions of why American society was willing to elect the boorish Donald Trump[48] and why "traditional masculinity" should be treated as a psychological illness by the American Psychological Association, as suggested in its 2018 "Guidelines for Psychological Practice with Men and Boys."[49] One suspects that Michel Foucault is rolling in his grave over this development.

Although some scholars—such as Nancy Dowd in *The Man Question* (2010)[50]—have attempted to complicate this association of masculinity with misogyny, domination, and violence, intersectionalism generally redeems men only when they also have some form of marginalized identity. For example, the "inclusive masculinity" developed by Eric Anderson in the mid-2000s was widely celebrated for its focus on homosexuality and feminism (until it was discovered that Anderson disagrees with Theoretical methods and favors a more rigorous empirical approach, at which point it was problematized).[51] Consequently, there has been very little study of those problems faced by men simply because they are men—outside of Theoretically sanctioned feminist, race, or sexuality issues.

SUMMARY OF THE SHIFT

The dominant form of feminism within gender studies, then, is intersectional feminism, which draws on critical race Theory, queer Theory, and postcolonial Theory. Gender studies rapidly moved away from its origins in "women's studies" and its roots in materialist analyses, with the development of Theory and the applied postmodern turn. Following this shift, by 2006, feminism within gender studies came to rely on four main tenets:

1. Gender is highly significant to the way power is structured in society;

2. Gender is socially constructed;

3. Gendered power structures privilege men;

4. Gender is combined with other forms of identity, which must be acknowledged and that knowledge is relative and attached to identity.

By the early 2000s, feminism had been almost completely subsumed by gender studies, which had adopted both the postmodern knowledge principle—that objective knowledge cannot be obtained—and the postmodern political principle—that society is structured into systems of power and privilege. Furthermore, it largely abandoned its radical and materialist scholarly roots and liberal activism, and replaced them with a postmodern blurring of categories and cultural relativism—the inevitable effects of gender studies' heavy reliance on both intersectionality and queer Theory. As much of the analysis in gender studies is discourse analysis, there is also an intense focus on language. The focus on group identity and intersectional standpoint theory that now forms the backbone of Social Justice thought leaves no room for the concepts of universality and individuality. The phrase *there is no universal woman* could be gender studies' motto.[52]

This analytical framework has had some benefits. It complicated the simplistic radical and materialist feminist metanarratives—in which women were an oppressed class and men their oppressors—by recognizing that power does not work in such a simple and intentionally binary way. This opened the door to a more nuanced analysis. This was particularly valuable to African American feminists, who were able to show that they faced very different stereotypes and barriers than white American feminists, and who expanded feminist scholarship to include them. It also encouraged the exploration of gender as something more complicated than roles imposed on men and women by patriarchy, by incorporating the prejudice and discrimination faced by trans men and women.

However, the problems within gender studies since its turn towards intersectionality have been considerable. The assumption that gender imbalances underlie all interactions between people perceived as belonging to a dominant gender and people perceived as belonging to a marginalized one—and that these imbalances always favor the masculine—has severely limited the ability to conduct rigorous scholarship on sex and gender. The current analytical framework does not allow for the possibility of a situation in which gender power imbalances do *not* exist or one in which they disadvantage men. While it is frequently argued that "patriarchy harms men too," it is simply impossible to argue that male dominance is not a factor in *any* given disparity. It is also impossible to say that men can be systematically disadvantaged as a sex by anything other than the unintended consequences of their own dominance—say, for instance, by the social prestige of intersectional feminism and the lack of a comparably well-regarded movement that addresses men's issues.

The problems with the assumption that all gender differences can be explained by social constructivism are also profound. By centralizing social constructivist ideas of gender from radical feminism and queer Theory, biological explanations for why, on average, men and women make different life choices, display different degrees of psychological traits, have different interests, or exhibit different sexual behaviors cannot be included within intersectional feminist analysis. As there is considerable evidence that such differences exist[53] and that they actually increase when women are free to make their own choices[54]—and it would be remarkable if we were the only primates without such differences—this also limits the ability to do rigorous and valuable scholarship within gender studies, while undermining the credibility of any rigorous and valuable scholarship that has been done in the field.

Finally, the attempt to make all analyses of gender intersectional, to focus relentlessly on a simplistic concept of societal privilege, rooted overwhelmingly in identity (and not in economics) and to incorporate elements of critical race Theory and queer Theory, results in a highly muddled, Theoretical, and abstract analysis that makes it difficult—if not impossible—to reach any conclusions other than the oversimplification that straight white men are unfairly privileged and need to repent and get out of everyone else's way. Because of the focus on the relevance of one's standpoint to one's access to knowledge, scholars are severely limited in the extent to which they can even do gender studies unless they are trans women of color, which few scholars are. This results in large sections of academic papers dedicated to scholars performatively acknowledging their positionality and problematizing their own work, rather than doing something useful. Gender studies' own Theoretical frameworks currently hinder it from producing scholarship of value to the cause of social justice. This is the price it pays for its "increasing sophistication."

7 DISABILITY AND FAT STUDIES

Support-Group Identity Theory

As Theory has developed, it has become increasingly obsessed with identity and positionality. The postmodern knowledge principle insists that objective knowledge is not possible and favors specialized "knowledges" that arise from the lived experience of individuals of a certain identity, positioned in a specific way by society. The postmodern political principle is, in essence, a call to identity politics, which requires adopting an identity as part of some marginalized group or being assigned to a relatively privileged one. This is supported by the postmodern theme of fragmenting the universal and replacing the individual with the group. We see this tendency in postcolonial Theory, where the "other" needs to be rescued from Western ways. We see it in queer Theory, in which "queer" sexual, gender, and other identities are a peculiar fascination, while "normal" identities are problematized for the alleged implications of their very existence. We see this in critical race Theory, which advocates identifying with one's socially constructed racial status and adopting, promoting, and protecting specific cultures. We see it in intersectional feminism, which continually examines how various identities intersect to create ever more niche identity statuses. We also see it in the postmodern study of disability and fatness, which focuses on social constructions to such an extent that the objective realities of the disabilities and excess weight they examine are Theorized almost out of existence. This is a kind of kabuki theater, in which Theory is used to turn support-group initiatives into scholarship and ill-informed activism.

As with gender studies, critical approaches to studying disability and fatness as identities began with the applied postmodern turn of the late 1980s and early 1990s, which led to the creation of two related postmodern identity studies fields: disability studies and fat studies. Like gender studies, these have largely displaced other approaches to scholarship and activism, which tend to be more practical and less apt to believe everything is best seen as a purely social construct and engaged through highly emotional appeals to identity politics. Though similar in many respects, these two fields have different histories, so they will be considered separately here.

DISABILITY STUDIES

Disabled activism began in the 1960s, at around the same time as and with similar goals to the Civil Rights Movement, second-wave feminism, and Gay Pride. Its original aim was to make society more accommodating and accepting of disabled people, and thereby improve their quality of life. Much of this was to be achieved by increasing disabled people's access to the opportunities available to the nondisabled and the movement enjoyed much success in this. On the whole, this was excellent progress.

This perfectly reasonable goal began to change in the 1980s. After the turn towards applied postmodernism and the incorporation of intersectional feminism, queer Theory, and critical race Theory, disability studies began to view ability as a social construct, and has since become increasingly radical and in denial about reality. Various forms of disability are considered to be cultural constructs—as is the condition of being able-bodied (lacking a disability). Disability (including certain treatable mental illnesses) came to be valorized as a set of related marginalized identity groups, and these were placed in contrast to "normal" able-bodied identities. As a result, disability studies has taken on an increasingly intersectional and queer Theoretic approach, which has made it steadily more obscure, abstract, and unsuited to improving the opportunities and quality of life of disabled people.

The changes to "dis/abled"[1] scholarship and activism in the 1980s can be best understood as a shift from understanding disability as something that resides in the individual to viewing it as something imposed upon individuals by a society that does not accommodate their needs. Before this shift, disabled people were considered to be people with some form of disability; afterwards, disability was viewed as a status imposed upon them by a relatively unwelcoming and uninterested society. For example, a person with deafness was previously considered to be a person who cannot hear, and who is disabled to some extent by her impairment. After the shift, she was seen as a Deaf person, someone who cannot hear and whom society has "disabled" by failing to be equally accommodating to those without hearing as it is to those with hearing (by default). In other words, a person is only *disabled* because of society's expectations that people are generally able-bodied and benefit from being so. It is a status imposed upon those with impairments.

This shift to a social constructivist view of disability seems to have taken place in two stages. In the first, what is commonly called the "social model of disability" replaced the "medical model of disability," sometimes called the "individual model." This occurred in the 1980s and is widely credited to the British social work scholar and sociologist Michael Oliver. Within the medical or individual model (some people conflate these and others distinguish them), disability is something that affects a person, and the solution is to fix the disabling condition or mitigate their impairments, so they can engage with the world more like able-bodied people do.[2] Within the social model of disability, the onus is on society to accommodate the individual with impairments. Oliver writes,

> Th[e] social model of disability acknowledges impairment as being a cause of individual limitation, but disability is imposed on top of this. This may be summed up this way: Disability is the disadvantage or restriction of activity caused by the political, economic and cultural norms of a society which takes little or no account of people who have impairments and thus excludes

them from mainstream activity. (Therefore disability, like racism or sexism, is discrimination and social oppression). . . . This social model of disability, like all paradigms, fundamentally affects society's world-view and within that, the way particular problems are seen.[3]

Oliver aimed to effect a conceptual shift: from a binary understanding of disabled versus able-bodied *people* to the idea of a spectrum of capabilities, whose meanings have been understood differently in different times and cultures. The understanding of disability that existed in the 1980s, in Britain in particular, changed to one that placed the responsibility for enabling or disabling people onto society. This conceptual shift demands that society must adjust to the individual, not the other way around.

There is no sign that Oliver originally took a particularly postmodernist approach, and his view of disability as a social construct is not radical. That has since changed. His book *Social Work with Disabled People*, first published in 1983, is currently in its fourth edition and includes significant references to later work from within identity studies. For example, in the most recent edition, the language has clearly been influenced by intersectionality:

[E]xperiences will undoubtedly be culturally located and reflect differences of class, race, gender and so forth, and so discourse may well be culturally biased. When using the social model, understanding also comes from recognising that historically experiences of disability have been culturally located in responses to impairment. The social model can be used by those in different cultures and within ethnic, queer or gender studies to illustrate disability in those situations. Equally these disciplines all need to take account of disableism with their communities.[4]

Disability studies currently relies strongly on the two postmodern principles: knowledge is a social construct, and society consists of systems of power and privilege. This orientation within disability studies frequently draws on critical race Theory. Disability studies as a whole relies heavily on both Michel Foucault and Judith Butler, and consequently its most frequent postmodern themes are the blurring of boundaries and the importance of discourse—accompanied by a radical distrust of science. The concept of the individual is also frequently disparaged within disability studies, due to the belief that individualism enables a "neoliberal expectation" to adapt to one's disabilities and become a productive member of capitalist society.

ABLEISM

Within disability studies, "ableism" is largely understood as the acceptance of the (Theoretically problematic) assumptions that it is generally better to be able-bodied than disabled and that it is "normal" to be able-bodied. "Disableism," on the other hand, denotes prejudice against disabled people, including the idea that their disabled status exists outside of the usual understanding of "normal" and the belief that an able-bodied person is superior to a disabled person. This oppression is part of a constellation of different forms of bigotry. As the self-described autistic, disabled, asexual, and genderqueer activist Lydia X. Y. Brown defines it,

> [A]bleism might describe the value system of ablenormativity which privileges the supposedly neurotypical and ablebodied, while disableism might describe the violent oppression targeting people whose bodyminds are deemed deviant and thus disabled. In other words, ableism is to heterosexism what disableism is to queerantagonism.[5]

Accordingly, queer Theory, with its focus on deconstructing the normal, has proven particularly compatible with disability studies. Just as queer Theorist Judith Butler evoked Adrienne Rich's concept of "compulsory heterosexuality"—the social enforcement of heterosexuality as the normal, default sexuality—so does Robert McRuer in disability studies. In his 2006 book, *Crip Theory: Cultural Signs of Queerness and Disability*,[6] which examines how queer Theory and disability studies inform each other, he argues,

Like compulsory heterosexuality, then, compulsory able-bodiedness functions by covering over, with the appearance of choice, a
system in which there is actually no choice. . . . Just as the origins of
heterosexual/homosexual identity are now obscured for most people so that compulsory heterosexuality functions as a disciplinary
formation seemingly emanating from everywhere and nowhere, so
too are the origins of able-bodied/disabled obscured . . . to cohere
in a system of compulsory able-bodiedness that similarly emanates
from everywhere and nowhere.[7]

Foucault's influence is evident here. This passage echoes his notion
of power operating on all levels, to control and constrain people into
conforming with expectations.[8] The solution is to blur the boundaries of
categories to the point of erasing them. Foucault and the queer Theorists who drew on him argued that sexualities and madness were merely
constructs of medical discourses that unjustly sought to categorize people as "normal" and "abnormal" and to exclude the "abnormal" from
participation in the dominant discourses of society. The view of ability
status as something that is unjustly constructed as "normal" (able-bodied) or "abnormal" (disabled) has consequently dominated and confused
disability studies ever since its adoption of queer Theoretic approaches.

This new, postmodernist approach fit the social model of disability exceptionally well and formed the basis of the second stage of its
shift toward applied postmodernism. It is central to Dan Goodley's 2014
book, *Disability Studies: Theorising Disablism and Ableism*. Borrowing directly from Foucault, Goodley writes, "Disability is normatively understood
through the gaze of medicalization: that process where life becomes
processed through the reductive use of medical discourse."[9] He applies
Foucault's concept of "biopower," in which scientific discourses have
particularly high prestige and are accepted as truth and perpetuated
through society, where they create the categories they seem to describe.[10]
Goodley's adoption of the postmodern knowledge and political principles—he understands scientific discourses as oppressive and no more
rigorous than other ways of knowing—is clear when he likens science
to colonialism:

We know that colonial knowledges are constructed as neutral and universal through the mobilisation of associated discourses such as humanitarian, philanthropic and poverty alleviation measures. We might also ask: how are ableist knowledges naturalised, neutralised and universalised?[11]

Alarmingly, Goodley considers diagnosing, treating, and curing disabilities as cynical practices, dependent upon corrupt ableist assumptions and upheld by a "neoliberal system," in which people are forced to be fully autonomous, high-functioning individuals so they can contribute their labor to capitalist markets. Even more worryingly, he claims that "autonomy, independence, and rationality are virtues desired by neoliberal-ableism."[12]

The postmodern political principle, which sees the world as constructed of systems of power, pervades Goodley's book. He describes society in intersectional terms, as "merging overlapping discourses of privilege" and writes,

I argue that modes of ableist cultural reproduction and disabling material conditions can never be divorced from hetero/sexism, racism, homophobia, colonialism, imperialism, patriarchy and capitalism.[13]

For Goodley, Oliver's social model isn't intersectional enough. He argues that it does not include analyses of race and gender and that it fails to regard disability in queer Theory terms—as "an identity that might be celebrated as it disrupts norms and subverts values of society."[14]

This idea that disabled people have a responsibility to use their disabilities to subvert social norms—and even to refuse any attempts at treatment or cure—in the service of the postmodern disruption of categories is yet another alarming feature of disability studies—and it isn't peculiar to Goodley. It also appears in Fiona Campbell's much-cited *Contours of Ableism: The Production of Disability and Ableness*.[15] Like Goodley, Campbell regards it as problematic that disabilities are seen as problems to be cured, if possible:

[A] chief feature of an ableist viewpoint is a belief that impairment or disability (irrespective of "type") is inherently negative and should opportunity present itself, be ameliorated, cured or indeed eliminated.[16]

Within scholarship and activism, the express wish to prevent or cure disability is shockingly often reframed as wishing *disabled people* (rather than their disabilities) did not exist—a cynical ploy that abuses a play on words. Campbell goes even further. Drawing on the queer Theory of Judith Butler, she characterizes able-bodiedness and disability as performances that people learn from society. They "co-constitute" each other in a binary that must be overthrown:

Whether it be the "species typical body" (in science), the "normative citizen" (in political theory), the "reasonable man" (in law), all these signifiers point to a fabrication that reaches into the very soul that sweeps us into life and as such is the outcome and instrument of a political constitution. The creation of such regimes of ontological separation appears disassociated from power. . . . Daily the identities of *disabled* and *abled* are performed repeatedly.[17] (emphasis in original)

This isn't merely insane, nor is it just fetishism of the underdog. It's applied postmodernism. This tendentious passage bears clear marks of the influences of Jacques Derrida and Judith Butler. The Derridean view posits that our understandings of disability and able-bodiedness create each other by means of a hierarchical dichotomy—that is, we understand each concept only as not being the other, and the two concepts are not viewed equitably. This is interpreted through the Butlerian notion of *performativity*, which she derived from applying Derrida and Foucault to her own interpretation of John Austin's concept of the same name in the philosophy of language.

Campbell also calls upon critical race Theory, especially its tenet that racism is such a normal, ordinary, and natural part of Western life that no one sees or questions it.[18] She adapts this to disability studies to argue that ableism is also such an ordinary form of prejudice that we do not question why we believe it is better to be able-bodied than to have an impairment. She even criticizes disabled people for having "internalized ableism"—a false consciousness that leads them to accept ableism, despite being disabled—if they express any wish not to be disabled. She writes, "By unwittingly performing ableism, disabled people become complicit in their own demise, reinforcing impairment as an undesirable state."[19]

These ideas are fairly typical of disability studies. Lydia X. Y. Brown, for example, also depicts disability as a performance and having a disability as an identity to be celebrated. This is apparent in this account of a discussion with a Muslim convert friend, who explains why she wears hijab, although she does not believe in the modesty concept behind it:

> Wearing hijab is an outward sign of being Muslim. She was performing "being Muslim" and wanted to be associated with being Muslim, and chooses to wear the hijab so that other people—Muslim or not—can identify her, similarly to how I, as an Autistic person who doesn't instinctually or innately flap my hands or arms—it was never a stim that I developed independently—will deliberately and frequently choose to flap, especially in public, in order to call attention to myself, so that other people—whether autistic or not—might identify me as autistic. I use this as an outward sign, [just as some Muslim women might choose to wear hijab even in the absence of religious convictions about head coverings].[20]

It is unlikely that this openly attention-seeking performance would be universally appreciated by autistic people (or the Muslim performance by Muslims). Nevertheless, some activists insist that their disabilities—including treatable mental illnesses, like depression, anxiety, and even being suicidal[21]—are positives and liken them to other aspects of identity, which can be used for empowering forms of identity politics.

This politicized approach should be distinguished from accepting one's impairments and embracing their reality in a psychologically positive way. It parallels the identity-first "I am Black"/"I am a person who happens to be Black" distinction made by critical race Theorists (see chapter 5). For instance, in his book *No Pity: People with Disabilities Forming a New Civil Rights Movement,* Joseph Shapiro objects to the idea that it is a compliment when an able-bodied person doesn't think of a disabled person as disabled. He writes,

> It was as if someone had tried to compliment a black man by saying "You're the least black person I ever met," as false as telling a Jew, "I never think of you as Jewish," as clumsy as seeking to flatter a woman with "You don't act like a woman."[22]

Shapiro likens Disabled Pride to Gay Pride. Having a disability, he feels, should be seen as laudable:

> Like homosexuals in the early 1970s, many disabled people are rejecting the "stigma" that there is something sad or to be ashamed of in their condition. They are taking pride in their identity as disabled people, parading it instead of closeting it.[23]

While no one should be made to feel ashamed of their sexuality, race, religion, gender, or ability status, many disabled people probably disagree with the view that having a disability should be celebrated—and this is unlikely to help them find an effective treatment or remedy, if that's what they want. And, despite what disability studies claims, this is not something they should be ashamed of wanting.

An additional problem arises when activists wish to take on a disability as an identity for the purposes of celebration or political empowerment, but do not wish medical practitioners to label them. This often arises from the postmodern knowledge principle, which rejects the idea that doctors are any more qualified to diagnose disability than anyone else. This encourages people to self-diagnose, for the purpose of belonging to an identity group. A documented conversation between Lydia X. Y. Brown and Jennifer Scuro provides an example (LB and JS, respectively):

> LB: People do say to me, "I think I'm Autistic but I don't really want to say that because I've never been diagnosed," that is, given a diagnosis by someone with letters after their name. My response

is: "Well, it's not up to me to tell you how you should or should not identify," but I don't believe in giving power to the medical-industrial complex and its monopoly over getting to define and determine who counts and who does not count as Autistic . . .

JS: Yes, once I started to get into the territory of diagnosis, once I started playing around with the problem of diagnostic thinking when it is only left to trained diagnosticians, this allowed me to challenge how all of us must contend with thinking diagnostically.[24]

This exchange seems to advocate that people self-identify as disabled for the purposes of gaining a group identity (postmodern theme), to engage in postmodern disruption of the knowledge-production capacity of medical science (postmodern knowledge principle), or as a politically motivated disruption of the dominant belief that disability is a thing to be avoided or treated (postmodern political principle). It is unclear how any of this can be helpful to disabled people.

HELPFUL ADVOCACY DERAILED

Disability studies and activism and the social model of disability started off well. Despite some worrying conceptual shifts, their initial aims were to place less onus on disabled people to adapt themselves to society and more on society to accommodate them and their disabilities. This change of emphasis, which has been incorporated into various laws, is likely to increase disabled people's access to employment and social opportunities from which they have historically been barred. This was a similar goal to those of second-wave feminism, the Civil Rights Movement, and Gay Pride, and it was fitting that scholarship should continue this work by studying social attitudes towards disability with a view to improving them.

Unfortunately, the incorporation of applied postmodern Theory into disability studies scholarship seems to have derailed it. This identity-obsessed approach pressures disabled people to identify with, celebrate, and politicize their disabilities. While disabled people *can* be constrained by an overuse of medical labels, a deep suspicion of medical science in itself is unlikely to benefit disabled people or anyone else. Intersectionality is likely to confuse and complicate the issue of prejudice against the disabled—entirely unnecessarily—by burying it under a mountain of "overlapping discourses of privilege." The use of critical race Theory as a model to insist that disabilities are ultimately social constructions is particularly unhelpful, given that—unlike social categories of race—physical and mental impairments are objectively real and people often dislike having them because of the way they materially affect their lives (and not because they have been socialized to believe they should dislike them).

It is especially unethical to demand that disabled people take on their disability as an identity and celebrate it in order to disrupt ableist cultural norms, in an application of the postmodern political principle. While some disabled people may find comfort and empowerment in identity-first politicking, many won't. Many disabled people wish they weren't disabled—which is perfectly reasonable—and seek ways to improve or mitigate their condition for themselves and others. This is their right. Accusations of "internalized ableism" are presumptuous and insulting. Disabled people may not wish to be identified primarily by their disability but by other aspects of themselves they feel better represent who they are. Worthwhile disability activism would support this, rather than problematizing it.

One problem with taking on a physical or mental disability as an identity is that it disincentivizes any possible mitigation of the disability. This might, for example, lead people to problematize or refuse technology that allows deaf people to hear, because they can no longer identify as deaf afterwards. While individuals should do as they wish, this suggests a profound confusion of priorities. Most deaf people whose hearing impairment could be straightforwardly[25] remedied by a hearing aid would not consider rejecting that intervention, and they are unlikely to be helped by people calling them identity-traitors for taking it. Disability studies and activism therefore fail to speak for the people for whom they claim to advocate, and inhibit disabled people's ability to get the diagnoses and treatments they desire. Furthermore, focusing on one's identity as a disabled person can devalue other aspects of an individual, which could lead to greater fulfillment and quality of life. Given the current problem with the rise of victimhood culture, which assigns superior status to marginalized identities,[26] there may be an increased temptation to become more rather than less disabled and to focus overwhelmingly on one's disability. This is particularly troubling if people can self-identify as disabled without a professional diagnosis or medical care. In this regard, disability studies is a well-intentioned failure.

FAT STUDIES

The problems in disability studies are mirrored in a related field called fat studies. Like disability studies, fat studies began in the United States in the 1960s, as fat activism, and has appeared in many forms since, but it has only recently established itself as a distinct branch of identity studies. It also draws strongly on queer Theory and feminism, especially as it has developed in the United Kingdom, and has a strongly intersectional focus. It attempts to portray negative perceptions of obesity as akin to racism, sexism, and homophobia, and it explicitly rejects science. In postmodern fashion, it focuses on the social construction of obesity and seeks to empower obese people to reject medical advice and embrace a supportive community "knowledge" that sees obesity favorably. Fat studies relies strongly on the postmodern knowledge principle, which sees knowledge as a construct of power, perpetuated in discourses—here, discourses that are rooted in the "hatred" of fat people (*fatphobia*), combined with misogyny and racism. Fat studies is therefore prone to Theorizing highly complex frameworks of oppression, evincing a radical skepticism of science, and advocating "other ways of knowing," which include personal experiences, Theory, feminism, and even poetry.

Though it is most popular in the United Kingdom, fat activism probably began in the United States, with the founding of the National Association to Advance Fat Acceptance (NAAFA)[27] in 1969 and the development of the Fat Underground[28] in the 1970s. Fat activism originated squarely within the set of social, cultural, and political changes that began to elevate cultural and identity studies, and postmodernism, in around the 1970s. However, fat activism seems to have taken on postmodern traits much more recently than the other types of identity studies that rely on applied postmodern Theory. This is probably because fat studies did not become a scholarly field in its own right until quite recently, although feminist scholars had long Theorized about pressure on women to be slim. Fat studies insists that pervasive and societally accepted "fatphobia" prevented it from being taken seriously and regards as fatphobic any study of obesity as a dangerous and (usually) treatable medical condition.

Historically, the scholarship and activism that would go on to become fat studies was called fat feminism. This was strongly associated with the radical and radical-lesbian branches of feminism and consequently had a limited following. This did not change much until the 1990s, when the body positivity movement, which focused on acceptance and celebration of "fat bodies," emerged from within liberal currents in society. A related Health at Every Size movement, which seems to have existed in various forms since the 1960s, became prominent in 2003 when the Association for Size Diversity and Health trademarked the phrase.[29] In 2010, Linda Bacon, a scholar of physiology and psychotherapy, wrote a popular book called *Health at Every Size: The Surprising Truth About Your Weight*,[30] which argues that bodies of all dimensions can be healthy.[31] The medical consensus opposes this idea.[32]

Fat studies developed rapidly, began taking on an applied postmodern approach, and soon became thoroughly intersectional, making illogical claims like: "we cannot dismantle weight/size oppression without addressing the intersectionality of all oppressions."[33] Fat studies' claim to be an independent discipline was strengthened in 2012, when the journal *Fat Studies* was founded. The journal explicitly likens negative opinions about obesity—including concerns about possible health implications of being overweight or obese—to prejudice against people for their immutable characteristics, claiming, "*Fat Studies* is similar to academic disciplines that focus on race, ethnicity, gender, or age."[34]

The development of fat studies has been comprehensively detailed by Charlotte Cooper, arguably the leading fat scholar and the author of *Fat Activism: A Radical Social Movement* (2016). Cooper, who is British, notes the virtual abandonment of fat activism by radical feminism and its revival by postmodern feminism:

The origins of fat feminism are immersed within a feminism that is problematic, maligned, unfashionable and obscure, that is, radical lesbian feminism, including, at times, lesbian separatism. Critiques of this feminism surfaced within queer, third wave and postmodern feminisms because of, for example, its essentialism and its fundamentalism.[35]

Within fat studies, it is common to address negative attitudes towards obesity alongside racism, sexism, homophobia, transphobia, disableism, and imperialism, even though there is strong evidence that obesity is a result of consistently consuming more calories than are needed and carries significant health risks. Fat activism and fat studies are now predominantly intersectional and feminist, and draw heavily on queer Theory and the Butlerian politics of parody.[36] In her book, Charlotte Cooper describes a fat-activism event that was staged in response to the 2012 London Olympic Summer Games—which are deemed intrinsically fat-phobic in the extreme—called "Fattylympics," in which deliberately silly quasi-athletic events were mockingly engaged in at a London park as an act of strategic resistance and protest.

Queer Theory and Judith Butler have been particularly influential in the development of fat studies. Charlotte Cooper begins her book, for example, by declaring it to be "openly queer" and by "encouraging fat activists to resist the pull of access and assimilation, if they can, and consider queer strategies to reinvigorate the movement."[37] Again, Foucault's concept of "biopower"—in which scientific discourses are argued to have undue power as producers of knowledge, which is then perpetuated at all levels of society via discourse (ways of talking about things)— is utilized, in a rather paranoid fashion. As Cooper writes,

> In *The History of Sexuality*, and elsewhere, power is not enshrined within authorities feeding down to the lowliest subject, it is a dynamic field in which everyone is implicated.[38]

She also claims,

Michel Foucault's work on governmentality is commonly used to theorise bodies in relation to power and has been used by people interested in how fat people are socially controlled, stratified, surveilled, regimented, patrolled, and self-governing.[39]

This isn't merely a quirk of Charlotte Cooper's. Kathleen LeBesco, senior associate dean of academic affairs at Marymount Manhattan College, takes a similar stance in *The Fat Studies Reader*.[40] This belief in hidden discourses, through which power is conveyed and discipline upheld, runs through Fat Activism texts at all levels and calls upon, not only Foucault but also Judith Butler.[41] For Cooper, "Obesity discourse is totalitarian, by which I mean it presents itself as the only authority on fat, nothing else counts."[42] For fat scholar Marilyn Wann,

> Every person who lives in a fat-hating culture inevitably absorbs anti-fat beliefs, assumptions, and stereotypes, and also inevitably comes to occupy a position in relation to power arrangements that are based on weight. None of us can ever hope to be completely free of such training or completely disentangled from the power grid.[43]

Let's take a broader view for a moment. Visualize a power grid. This is the conception of human society that constitutes the postmodernist worldview. It posits that we are born and positioned by elements of our identity, such that we have different levels of access to power—privilege is like being plugged in to the network—and we learn to perform our position and thus "conduct" the power through ourselves as part of the system, often without ever knowing that the grid is there. This learning is achieved mostly by socialization into "hegemonic" identity roles constructed and accepted by society and is rarely intentional. By performing our roles, we uphold the social and cultural assumptions that grant and deny access to power. Furthermore, access to power has an automatically corrupting influence, which leads us to perform our roles, thus socializing ourselves and others into accepting the inequities of the system, justifying our own access, and rationalizing the exclusion of others. This is all done through discourses—ways we speak about things, including how we represent them in nonverbal media. As this conception of society, which originated in the obscure and complex language of the original postmodernists, has evolved, it has consolidated into a belief system. Thus, we frequently see Theorists state this explanation with the confidence of an objective belief—something that would not have been possible for the first postmodernists.

THEORY—A PARANOID FANTASY

In order to navigate this complex grid of power-laden discourses, one has to first be trained to detect it. This is what critical Theory was invented to do. So, in a circular, self-justifying argument, Theory insists that we need Theory. For some fat studies scholars, gender—thus intersectional feminism and queer Theory—is most significant:

> Sexism has become a deeply coded set of behaviors that are difficult to unlock if you don't know how to see them. It can take special access to education and language in order to unveil sexist behavior. Often, that critical language is cast as suspect, overly intellectual, or a product of paranoid fantasy.[44]

For others, although the intersectional and queer approach to evaluation and disruption is both productive and appropriate, everything ultimately comes back to capitalism. Charlotte Cooper, for instance, makes a very similar argument to that made by Goodley in *Disability Studies*. For Cooper, the forces of "neoliberalism" (approximately: capitalist society) pressure people to adapt themselves to society, instead of requiring society to accommodate them. Cooper is therefore deeply critical of the body positivity movement, which she considers a form of "gentrification" in its "emphasis on individualism rather than collectivity."[45] Her issue is that body positivity places the responsibility on individuals to love their own bodies and be happy in them, rather than on society to stop viewing obesity negatively—a problematic approach, which is sometimes referred to as *responsibilizing* them. As one member, "Liz," of what Cooper called her "fat community," who she interviewed for *Fat Activism*, argues, "Fat hatred is fuelled by capitalism because these companies create products that are all about making fat people skinny,"[46] and "using capitalism as a basis for activism illustrates how, within the gentrification of fat activism it is access rather than social transformation that has become the main motivator."[47]

If this sounds like a paranoid fantasy, it's because it is. The idea of an intersectional power grid surrounding fat activism is needlessly messy. Biology and the science of nutrition are misunderstood as a form of Foucauldian "biopower," which constrains and disciplines people. Medical science around obesity is misunderstood to impose an oppressive, disciplinary narrative on people. "[C]alling fat people 'obese' medicalizes human diversity"[48] and "Medicalizing diversity inspires a misplaced search for a 'cure' for naturally occurring difference,"[49] Marilyn Wann tells us in the foreword to the *Fat Studies Reader*, echoing Foucault. Kathleen LeBesco likens obesity to homosexuality and reasons that, just as homosexuality has now been recognized as a naturally occurring phenomenon that does not need a cure, so too must obesity be similarly recognized. Despite the ample evidence that obesity increases the risk of serious diseases and early death, while homosexuality in itself does not, LeBesco also speculates that obese people who think their weight is a problem have been conditioned into accepting their oppression:

> That fat and queer people would heartily embrace science and medicine as a solution to their socially constructed problems is redolent of Stockholm syndrome—after all, science and medicine have long been instrumental in oppressing fat and queer people, providing argument after argument that pathologize the homosexual or "obese" individual (whether the mind or the body).[50]

One answer to this is to embrace or even increase one's fatness. "It takes time to make a fat body," fat studies scholar Allyson Mitchell writes; "it takes even more time to make a politicized fat body."[51] LeBesco goes even further, arguing that "scientific knowledge doesn't reveal all there is to know,"[52] hinting that fatphobia is motivated by eugenics, and advocating the use of social and political tools to deal with fat hatred. By contrast, emphasizing the value of health is cast as a problematic ideology called *healthism*.

Healthism is bolstered by *nutritionism*, which is an allegedly excessive focus on the relevance of the nutritional value of foods to the study of nutrition and dietetics (diet and its impacts on health). There are parallel "critical" fields of dietetics and nutrition studies, which seek to make those fields about Social Justice instead of about diet and nutrition. Lucy Aphramor and Jacqui Gingras, for instance, deplore the way studies of diet and nutrition are typically based on science:

> Dietetics recognizes knowledge as that which can be supported by dominant scientific literature developed around rigorous, quantifiable scientific methods. Such rational knowing has implications for how dietetics is taught and practiced.[53]

And

> But to uphold the rigor of the scientific convention limits engagement with meaning making: language is not a neutral tool but rather a powerfully charged political vector. The words that we use here influence our ability to generate possibilities.[54]

Rather than using science to understand diet and nutrition and their health implications, these critical dieticians "have instead chosen to engage poetry as a way of 'crafting a praxis-oriented culture' and troubling the status quo."[55] They urge a "rethink of how dietetic attitudes toward fatness and gender play a role in legitimating and constructing science."[56] This seems unlikely to advance any of the relevant fields of study or to help anyone do anything other than temporarily feel special.

The book *Critical Dietetics and Critical Nutrition Studies*, aimed at undergraduates, is therefore extremely troubling. While the Health at Every Size approach stopped short of denying medical science and instead used dubiously interpreted medical studies to claim one could be healthy at any weight, *Critical Dietetics* describes science as no more useful than any other approach to understanding food, nutrition, diet, and fatness:

Although we do not wholly reject the scientific method as a means of creating knowledge about the world, a critical orientation rejects the notion that it is even possible to produce knowledge that is objective, value-free, and untouched by human bias. A critical orientation similarly rejects the idea that any one way of creating knowledge about the world is superior to another or is even sufficient. . . . As such, [Critical Dietetics] draws on post-structuralism and feminist science (two other windows) that hold that there is not one truth that can be generated about any single thing, that multiple truths are possible depending on who is asking and for what purpose, and that knowledge is not apolitical even if it is considered positivist (i.e. value neutral or unbiased).[57]

This is as explicit a rejection of objective reality as it is possible to get. "Post-structuralism and feminist science" are used to dismiss the overwhelming evidence that nutrition plays a significant role in health and that obesity increases the risk of heart disease, several cancers, and diabetes—not to mention polycystic ovary syndrome, joint problems, mobility problems, and respiratory problems—and is strongly correlated with early death. This "fatphobic" health denialism is the approach taken by Cooper too. She advocates "research justice," in which empirical studies of obesity can be swapped out at will for "embodied community knowledge"[58] in order to "unlock knowledge that has already been generated by fat people."[59]

SUPPORT-GROUP SCHOLARSHIP

Fat studies and fat activism seem to have started in various different places at different times and have many strands. In addition to its radical lesbian feminist origins, fat activism includes a celebratory body positivity movement, a dubious but popular Health at Every Size model, and (recently) an intersectional queer feminist branch with its associated scholarship—which is to say Theory. The proliferation of these approaches strongly suggests that there is a need for some kind of advocacy and community for obese people. Fat activism could have a valuable role to play in society, if it could counter discrimination and prejudice against obese people and provide a support network, without descending into radical social constructivism, paranoia, and science denial.

Sadly, fat studies is currently among the most irrational and ideological forms of scholarship-activism in identity studies. A latecomer to the party, it has had to incorporate so many existing forms of identity-driven Theory, without having an internally consistent framework of its own, that it has become highly messy and confusing—veering from critical race to feminist to queer Theory, while weaving in anticapitalist rhetoric and ideas taken from disability studies. Fat studies spends a great deal of time trying to associate itself with forms of activism and scholarship that address prejudice against people on the grounds of immutable characteristics like race, sex, and sexuality, although this is frequently unconvincing due to the evidence that obesity is a result of overeating. Again, a productive form of activism could work against the idea that overeating is simply the result of a lack of self-discipline or of greed and look at the psychological and physiological issues that make this problem hard to overcome for so many people—but this is not the approach fat studies takes. Instead, it has adopted the postmodern knowledge and political principles, applies the four postmodern themes, and integrates these into an approach that otherwise very much resembles that of a support group that asserts itself as rigorous.

This also leaves fat activism vulnerable to the criticism that it undermines other forms of activism by attempting to claim too close a kinship with them. The idea that obesity is just like homosexuality, for example, could threaten the hard-won recent consensus that homosexuality is innate, value-free, and perfectly healthy. It is also clearly unethical to accuse obese people of Stockholm syndrome or internalized fatphobia if they are unhappy being overweight. But, as erasing the individual in favor of group identity and focusing on the power of language are primary concerns in fat studies, it considers this gambit both necessary and virtuous.

Above all, this form of fat activism is potentially dangerous. People who find it very difficult to manage their weight and suffer from low self-esteem as a result can be motivated to reject the medical consensus that obesity is a serious health problem of epidemic proportions. If fat activism succeeds in attaining the status currently assigned to feminist and antiracist activism, doctors, scientists, and researchers could feel intimidated to provide factual information to the obese—which would limit the ability of obese individuals to make informed choices about their health.

In sum, fat studies is hardly a rigorous approach to studying any-thing and yet it has found a home within the various fields of study that might collectively be called *Social Justice scholarship*. These fields vary widely, though they have enough in common to be readily identifiable: they are usually entitled "critical X" or "X studies," where X is whatever they want to complain about, disrupt, and modify, in accordance with the postmodern knowledge and political principles. Despite addressing a range of concerns, which encompass almost all human endeavors, they share one common element: Theory, applied in a form that treats the underlying postmodern assumptions as *objectively real*. It is to this Theory that we must now turn our attention.

8 SOCIAL JUSTICE SCHOLARSHIP AND THOUGHT

The Truth According to Social Justice

Reified means "made into a real thing," and it refers to abstract concepts that are treated as though they were real. Beginning in around 2010 and steadily gaining steam ever since, the scholarship undertaken under the broad banner of "social justice"—which we'll call *Social Justice scholarship*—took shape within a new, third phase in the postmodern project. In this phase, scholars and activists have come to take for granted a reification of the once abstract and self-doubtful postmodern knowledge principle and postmodern political principle.

As we discussed in chapter 1, these foundational postmodern principles held that objective knowledge is impossible, that knowledge is a construct of power, and that society is made up of systems of power and privilege that need to be deconstructed. As we discussed in chapters 2–7, this view was made actionable in the applied phase in the 1980s and 1990s, which saw postmodernism fragment into postcolonial Theory, queer Theory, critical race Theory, intersectional feminism, disability studies, and fat studies. Subsequently, especially since 2010, these post-

modern ideas have become fully concretized in the combined intersectional Social Justice scholarship and activism and have begun to take
root in the public consciousness as allegedly factual descriptions of the
workings of knowledge, power, and human social relations.

The postmodern knowledge principle and the postmodern political principle were used primarily for deconstructive purposes in the first
phase (roughly 1965–1990) and made applicable for reconstruction during the second phase in the form of applied postmodernism (roughly
1990–2010), yet they were confined principally to specific academic
fields and activist circles. In this third phase of postmodernism, these
principles are treated as fundamental truths both within these two settings and beyond. After decades of being treated like knowns within sec-
tors of academia and activism, the principles, themes, and assertions
of Theory became *known-knowns*—ideas taken for granted as true statements about the world that people "just know" are true. The result is
that the belief that society is structured of specific but largely invisible
identity-based systems of power and privilege that construct knowledge
via ways of talking about things is now considered by social justice scholars and activists to be an objectively true statement about the organizing principle of society. Does this sound like a metanarrative? That's
because it is. Social Justice scholarship and its educators and activists
see these principles and conclusions as *The Truth* According to Social
Justice—and they treat it as though they have discovered the analogue of
the germ theory of disease, but for bigotry and oppression.

The reification of the two postmodern principles means that the
original postmodern radical skepticism that any knowledge can be reliable has been gradually transformed into a complete conviction that
knowledge is constructed in the service of power, which is rooted in
identity, and that this can be uncovered through close readings of how
we use language. Therefore, in Social Justice scholarship, we continually
read that patriarchy, white supremacy, imperialism, cisnormativity, heteronormativity, ableism, and fatphobia are literally structuring society
and infecting everything. They exist in a state of immanence—present
always and everywhere, just beneath a nicer-seeming surface that can't
quite contain them. That's the reification of the postmodern knowledge principle. This "reality" is viewed as profoundly problematic and

thus needs to be constantly identified, condemned, and dismantled so that things might be rectified. Consequently, we now have Social Justice texts—forming a kind of Gospel of Social Justice—that express, with absolute certainty, that all white people are racist, all men are sexist, racism and sexism are systems that can exist and oppress absent even a single person with racist or sexist intentions or beliefs (in the usual sense of the terms), sex is not biological and exists on a spectrum, language can be literal violence, denial of gender identity is killing people, the wish to remedy disability and obesity is hateful, and everything needs to be decolonized. That is the reification of the postmodern political principle.

This approach distrusts categories and boundaries and seeks to blur them, and is intensely focused on language as a means of creating and perpetuating power imbalances. It exhibits a deep cultural relativism, focuses on marginalized groups, and has little time for universal principles or individual intellectual diversity. These are the four themes of postmodernism, and they remain central to the means and ethics of Social Justice scholarship. There has, however, been a change of register and tone. Within the new Social Justice scholarship, Theory's principles and themes have become much simpler and much more straightforwardly expressed as its Theorists have grown more confident of their fundamental tenets. Social Justice scholarship represents the evolution of postmodernism into a third stage: its culmination as a *reified postmodernism*. A moral person aware of The Truth According to Social Justice must serve its metanarrative by actively asserting a Theoretical view of how the world works and how it ought to work instead.

Because of the reification of the underlying principles, which began as postmodernism began to be applied, Social Justice scholarship does not neatly fit into any one category of Theory. It has become so intersectional that it calls upon all of them according to need, continually problematizing society and even aspects of itself, and abiding by only one golden rule: Theory itself can never be denied; Theory is real. Social Justice scholarship has become a kind of Theory of Everything, a set of unquestionable Truths with a capital T, whose central tenets were taken from the original postmodernists and solidified within the derived Theories.

POSTMODERNISM EVOLVING

If we think of the first postmodernists of the late 1960s as a manifestation of radical skepticism and despair and the second wave, from the late
1980s, as a recovery from hopelessness and a drive to make core ideas
politically actionable, this third wave, which became prominent between
the late 2000s and the early 2010s, has fully recovered its certainty and
activist zeal. The first postmodernists were reacting largely to the failure of Marxism, the longstanding analytical framework of the academic
left, and suffering from major disillusionment. Because their theoretical
framework of choice was falling apart, they adopted the cynical attitude
that nothing could be relied upon anymore. The metanarratives they
were skeptical of included Christianity, science, and the concept of progress, among others—but, with the loss of Marxism, came a loss of hope
of restructuring society towards "justice." They therefore sought only to
dismantle, deconstruct, and disrupt existing frameworks ironically, with
a kind of joyless playfulness. This was the state of cultural thought in
the 1970s.

By the time this first wave of despairing skepticism—the *high deconstructive phase* of postmodernism—had worn itself out twenty years
later, the academic left had somewhat recovered hope and was looking
for more positive and applicable forms of Theory. It took postmodernism's two key principles and four themes, and tried to do something with
them. Thus, postmodern Theory developed into the applied postmodern Theories, plural. Within postcolonial Theory, there were attempts
to reconstruct the East's varied senses of itself (although Bhabha and
Spivak remained highly pessimistic about this). It would, if it could, res-
cue the "other" from the West, mostly by tearing the West down. Within
queer Theory, the belief that all categories are socially constructed and
performative produced a kind of activism. By continuing to deconstruct
categories, blur boundaries, and see everything as fluid and changeable,
queer Theory sought to "liberate" people who did not fit into those categories of sex, gender, and sexuality from expectations that they should.
Critical race Theory was more concrete and applicable due to its beginnings in law, but it drew on black feminist scholars to form intersectional
approaches that ultimately came to dominate feminism. Above all else,

intersectional feminism sought empowerment through identity politics and collective action, which largely define the current cultural mood. Disability studies, and the newcomer, fat studies, produced some densely Theoretical work that relies heavily on queer Theory, but their approach and premises were quite straightforward—regard medical science as a social construct and be proud of and militant about disabled and fat identities. So, by the 1990s, the applied postmodern turn had arrived, made postmodern Theory actionable, and focused on identity and identity politics.

As these Theories developed through the late 1990s into the 2000s within various forms of identity studies—such as gender studies, sexuality studies, and ethnic studies—they increasingly combined their aims, to become steadily more intersectional. By the mid-2000s, if you studied one of the key topics—sex, gender identity, race, sexuality, immigration status, indigeneity, colonial status, disability, religion, and weight—you were expected to factor in all the others. While scholars could—and still can—have particular focuses, there was much mixing and merging. This resulted in a form of general scholarship that looks at "marginalized groups" and multiple systems of power and privilege.

One startling omission in this list of intersectional identities is any meaningful mention of economic class—they sometimes raise the point but almost never substantively. Traditional Marxists could be criticized by focusing so single-mindedly on economic class as the key factor in society that they sometimes overlooked or underestimated other axes of oppression, notably those against women and sexual minorities. The feminist movement starting in the early 1970s, and the gay rights movement shortly thereafter, provided useful correctives to this sole focus on class. Nowadays, however, economic class is barely mentioned unless combined "intersectionally" with some other form of marginalized identity. It is therefore no surprise that many working-class and poor people often feel profoundly alienated from today's left—Marxists rightly identify it as having adopted very bourgeois concerns. It is profoundly ironic that a movement claiming to problematize all sources of privilege is led by highly educated, upper-middle-class scholars and activists who are so oblivious to their status as privileged members of society.

As so many of these marginalized groups united and the various streams of thought merged to create a single large pool of similar, competing issues, Social Justice scholars and activists also became much more confident in their underlying assumptions. As the 2010s began, the ambiguity and doubt that had characterized postmodernism up until then had almost entirely disappeared, and, with them, the dense, obscure language that Alan Sokal and Jean Bricmont famously called "fashionable nonsense" in the mid-1990s.[1] By the 2010s, the language, while still technical, was far clearer. These were stronger words, words of conviction.

This certainty has its roots in the previous applied postmodern stage, in which scholar-activists distanced themselves from radical skepticism, to assert that systematic oppression must be accepted as objectively true in order to combat it. In Kimberlé Crenshaw's 1991 "Mapping the Margins," the foundational intersectionality text, for instance, significant attention is paid to the importance of distinguishing "I am Black" from "I am a person who happens to be Black." Other scholars in critical race Theory, such as bell hooks, echoed this sentiment, and queer Theorists made similar statements about gay, lesbian, bisexual, trans, gender nonconforming, and queer identities. Identities based on national origin and history rapidly gained prominence through postcolonial Theory, and fat and disabled identities—including identities based on mental illnesses like depression and anxiety—became commonplace due to the influence of fat and disability studies. By the 2010s, both this approach and the postmodern principles and themes used to interact with these "realities" had become articles of belief, and activists and Theorists were unafraid to assert them.

Social Justice scholarship is now heavily invested in identity, which it uses as a lens through which to determine what is true, and identity politics, which it uses to act for change in the world. Much of the scholarship since 2010 is therefore labeled "feminist," "queer," etc., *epistemology* (the study of knowledge and how it is produced) or *pedagogy* (theory of education). Even when it does not use the words "epistemology" or "pedagogy," nearly all Social Justice scholarship is concerned with what is said, what is believed, what is assumed, what is taught, what is conveyed, and what biases are imported through teaching, discourses, and stereotypes. All this scholarship starts from the Theoretical premise that society works through systems of power and privilege maintained in language, and these create knowledge from the perspectives of the privileged and deny the experiences of the marginalized. Social Justice scholarship therefore targets science[2] and any other analytical methods that contradict these assumptions or claims made under them.

As a result, Social Justice scholarship takes umbrage with anything that foregrounds reason and evidence as the way to know what is true and demands "epistemic justice" and "research justice" in their place. By this, it means that we should include the lived experiences, emotions, and cultural traditions of minority groups, consider them "knowledges," and privilege them over reason and evidence-based knowledge, which is unfairly dominant. Research justice often involves deliberately avoiding citing white, male, and Western scholars in favor of those with some intersectionally marginalized status. This can even involve glossing over the contributions of those from privileged identity groups, a practice that makes it difficult to track ideas back to the white male founding fathers of postmodernism. In a rather stunning, but typical, example, black feminist philosopher Kristie Dotson cites Gayatri Spivak copiously on "epistemic violence," but never mentions Spivak's reliance on Michel Foucault.[3] This is unlikely to be simply an example of lazy scholarship or oversight (Dotson is thorough, and Spivak mentions the Foucauldian origins of the idea on nearly every page of "Can the Subaltern Speak?"), and much more likely to be a deliberate erasure of the earlier postmodernist in accordance with research justice. As has been noted in a similar case,

> One of the friendly critiques I made about the paper regarded its engagement with intersectional theory, specifically its use of Michel Foucault's conceptualization of power instead of Patricia Hill Collins's articulation from *Black Feminist Thought*. My claim was twofold: if the author intended to meaningfully engage issues of diversity and feminist thought in an intersectional way, then using the work of a leading Black Feminist theorist's formulation of intersectional power would make sense. Second, it was not clear to me that the reliance on Foucault could meaningfully contribute to advancing intersectionality scholarship specifically, given the distinctions.[4]

In other words, regardless of where the concepts originated, the only intersectionally responsible way to do research is to cite the work of a black feminist Theorist.

A MENAGERIE OF NEW TERMS

When an ideology—that is, a philosophy plus a moral imperative—reifies its central tenets, its adherents often develop a keen interest in knowledge and its production. This is because the ideology needs to prove that its assumptions are based on reality. Usually, this is a primarily philosophical endeavor—the work of theologians, metaphysicians, and theorists, who tinker with the concept of knowledge to make sure their moral beliefs qualify as such. (This is why Plato described knowledge as *justified true beliefs*.) Thus, Social Justice scholarship is profoundly interested in the relationship between identity and knowledge. This means identifying, demonstrating, and attempting to disrupt alleged injustices characteristic of systems of knowledge and knowledge production (sciences, construed broadly) and the way they are passed on through education.

This is a timeworn habit of ideologues. Even before the influence of postmodernism, identity studies have always focused on the relationship between one's identity and what one is able to know. For instance, feminist philosophy devised various epistemologies—theories of how knowledge is produced and understood—in the 1980s. Three primary methods were used to justify feminist claims: feminist empiricism, standpoint theory, and postmodern radical skepticism. Feminist empiricism asserts that science, as a process, generally operates correctly except that, before feminism, it was plagued with male-centered biases that prevented it from being truly objective. This method fell out of fashion in the 1990s, during the applied postmodern turn and as a casualty of the "science wars"[5] of that era. The second and third methods are of considerably greater interest to Social Justice scholarship, because they accord with the postmodern knowledge principle that knowledges flow from identity; they now form the backbone of the intersectional approach to epistemology. Above all, they are centrally concerned with how to connect knowledge and knowledge production to Theoretically derived notions of justice and injustice. They have also been mainstreamed throughout society since 2010.

To this purpose, the term *epistemic injustice* was coined by Miranda Fricker, in her 2007 book *Epistemic Injustice: Power and the Ethics of Knowing*.[6] Fricker describes epistemic injustice as occurring when someone is wronged in their capacity as a knower. According to Fricker, this can happen in a number of ways: when someone is not recognized as someone who *can* know something; when her knowledge is not recognized as valid; when she is prevented from being able to know something; or when her knowledge is not understood. Fricker divides epistemic injustice into *testimonial injustice*—when people are not considered credible because of their identity—and *hermeneutical injustice*—when someone's knowledge cannot be understood.

Fricker's analysis—which assumes that certain groups are intrinsically disadvantaged because of their identity—is not wholly without merit. People often do trust the knowledge of some individuals or groups more than others, and this may sometimes be due to social prejudices (e.g., racism) rather than to those people's actual degree of relevant expertise. Also, members of marginalized groups are sometimes impeded in their striving for knowledge: for instance, lesbians and gay men in small communities may find it hard to understand their own sexuality, and atheists may struggle to comprehend their own lack of faith if they have never heard these issues talked about before.

However, Fricker regarded these as problems created and faced by *individuals*, rather than *properties of groups*. Accordingly, she advocated that everyone cultivate certain "virtues," so they do not commit epistemic injustices. Her individualistic approach did not go down well with the Social Justice postmodernists, who believe that knowledge is intrinsically tied to identity, and who criticized her for being overly simplistic and neglecting the need for widespread structural change.[7] Since Fricker's work is directed at individuals, it does not primarily address *social* justice. Scholars have since drawn upon, expanded, and reoriented her work, to depict injustice as a property belonging to social groups and caused by the social power dynamics within which they operate. Since 2007, Social Justice philosophy, particularly in education and law, has focused heavily on how knowledge is treated unequally—always, allegedly, as a result of identity.[8]

This has spawned a vast specialized vocabulary. In 2014, Kristie Dotson expanded and recontexualized Fricker's concept of epistemic injustice, which she sees as a superficial aspect of a bigger, less tractable, identity-group-based problem she calls *epistemic oppression*.[9] This form of oppression is alleged to occur when the knowledges and knowledge-producing methods said to be used by marginalized groups—including folk wisdom and witchcraft—are not included within our prevailing understanding of knowledge. Influenced by both the postmodern knowledge and political principles, Social Justice scholars categorize the different approaches to knowledge as "marginalized" or "dominant," and of course they prefer the former. But they are not much interested in knowing whether these competing methods are *effective* in the sense of bringing beliefs into closer accord with reality; that is at best a secondary concern. On the other hand, because Critical Social Justice scholarship assumes that knowledge is dependent on power dynamics, it is deeply interested in the ways in which one's identity impacts whether and how one is understood and listened to and has coined many terms to describe this. Dotson's work on epistemic oppression was a continuation of her earlier (2011) work on *epistemic violence*—having one's cultural knowledge repressed by that of a dominant culture, which, for Dotson, is the result of *pernicious ignorance* on the part of hearers who refuse to understand.[10] These terms proliferated in the early and mid-2010s. *Epistemic exploitation* was coined by Nora Berenstain in 2016, for instance, to describe the injustice caused when marginalized people are expected to share their knowledge.[11] Thus, it is an act of oppression *not* to make an effort to understand a marginalized knower on her own terms, and it is an act of exploitation (read: oppression) to ask a marginalized knower to explain her knowledge on her own terms.

In 2013, Theorist José Medina coined the melodramatic term *hermeneutical death*, which describes a failure to be understood so profound as to destroy the person's sense of self. At the opposite end of this spectrum is the concept of *hermeneutical privacy*, which describes the right not to be understandable at all.[12] So, marginalized people can be oppressed to the point of psychic death by not being understood, but their right to be completely incomprehensible should also be respected. Negotiating this minefield must be very difficult for the well-meaning individual determined not to oppress anybody. Fricker's *testimonial injustice* has inspired a growing number of related ideas like *testimonial betrayal*,[13] *epistemic freedom*,[14] and *epistemic responsibility*.[15] While we could go on, we think you get the idea—"knowledges" and demands for respect for those "knowledges" are the point of focus throughout Social Justice scholarship.

WHO YOU ARE IS WHAT YOU KNOW

What are the reason and purpose behind this obsession with knowledges and knowers? To circumvent more rigorous methods when rigor stands between them and their ideological aims, theoretical or practical. Social Justice scholars attempt to justify this with an attitude that sees science and reason as unjustly privileged—regardless of their ability to accurately describe reality and make predictions about it—over the wide variety of identity-based "ways of knowing." The problem, for them, is that scientific forms of knowledge production aim to be objective and universal, and (at least in most people's view) frequently succeed at that aim. Because there are evidence-based scientific explanations for some of the social issues that impact identity groups, science often finds itself in direct contravention of the postmodern principles, especially the belief that everything important is socially constructed. In addition, many philosophers, scientists, and other scholars have offered reasoned arguments that identify flaws in Theory and in Social Justice scholarship's assumptions, methods, and conclusions. This type of criticism does not tend to go down well with the postmodernism at the heart of Social Justice scholarship and activism, so Social Justice–based attacks on science and reason are usually open and direct. This is not only because science and reason have an irritating habit of revealing the flaws in Theoretical approaches; it is also because they are *universal* and thus violate the postmodern knowledge principle and the postmodern theme of centering group identity, around which Social Justice scholarship is organized.

This violation is dealt with through the postmodern political principle. Because science has such a high prestige as a reliable producer of knowledge—and because postmodernists from Lyotard to Foucault have disparaged it as a discourse of power for the last fifty years—it is com-

monly regarded with deep suspicion by Social Justice scholars and activists. Often, this is rationalized by pointing to the fact that people have
sometimes attempted to use science and reason to prop up injustices—
especially if you read the history as cynically as possible.[16] Claims like
this often refer to much earlier periods of science—citing, for example,
nineteenth-century arguments in support of colonialism that would now
be dismissed as pseudoscience. At other times, the suspicions result from
the fact that science has discovered things that do not conform to social-
constructivist ideas, such as that differences between the sexes exist. And
sometimes these objections are based on alleged discrimination: "formal
and informal barriers to the participation of women and racial minorities in scientific enterprises [that] have had the effect of disproportion-
ately favoring white males' presence and influence in science."[17] These
complaints, however, are often vague, begin with the cultural constructivist assumption that all inequalities must be the result of oppression
rather than, say, men and women having different interests on average,
and are typically accompanied by appeals to attitudes and problems that
have not been much in evidence for decades.

Instead of science, Social Justice scholarship advocates for "other
ways of knowing," derived from Theoretical interpretations of deeply
felt lived experience. It argues that reason and evidence-based knowledge are *unfairly* favored over tradition, folklore, interpretation, and emotion because of the power imbalances baked into them. Without the
slightest awareness of the racist and sexist implications, Theory views
evidence and reason to be the cultural property of white Western men.

Examples of this are common. Dotson famously called the dominance of reason and science a "culture of justification" in 2012 and argued instead for a "culture of praxis," which would incorporate multiple
ways of knowing in order to include more diverse groups of people in
philosophy.[18] Other scholars have argued that rational and scientific approaches limit Anglo-American epistemologists from accepting broader
and multiple ways of knowing.[19] Still others recommend emotion, as an
unjustly neglected means of arriving at reliable knowledge. Allison Wolf
calls this the "reason/emotion divide" and describes it as a construct of
the Western philosophical tradition. She advocates foregrounding feelings as a way of knowing.[20]

This approach is alarming, patronizing, and potentially dangerous. Nevertheless, the underlying concept of experiential knowledge is not entirely without merit. Quite often, it is more important to know how things are experienced than what the facts of the matter are. For example, if a friend's father has died of a heart attack, we generally want to know how she is feeling and how we can help her through her grief. Factual information about myocardial infarctions is probably of less importance at that time. Nevertheless, there are facts that can be known about heart attacks, and it is important that these facts be accurate. Such knowledge cannot be gleaned simply by the experience of a heart attack or of losing a loved one to a heart attack. Sometimes we need to empathize with the person who has lost her loved one to a heart attack and sometimes we need to consult a cardiologist.

Despite postmodernists treating it as though it is novel and profound, this divide between facts and experience is not particularly mysterious to philosophers outside of postmodernism: it is the difference between knowing *that* and knowing *how*. "Knowing that" is propositional knowledge, while "knowing how" is experiential knowledge. The trouble is not that this divide exists or that there is valuable information on both sides of it. The problems arise when we fail to recognize that interpretation colors, biases, and distorts experiential knowledge—at times profoundly—and makes it an unreliable guide to understanding the associated phenomena.

This confusion nevertheless forms the basis of the argument of another Social Justice–oriented Theorist, Alexis Shotwell, who argues that "focusing on propositional knowledge as though it is the only form of knowing worth considering is itself a form of epistemic injustice. Such a focus neglects epistemic resources that help oppressed people craft more just worlds."[21] Here, we see the assumption that the experiential knowledge of oppressed people is of paramount importance in dealing with the associated real-world phenomena. And of paramount value because of the postmodern political principle—it provides "resources that help oppressed people craft more just worlds." There is also the assumption that "oppressed people" all have the same experiential knowledge, presumably defined by their identities. Shotwell's commitment to the postmodern principles is confirmed when she writes, "A richer account of forms of knowing and a richer attention to people's lived experiences in

the world helps us identify, analyze, and redress epistemic injustices."[22]
This is not just a concern about "the unlevel knowing field."[23] This is
standpoint theory.

A DIFFERENT KIND OF COLOR BLINDNESS

Standpoint theory operates on two assumptions. One is that people occupying the same social positions, that is, identities—race, gender, sex,
sexuality, ability status, and so on—will have the same experiences of
dominance and oppression and will, assuming they understand their
own experiences correctly, interpret them in the same ways. From this
follows the assumption that these experiences will provide them with a
more authoritative and fuller picture. The other is that one's relative
position within a social power dynamic dictates what one can and cannot know: thus the privileged are blinded by their privilege and the oppressed possess a kind of double sight, in that they understand both the
dominant position and the experience of being oppressed by it. As the
feminist epistemologist Nancy Tuana puts it:

> Standpoint theory was designed to be a method that would render
> transparent the values and interests, such as androcentrism,
> heteronormativity, and Eurocentrism, that underlie allegedly
> neutral methods in science and epistemology, and clarify their
> impact. Such attention to the subject of knowledge illuminated
> the various means by which oppressive practices can result in or
> reinforce epistemic inequalities, exclusions, and marginalizations.
> In this way, feminist and other liberatory epistemologists aimed
> to transform the subject of knowledge in the sense of focusing on
> knowledge obscured by dominant interests and values and thereby
> to identify and provide tools for undermining the knowledges and
> practices implicated in oppression.[24]

Roughly, the idea is that members of dominant groups experience
a world organized by and for dominant groups, while members of oppressed groups experience the world as members of oppressed groups

in a world organized by and for dominant groups. Thus, members of oppressed groups understand the dominant perspective and the perspective of those who are oppressed, while members of dominant groups only understand the dominant perspective. Standpoint theory can be understood by analogy to a kind of color blindness, in which the more privileged a person is, the fewer colors she can see. A straight white male—being triply dominant—might thus see only in shades of gray. A black person would be able to see shades of red; a woman would be able to see shades of green; and a LGBT person could see shades of blue; a black lesbian could see all three colors—in addition to the grayscale vision everyone has. Medina refers to this as a "kaleidoscopic consciousness" and "meta-lucidity."[25] Thus, having oppressed identities allows extra dimensions of sight. This gives the oppressed a richer, more accurate view of reality[26]—hence we should listen to and believe their accounts of it.

Standpoint theory often finds itself criticized for essentialism—for thinking something like "all black people feel like this."[27] This isn't quite wrong because it rests, in a way, on a concept we've encountered before: *strategic* essentialism, wherein members of an oppressed group can essentialize themselves (or, here, the authenticity of their lived experience in relationship to power) as a means of achieving group political action. Its advocates don't defend it that way, however. They generally get around this accusation by arguing that the theory does not assume all members of the same group *have the same nature* but that *they experience the same problems in an unjust society*, although they can choose which discourses they wish to contribute to. Members of these groups who disagree with standpoint theory—or even deny that they are oppressed—are explained away as having internalized their oppression (false consciousness) or as pandering in order to gain favor or reward from the dominant system ("Uncle Toms" and "native informants") by amplifying Theoretically dominant discourses.

Standpoint theory is at the root of identity politics and it is the main thing that fundamentally differentiates it from the liberal civil rights movements. For influential black feminist Patricia Hill Collins, the relationship between standpoint theory and identity politics was explicit and represented a crucial element of progress.[28] Similarly, but perhaps more profoundly, Kristie Dotson, arguably the most influential black feminist Theorist of knowledge, argues that it is almost impossible for dominant social groups to see outside of their own system of knowledge, which is simply considered knowledge *per se* by mainstream society. In her 2014 paper "Conceptualizing Epistemic Oppression," she sets out orders of oppression. The first two are Fricker's two forms of epistemic injustice. The third and most profound order is "irreducible." By this, she means it is an epistemic injustice that cannot simply be attributed to an unjust social system but that exists within the system of knowledge itself. Hence, changing it from within is almost—if not entirely—impossible.[29] For Dotson, the systems of knowledge—"schemata"—have been specifically set up to work for dominant groups and exclude others, but, because they work for the dominant groups so smoothly, they do not even realize that there are things they don't know, things that can only be known from within the knowledge systems that they oppress.[30]

Dotson ultimately asserts that knowledge is inadequate unless it includes the experiential knowledge of minority groups. This knowledge is assumed to be consistently different from that of dominant groups because of the power dynamics between the groups. Furthermore, the knowledge produced by dominant groups—including science and reason—is also merely the product of their cultural traditions and is not superior to the knowledge produced by other cultural traditions. Dotson explicitly proceeds from the two postmodern principles. Her argument, which is central to standpoint theory, denies that science and reason belong to all humans and are the same for all humans and, in effect, assigns them to white Western men. Dotson goes further than this. The logical implication of her third-order oppression is that if someone from a dominant group does not agree that her knowledge-producing systems are limited by their failure to include experiential knowledge from outside them, that is because she is unable to step outside of her own culture. In other words, legitimate disagreement is not an option.

José Medina sets this view out in an accessible and seemingly rigorous way in his 2013 book, *The Epistemology of Resistance.* Medina characterizes the members of privileged groups as "epistemically spoiled" and argues that they "have a hard time learning their mistakes, their biases, and the constraints and presuppositions of their position in the world and their perspective."[31] The study of knowledge within Social Justice scholarship is based on a premise that privilege spoils people and makes them unable to appreciate other ways of knowing. Medina argues that this spoiled state generates the "epistemic vices" of *epistemic arrogance, epistemic laziness*, and *active ignorance*. Being oppressed, for Medina, confers the converse "epistemic virtues" of *epistemic humility, epistemic curiosity/diligence*, and *epistemic openness*.[32] These vices and virtues, associated with relative privilege and oppression, feature prominently in critical race Theory and postcolonial Theory, where an oppressed standpoint allows a double or multiple consciousness, because oppressed people operate in different systems at the same time.

The line of thought, which grants double sight to the oppressed but not to her oppressor, is often attributed to Marxism, but it's more accurate to say that postmodernism and Marxism share a common philosophical ancestor in the work of German philosopher Georg Wilhelm Friedrich Hegel,[33] though Marx may have been a significant conduit of these ideas for the postmodernists. As always, postmodernism and Marxism exhibit significant and intentional differences. The key difference is whether the oppressed suffer from false consciousness as a result of a hidden imposition of power, as the Marxists believed, or whether it is the *oppressors* who suffer from false consciousness, due to their socialization into a system of knowledge that benefits them, as the postmodernists would increasingly have it. Theorist Charles Mills states this difference from the Marxist idea:

> The racially subordinated—victims, after all, of genocide, expropriation, and slavery!—are often quite well able to recognize their situation. It is not (or not always) that the imprisoned lack the concepts, the hermeneutical resources, to understand their situation, but that the privileged lack the concepts and find them incredible or even incomprehensible, because of their incongruity with white-supremacist ideology. Even if they were to "hear" what blacks were saying, they still would not be able to "hear" them because of the conceptual incoherence of the black framework of assumptions with their own dominant framework. Whites are imprisoned (reversing the metaphor) in a cognitive state which both

protects them from dealing with the realities of social oppression and, of course, disables them epistemically.[34]

What this means is that Social Justice scholarship reifies the postmodern knowledge principle—makes it "real"—and combines it with the postmodern political principle, which is a drive to change the underlying systems of power that it assumes are baked into every social interaction. It does this by utilizing the four postmodern themes with an unprecedented level of conviction.

THOU SHALT NOT DISAGREE WITH THEORY

Perhaps what is most worrying about Social Justice scholarship is the increasing difficulty of speaking about issues relevant to social justice—or about Social Justice scholarship itself—in any way other than under its own inflexible terms. This means doing so only with the approved terminology and accepting the validity of standpoint theory and identity politics. Disagreement is rarely tolerated, now that the postmodernist assumptions have been reified. This can be seen in the fact that disagreement is often regarded as, at best, a failure to have engaged with the scholarship correctly, as though engagement must imply acceptance, and, at worst, a profound moral failure. This kind of claim is more familiar from religious ideology—if you don't believe, you haven't read the holy text properly or you just want to sin—but applied to what is supposed to be rigorous academic scholarship. This is a more or less direct consequence of having reified postmodernism.

Many people (especially academics) remain unaware of the depth of this problem, which presents as ideological closedness, unwillingness to accept any disagreement, and an authoritarian will to enforce a Social Justice conception of society and moral imperative on others.[35] Caring about justice in society is not a problem—indeed, it's necessary to a healthy society. It is also not inherently a problem if bad ideas enter the academy and gain popularity. This is how knowledge advances—by giving space to all kinds of ideas within our centers of learning, where they can be examined, tested, and criticized. (Some of the most well-established ideas of today—like the "Big Bang" theory of cosmology—were considered mad and unethical at one time.) A problem arises, however, when any school of thought refuses to submit its ideas to rigorous scrutiny, rejects that kind of examination on principle, and asserts that any attempts to subject it to thoughtful criticism are immoral, insincere, and proof of its thesis. To get a sense of the severity of this problem, let's look at three examples from the 2010s.

Example 1: *Being White, Being Good: White Complicity,*
White Moral Responsibility, and Social Justice Pedagogy
by Barbara Applebaum (2010)

In this 2010 book, Social Justice educator Barbara Applebaum uses the postmodern knowledge and political principles to argue that all white people are complicit in racism, because of their automatic participation in the system of power and privilege described by critical race Theory. Though this book is not well-known among the general public, it is a landmark text in critical whiteness and critical education Theory circles, because it represents an advance on the idea that all white people have privilege (a concept that dates to 1989 and the applied postmodern turn) to insist that all white people are therefore actively complicit in racism. She writes,

> White students often assume that responsibility begins and ends with the awareness of privilege. By admitting to or confessing privilege, however, white students are actually able to avoid owning up to their complicity in systemic racism.[36]

This really does say that confessing to white privilege is far from sufficient. White students must accept their ongoing complicity in perpetuating systemic racism simply by being white. It is assumed that they must have learned, internalized, and been perpetuating racism even if they do not know it. If this reminds you of Foucault's notion of powerful discourses working through everyone in society—you're right. "Integral to the understanding of how discourse works," Applebaum informs us, "is the Foucaultian notion of power."[37] "Not only is discourse the prism through which reality is given meaning," she tells us, "but also power works through discourse to constitute subjects."[38] Again, we get this image of power working as a grid, through the people positioned on it, each performing and speaking according to its directives—rather like (nerd alert!) a Borg hive.

Applebaum demands people believe this paradigm—even though she is quick to point out that she is not *technically* forbidding disagreement. She writes,

> One can disagree and remain engaged in the material, for example, by asking questions and searching for clarification and understanding. Denials, however, function as a way to distance oneself from the material and to dismiss without engagement.[39]

So, one can ask questions about Applebaum's thesis and try to understand it, but denial of "The Truth" (what we usually think of as disagreement) can only mean one has not engaged with the material enough or in the right way. In other words, Applebaum proceeds upon an assumption that her thesis is true. She is certain that she is in possession of The Truth (According to Social Justice)—and scolds those who disagree: "[T]he mere fact that they can question the existence of systemic oppression is a function of their privilege to choose to ignore discussions of systemic oppression or not."[40] One might be forgiven for thinking that Applebaum is not really open to the possibility that people might disagree with her. Her students certainly appear to think so:

> [S]tudents in courses that make systemic injustice explicit often complain in teacher evaluations that they have not been allowed to disagree in the course. Students often maintain that such courses indoctrinate a particular view about racism that they are not willing to accept.[41]

Applebaum advocates shutting down such student disagreement. She gives the example of a male student, who questioned the gender wage gap:

Allowing him to express his disagreement and spending time trying to challenge his beliefs often comes at a cost to marginalized students whose experiences are (even if indirectly) dismissed by his claims.[42]

Critical education Theory holds that it is dangerous to allow students to express such disagreement. This is because of its reliance on the postmodern knowledge principle—social reality and what is accepted as true are constructed by language. Disagreement would allow dominant discourses to be reasserted, voiced, and heard, which Theory sees as not safe. As Applebaum explains, "language constitutes our reality by providing the conceptual framework from which meaning is given."[43] She adds, "Even if one retreats to the position where one only speaks for oneself, one's speech is still not neutral and still reinforces the continuance of dominant discourses by omission."[44] Given this understanding of the power of language (a postmodern theme) and its impacts on social justice (through the postmodern political principle), it is essential to control what may and may not be said. This imperative permeates Social Justice scholarship.

Having already defined the only legitimate form of "disagreement" as putting in more effort to understand (read: agree) and dismissed actual disagreement as refusal to engage with The Truth, Applebaum continues,

> Resistance will not be allowed to derail the class discussions! Of course, those who refuse to engage might mistakenly perceive this as a declaration that they will not be allowed to express their disagreement but that is only precisely *because* they are resisting engagement.[45] (emphasis in original)

Resistance is indeed futile.

Example 2: "Tracking Privilege-Preserving Epistemic Pushback in Feminist and Critical Race Philosophy Classes" by Alison Bailey (2017)

In this essay, Bailey argues that anyone who disagrees with Social Justice scholarship is insincere and simply trying to preserve unjust power structures, in the service of a knowledge-producing system that privileges straight white men and prevents Social Justice. She defines it thus: "Privilege-preserving epistemic pushback is a variety of willful ignorance that dominant groups habitually deploy during conversations that are trying to make social injustices visible."[46] She assumes that criticisms of Social Justice scholarship are simply attempts to deliberately ignore The Truth According to Social Justice. Furthermore, criticism of Social Justice work is immoral and harmful, Bailey tells us:

> I focus on these ground-holding responses because they are pervasive, tenacious, and bear a strong resemblance to critical-thinking practices, and because I believe that their uninterrupted circulation does psychological and epistemic harm to members of marginalized groups.[47]

Since Social Justice scholars like Bailey assume that disagreement with their work must be a result of intellectual and moral failings, no such disagreement can ever be brooked:

> Treating privilege-preserving epistemic pushback as a form of critical engagement validates it and allows it to circulate more freely; this, as I'll argue later, can do epistemic violence to oppressed groups.[48]

It should therefore be shut down and replaced with Social Justice scholarship. In fact, for Bailey, critical thinking itself is a problem: it needs replacing with "critical pedagogy" (in which the word "critical" means something different). She explains:

> The critical-thinking tradition is concerned primarily with epistemic adequacy. To be critical is to show good judgment in recognizing when arguments are faulty, assertions lack evidence, truth claims appeal to unreliable sources, or concepts are sloppily crafted and applied. . . . Critical pedagogy regards the claims that

students make in response to social-justice issues not as propositions to be assessed for their truth value, but as expressions of power that function to re-inscribe and perpetuate social inequalities. Its mission is to teach students ways of identifying and mapping how power shapes our understandings of the world. This is the first step toward resisting and transforming social injustices.[49]

This is an explicit admission that Bailey's aim is not to seek truth, but to teach a specific understanding of Social Justice, for the purposes of activism. Although this essay has not been very influential, it is worth looking at because it is a very clear example of how philosophy classes can be used to instruct students in The Truth According to Social Justice. That this paper was published in *Hypatia*, the leading feminist philosophy journal, gives us an alarming indication of what is considered acceptable in the fields of Social Justice scholarship, how it can influence education, and how confident and clear this current manifestation of reified post-modernism is.[50]

Bailey refers to disagreements with Social Justice approaches as "shadow texts," to suggest that written criticisms of Social Justice are neither sincere nor helpful, and should not be regarded as genuine scholarship. The image of *shadow texts*, she tells us, comes from the idea of an investigator shadowing her mark: "The word 'shadow' calls to mind the image of something walking closely alongside another thing without engaging it."[51] The two examples of shadow texts she gives involve a male student pointing out that men can be victims of domestic violence too, and a female student arguing that one can *mention* a racist slur in order to discuss it, without *using* it as a slur. Bailey responds,

> We are discussing institutional racism. Jennifer, a white philosophy major, shares a story about racist graffiti that uses the "n" word. She says the word, animating it with that two-fingered scare-quote gesture to signal that she is mentioning it. I ask her to consider the history of the word and how it might mean something different coming from white mouths. I ask her not to use it. She gives the class a mini lecture on the use–mention distinction, reminding me that it "is a foundational concept in analytic philosophy"

and that it's "perfectly acceptable to mention, but not to use the word in philosophical discussions."[52] . . . If Jennifer continues to press philosophical concepts into the service of a broader refusal to understand the dehumanizing history of the n-word, then "I mentioned but didn't use the word 'n-----'" is a shadow text.[53]

Rather than consider the validity of these arguments, or give the students the chance to discuss them, Bailey assumes that they are simply trying to preserve male and white privilege. She therefore uses them as object lessons of failures to genuinely engage. "Learning to spot shadow texts can offer epistemic friction: they help the class focus on what shadow texts do, rather than just on what they say," she writes.[54] That is, Bailey is instructing those in her philosophy classes not to engage with the argument but rather to recognize which discourse of power they could be feeding into. This is perfectly consistent with the two postmodern principles.

Students in Bailey's philosophy classes are taught to immediately identify counterviews as resistance to Social Justice's take on The Truth and as a kind of "ignorance." She thinks that, when people disagree, it's because something "triggered the resistance."[55] She writes,

> I ask our class to consider how identifying shadow texts might help track the production of ignorance. . . . It's essential for them to understand that tracking ignorance requires that our attention be focused not on a few problem individuals, but on learning to identify patterns of resistance and tying ignorance-producing habits to a strategic refusal to understand.[56]

It is hard to miss the militant activist tone here. Like Applebaum, Bailey has a priestlike certainty of her own rightness and the concomitant need to reeducate and shut down anyone who disagrees. This marks a significant change from the earliest postmodernists' radical skepticism, but it is in keeping with how the postmodern principles and their application have evolved over the last half-century.

Example 3: *White Fragility: Why It Is So Hard*
to Talk to White People about Race
by Robin DiAngelo (2018)

In this book, lecturer in "whiteness studies" Robin DiAngelo develops the concept of "white fragility" that she first laid out in a highly cited paper of that title from 2011.[57] She begins with a strong objective truth claim:

> White people in North America live in a social environment that protects and insulates them from race-based stress. This insulated environment of racial protection builds white expectations for racial comfort while at the same time lowering the ability to tolerate racial stress, leading to what I refer to as White Fragility.[58]

By itself this might be a useful insight, leading white people to reflect more deeply about their possibly unconscious prejudices. But DiAngelo goes on to insist that society is permeated by white supremacy and that any disagreement with her ideas is the result of a weakness that has been socialized into white people through their privilege:

> White Fragility is a state in which even a minimum amount of racial stress becomes intolerable, triggering a range of defensive moves. These moves include the outward display of emotions such as anger, fear, and guilt, and behaviors such as argumentation, silence, and leaving the stress-inducing situation.[59]

Any negative feelings about being racially profiled and held responsible for a racist society are taken as signs of being "fragile" and as evidence of complicity in—if not collusion with—racism. White people are complicit beneficiaries of racism and white supremacy. This is The Truth According to Social Justice—disagreement is not allowed. DiAngelo is quite explicit about this. If disagreeing, remaining silent, and going away are all evidence of fragility—mere "defensive moves"—the only way one can avoid being "fragile" is to remain put, show no negative emotions, and agree with The Truth—after which one must actively participate in discovering the Truth, that is, learning how to deconstruct whiteness and white privilege, which is billed as the necessary work of "antiracism."

This is quite staggering. DiAngelo, a white woman, contends that all white people are racist and that it is impossible not to be, because of the systems of powerful racist discourses we were born into.[60] She insists that we are complicit by default and are therefore responsible for addressing these systems. Like Applebaum, she argues that it does not matter if individual white people are good people who despise racism and are not aware of having any racist biases:

> Being good or bad is not relevant. Racism is a multilayered system embedded in our culture. All of us are socialized into the system of racism. Racism cannot be avoided. Whites have blind spots on racism, and I have blind spots on racism. Racism is complex, and I don't have to understand every nuance of the feedback to validate that feedback. Whites are / I am unconsciously invested in racism. Bias is implicit and unconscious.[61]

This personal approach pervades *White Fragility*. So do collectivism and rejection of individuality. DiAngelo writes as a white person addressing other white people and insists "we" should see the world the way she does,

> This book is unapologetically rooted in identity politics. I am white and am addressing a common white dynamic. I am mainly writing to a white audience; when I use the terms us and we, I am referring to the white collective.[62]

For Theorists like DiAngelo, white people are a collective because of their position within the power grid of society—they cannot help benefiting from racism and therefore must work through it. Moreover, white people are, according to DiAngelo, "socialized into a deeply internalized sense of superiority that we either are unaware of or can never admit to ourselves."[63] All white people can do is become more aware of their relationship to power and consciously address it—over and over again. This is the postmodern political principle at work.

DiAngelo also rejects the liberal principles of individualism and "color blindness"—that a person's race is irrelevant to her worth, as Martin Luther King, Jr., argued. Liberal values are, in The Truth According to Social Justice, racist because they enable white people to hide from the "realities" of their own racism and white supremacy. DiAngelo sermonizes,

> To challenge the ideologies of racism such as individualism and color blindness, we as white people must suspend our perception of ourselves as unique and/or outside race. Exploring our collective racial identity interrupts a key privilege of dominance—the ability to see oneself only as an individual.[64]

DiAngelo's is probably the purest manifestation of the postmodernist conception of society. Like her contemporaries, she displays an unshakable conviction in the postmodern principles and themes. This indicates that these have been reified as the foundation of the Social Justice metanarrative.[65] Worryingly, her ideas, more than any other, have successfully broken the bounds of academia and entered the mainstream. The book *White Fragility* was a New York Times best seller for over six months: DiAngelo was able to promote it on an extensive world tour. Another book by DiAngelo on confronting racism, as she sees it, is already on its way.

SUMMARY—MAKING THE POSTMODERN PRINCIPLES AND THEMES REAL

Social Justice scholarship does not just rely on the two postmodern principles and four postmodern themes: it treats them and their underlying assumptions as morally righteous known-knowns—as The Truth According to Social Justice. It therefore constitutes a third distinct phase of postmodernism, one we have called *reified postmodernism* because it treats the abstractions at the heart of postmodernism as if they were real truths about society.

To understand how the three phases of postmodernism have developed, imagine a tree with deep roots in radical leftist social theory.[66] The first phase, or *high deconstructive phase*, from the 1960s to the 1980s (usually simply referred to as "postmodernism"), gave us the tree trunk: Theory. The second phase, from the 1980s to the mid-2000s, which we call *applied postmodernism*, gave us the branches—the more applicable Theories and studies, including postcolonial Theory, queer Theory, critical race Theory, gender studies, fat studies, disability studies, and many critical *anything* studies. In the current, third phase, which began in the mid-2000s, Theory has gone from being an assumption to being The Truth, a truth that is taken for granted. This has given us the leaves of the tree of Social Justice scholarship, which combines the previous approaches as needed. The constant in all three phases is Theory, which manifests in the two postmodern principles and four postmodern themes.

Social Justice scholarship does not merely present the postmodern knowledge principle—that objective truth does not exist and knowledge is socially constructed and a product of culture—and the postmodern political principle—society is constructed through knowledge by language and discourses, designed to keep the dominant in power over the oppressed. It treats them as The Truth, tolerates no dissent, and expects everyone to agree or be "cancelled." We see this in the obsessive focus on who can produce knowledge and how and in the explicit desire to "infect" as many other disciplines as possible with Social Justice methods.[67] This is reflected in a clear wish to achieve epistemic and research "justice" by asserting that rigorous knowledge production is just a product of white, male, and Western culture and thus no better than the Theoretically interpreted lived experiences of members of marginalized groups, which must be constantly elevated and foregrounded.

The four postmodern themes are not generally treated by Critical Social Justice scholars as a reification of postmodernism. They are facets of The Truth According to Social Justice. The blurring of boundaries and cultural relativism typical of the applied postmodernist Theories are developed further, in an attempt to erase the boundary between rigorously produced knowledge and lived experience (of oppression). Group identity is treated as so integral to the functioning of society that those invested in Social Justice have elevated divisive group-identity politics to a fever pitch. Belief in the overwhelming power of language, which must be scrutinized and cleansed, is simply taken for granted.

This has had a number of consequences. Scholars and activists devote tremendous effort to searching for and inflating the smallest in-fractions—this being the "critical" approach. They scrupulously exam-ine people's current and past speech, particularly on social media, and punish purveyors of "hateful" discourses. If the person involved is con-sidered influential, the mob may even try to end her career altogether. Robin DiAngelo calls anything except deferential agreement "white fra-gility"; Alison Bailey characterizes disagreement as "willful ignorance" and a power play to preserve one's privilege; Kristie Dotson character-izes dissent as "pernicious"; Barbara Applebaum dismisses any criticism of Social Justice Theoretical methods as "color-talk" and "white ignore-ance."

Social Justice scholarship represents the third phase in the evolution of postmodernism. In this new incarnation, postmodernism is no longer characterized by radical skepticism, epistemic despair, nihilism, and a playful, though pessimistic, tendency to pick apart and deconstruct ev-erything we think we know. It now seeks to apply deconstructive meth-ods and postmodernist principles to the task of creating social change, which it pushes into *everything*. In the guise of Social Justice scholarship, postmodernism has become a grand, sweeping explanation for society—a metanarrative—of its own.

So let's return to the contradiction at the heart of reified postmod-ernism: how can intelligent people profess both radical skepticism and radical relativism—the postmodern knowledge principle—and at the same time assert the Truth According to Social Justice (Theory) with absolute certainty?

The answer seems to be that the skepticism and relativism of the postmodern knowledge principle are now interpreted in a more restric-tive fashion: that it is impossible for humans to obtain reliable knowl-edge by employing evidence and reason, but, it is now claimed, reli-able knowledge can be obtained by listening to the "lived experience" of members of marginalized groups—or what is really more accurate, to marginalized people's interpretations of their own lived experience, after these have been properly colored by Theory.

The difficulty with this sort of Social Justice "way of knowing" is, however, the same as that with all gnostic "epistemologies" that rely upon feelings, intuition, and subjective experience: what should we do when people's subjective experiences conflict? The overarching liberal principle of conflict resolution—to put forth one's best arguments and hash the issue out, deferring to the best available evidence whenever possible—is completely eliminated by this approach. Indeed, it's billed as a conspiracy used to keep marginalized people down. If different members of the same marginalized group—or members of different marginalized groups—give incompatible interpretations of their "lived experience," how can this contradiction be reconciled? The common-sense answer—that different people have different experiences and different interpretations, and that there is no logical contradiction in that—cannot suffice here, because Social Justice epistemology under the reification of postmodernism claims that these "lived experiences" reveal objective truths about society, not merely some people's beliefs about their experiences.

The radically relativist answer—that two or more contradictory statements can be simultaneously true—is sometimes attempted, but it does not, after all, make much sense. Instead, what Social Justice scholars seem in practice to do is to select certain favored interpretations of marginalized people's experience (those consistent with Theory) and anoint these as the "authentic" ones; all others are explained away as an unfortunate internalization of dominant ideologies or cynical self-interest. In this way the logical contradiction between radical relativism and dogmatic absolutism is resolved, but at the price of rendering the Social Justice Theory completely unfalsifiable and indefeasible: no matter what evidence about reality (physical, biological, and social) or philosophical argument may be presented, Theory always can and always does explain it away. In this sense, we are not so far, in fact, from the apocalyptic cults who predicted that the world would end on a specific day, but reaffirmed their beliefs with added fervor when that day passed uneventfully. (The spaceship coming to destroy the earth really did come, but the extraterrestrials changed their minds when they saw the cult members' devotion.)

It is therefore no exaggeration to observe that Social Justice Theorists have created a new religion, a tradition of faith that is actively hostile to reason, falsification, disconfirmation, and disagreement of any kind. Indeed, the whole postmodernist project now seems, in retrospect, like an unwitting attempt to have deconstructed the old metanarratives of Western thought—science and reason along with religion and capitalist economic systems—to make room for a wholly new religion, a postmodern faith based on a dead God, which sees mysterious *worldly* forces in systems of power and privilege and which sanctifies victimhood. This, increasingly, is the fundamentalist religion of the nominally secular left.[68]

Theory has not remained confined to the academy. First applied, then reified, postmodernism in the form of Social Justice has left the universities, spread—with evangelical zeal—by graduates and through social media and activist journalism. It has become a significant cultural force with a profound—and often negative—influence on politics. It may seem like an obscure and peculiar brand of academic theorizing—but it cannot be ignored. What does all this mean? What will happen next? And what needs to be done about it? The last two chapters of this book will address these questions.

9 SOCIAL JUSTICE IN ACTION

Theory Always Looks Good on Paper

Theory has broken the bounds of academia and exerts a profound influence on our culture. This might seem implausible. How can abstruse Theories about knowledge, power, and language survive outside the rarefied environment of the ivory tower and affect everyday life? Is the supermarket assistant really reading Gayatri Spivak on his tea break? Is your doctor devouring queer Theory on the train? How likely is it that your computer technician reads feminist epistemology in his spare time or that your favorite sports commentator is well versed in critical race Theory?

Not very. But that's not what we're arguing. Theory is obscure, and most people never engage with it directly. However, many of us are influenced by it, and no one is entirely safe from its abuses. In the United Kingdom recently, a disabled grandfather and bag packer named Brian Leach was sacked by his employer, the supermarket chain Asda, for sharing on Facebook a Billy Connolly comedy skit, which one of his colleagues felt was Islamophobic.[1] This follows from applications of postcolonial Theory. In the United States, software engineer James Damore was fired by Google for writing an internal memo that men and women differ psychologically on average—in an attempt to seek solutions to the four-to-one gender disparity in tech.[2] This follows from the assumptions underlying queer Theory and intersectional feminism. The British football commentator and comedian Danny Baker lost his job at the BBC for not realizing that a photograph of a chimpanzee in a smart coat and bowler hat that he tweeted could be construed as racist.[3] This follows from the way critical race Theory describes the world. Meanwhile, every major media event in Hollywood obsesses about identity and representation, while doctors across the Western world face the challenge of advising obese patients on their health without fat shaming them.[4]

Troubling examples like this crop up all the time, yet many people don't believe that there is very much to worry about. They will point out that Mr. Leach was reinstated, argue that Mr. Damore's views could encourage stereotyping, suggest that Mr. Baker should have realized the connotations of simian imagery, and agree that there are representation issues in Hollywood, while pointing out that doctors really could be more sensitive. Yes, they'll concede, we hear stories about campus protests, but students have always protested. They're young and idealistic. It's practically a rite of passage. Also, the accounts of intolerant students are over-hyped. It's mostly a few activists at elite universities[5] who demand trigger warnings, safe spaces, and the deplatforming of everyone who disagrees with them.[6] The majority of students continue to support freedom of speech. Mostly, they just keep their heads down, and focus on their work, particularly at community colleges and other working-class institutions. Why should we worry about the actions of a few entitled students at our most elite universities? Yale might as well be in Narnia, as far as many people are concerned.

From that viewpoint, these issues aren't impacting the real world enough to be a priority. Given the rise of demagoguery, populism, nationalism, and anti-intellectual currents on the right—who currently hold political power in the United States and the United Kingdom—and the growth of far-right movements all over Europe and beyond, should we really be worrying about a few people getting overzealous in their support of equality? Maybe there is some shouting, milkshake throwing, and the odd smashed window, but far-right terrorism is on the rise,[7] and online communities of the far right, "alt-right,"[8] and "incels"[9] are proliferating and fomenting vastly more serious acts of violence. Shouldn't liberal lefties focus their attention there, rather than worrying about a few mad academic papers and histrionic students?

To address this not wholly unreasonable objection, we will turn to popular sources. We will endeavor to convince you that what is happening in universities is a genuine problem, that these ideas are impacting the real world, and that fixing the problem in the universities is not a distraction from fighting the populist, anti-intellectual right but a vital part of it.[10]

WHAT IS HAPPENING IN OUR UNIVERSITIES, AND WHY DOES IT MATTER?

There is a problem that begins in our universities, and it comes down to Social Justice. The most immediate aspect of the problem is that Social Justice scholarship gets passed down to students, who then go out into the world. This effect is strongest within Social Justice fields, which teach students to be skeptical of science, reason, and evidence; to regard knowledge as tied to identity; to read oppressive power dynamics into every interaction; to politicize every facet of life; and to apply ethical principles unevenly, in accordance with identity. But Social Justice also materializes as a prevailing campus culture, which accepts many of these ideas as known-knowns. Most universities in the United States now have "diversity" requirements: these ideas are taught to everyone, as part of the general curriculum. It is common to underestimate this problem. We often encounter the assumption that, once they graduate, students will have to learn marketable skills and that this will resolve the problem: once they get into the "real world," they will have to leave behind these ideological positions in order to find employment. But what if they simply take their beliefs out into the professional world and remake that world to suit them?

Unfortunately, this is exactly what's happening. The real world is changing to absorb the skills of such students, and a Social Justice industry already worth billions of dollars is forming, all dedicated to training our companies and institutions to enact and police The Truth According to Social Justice. A new job entitled (some variation of) "Diversity,

Equity, and Inclusion Officer" has emerged. It is designed to change the organizational culture to accord with the ideology of Social Justice. These officers are the architects and enforcers of soft revolutions; they are inquisitors, seeking incidents of bias and imbalance. These also are not fringe jobs. They are, unsurprisingly, particularly concentrated within higher education, where, according to some reports in the United States, diversity officers are rapidly increasing in number and earn three times as much as the average American and more than the academic faculty.[11] Diversity, equity, and inclusion officers are not limited to the academy, however; they also crop up in administration and human resources departments, including in city governments. According to a major job search website in the United Kingdom, equality and diversity jobs are especially common in the Equality and Human Rights Commission, professional associations, the Law Society, schools and universities, the police, large private sector companies, local authorities, trade unions, and the Civil Service.[12] They have become the norm, not the exception, for many institutions and corporations of sufficient size. These officers therefore now wield significant institutional, social, and cultural power.

Within the universities, the problem is not confined to specific classes. "Bias response teams" are now thought to exist at over two hundred U.S. colleges, and they serve the entire campus by, as their name suggests, responding to reports of identity-based bias.[13] Although some are quick to point out that they do not have the power to *directly* inflict any kind of punishment for or control over speech and can only provide "education and persuasion,"[14] this is alarming, if not Orwellian, depending on what is considered bias and what education and training is provided to correct it. This is especially true since they can *indirectly* lead to sanctioning or firing by submitting bias reports to administrators such as heads of department, deans, and university presidents with recommendations for action. But what constitutes "bias" in these cases? Since the slights students have complained of include support for President Donald Trump, "phallic snow objects," and expressions of antiracism such as "I don't see color," and bias is operationally defined as a "state of mind," it appears that sensitivity detectors might be set rather high.[15] Although students who have been reported retain the right not to submit themselves for education, it is probable that many will not want to risk the accompanying opprobrium and will simply self-censor any problematic ideas. This is not conducive to the healthy debate and viewpoint diversity that are essential to knowledge production in universities. It's also divisive for campus communities and the workplaces graduates will be fit into, which all may become more dysfunctional as a result.

There have also been more overt attempts to silence certain views on campus. "No-platforming" policies for particular legal or political groups and certain public figures have become common,[16] though they often fly under the radar. Certain views—*academic* views shared by professionals—are considered too dangerous or even "violent" to be allowed a platform. Unlike deplatforming drives—in which someone who has been invited to speak has that invitation rescinded—policies that disallow certain views in the first place attract little attention. In the United Kingdom, more than 50 percent of universities restrict speech, especially certain views of religion and trans identity.[17]

This problem is expansive. One consequence is that once taken on, Social Justice scholarship and ethics completely displace reliable and rigorous scholarship into issues of social justice by condemning all other approaches as complicit with systemic bigotry and thus unthinkable—or, in practice, unpublishable and punishable. The cases of two scholars, Rebecca Tuvel and Bruce Gilley, immediately come to mind. Tuvel wrote a paper for the feminist philosophy giant *Hypatia*, exploring parallels between transracial and transgender identities and advocating transracial identity statuses. However, for Theory, race and gender are profoundly different. To claim transgender status, for queer Theory, is to break down the categories of sex and gender, which are Theorized to constrain people, but to claim a transracial identity, as we know from critical race Theory, would be to ignore the social significance of race and to make an illegitimate claim to a lived experience of oppression. This is seen as speaking over and erasing people of color. Tuvel—an untenured assistant professor—paid the price for this misstep. Not only was her paper retracted,[18] and not only did *Hypatia* suffer catastrophically for accepting it,[19] but so too was she subjected to a vicious witch hunt.[20] Her colleagues publicly blasted her for her insensitivity—even though some privately admitted that they secretly agreed with her.[21]

Bruce Gilley's case was, perhaps, even more extreme. After years researching postcolonial societies, mostly drawing upon scholars in genuine postcolonial contexts, he wrote "The Case for Colonialism": a nuanced counterbalance to the central thesis of postcolonial Theory that colonialism is always and only bad for the colonized. His paper was reviewed and accepted for publication in the scholarly journal *Third World Quarterly*—with explosive consequences. Immediately, accusations were filed against Gilley at Portland State University, where he works, and calls were made for the paper to be unpublished, for him to lose his job, and even for his doctorate to be revoked.[22] The editors of the journal that published the paper were similarly pilloried. Protests including death threats led to the paper's retraction.[23] These two cases, and a handful of others show that Social Justice scholarship censors academic ideas it disapproves of.

While some scholarship on gender, race, and sexuality is empirical and rigorous and could help redress imbalances in society, it is undermined by that which is not. This creates a crisis of confidence around some of the most important topics of our current political moment. Some scholars mischaracterize criticisms of shoddy and unethical scholarship as motivated by a hatred of minority groups or women. This is astonishing. Try to imagine a parallel in other fields. Would it seem reasonable to argue that people who object to unevidenced and unethical scholarship in medicine just hate sick people and don't care about their suffering? Do people say, "Yes, some bad papers get added to the body of medical knowledge but there are good ones too!" rather than trying to weed out the bad papers so that people don't receive dangerous or ineffective treatments? No, because we recognize that safe and effective medicine is essential to human thriving. But so is rigorous scholarship on social (justice) issues. Scholars within that field should know this better than anyone. In no serious discipline do we so plainly see a drive to be morally right (or righteous) instead of factually and theoretically correct. This drive is, perhaps, the most obvious feature of Social Justice scholarship.

These problems have also affected disciplines other than identity studies, especially in the humanities and arts. Literature, philosophy, and history have long accepted and, at times, even required the inclusion of Theory within their courses. Postcolonial Theory and feminist analysis—both materialist and postmodern—are particularly common. Other forms of analysis simply aren't allowed, at best, and are treated as intolerably biased, offensive, or violent, at worst. Even science, technology, engineering, and mathematics (STEM) subjects have been affected. Since 2010, there have been an increasing number of proposals from within *engineering*, arguing for the use of Social Justice concepts in that profession. One 2015 paper proposes that an engineer should "demonstrate competence in the provision of sociotechnological services that are sensitive to dynamics of difference, power, and privilege among people and cultural groups."[24] In the book *Engineering and Social Justice*, published by Purdue University Press, we read many variations on the same theme and a worrisome recommendation: "getting beyond views of truth as objective and absolute is the most fundamental change we need in engineering education."[25] Meanwhile, arguments have been made that mathematics is intrinsically sexist and racist because of its focus on objectivity and proof and because of disparate outcomes in mathematics education across racial groups. One 2018 paper asserts,

> Drawing upon Indigenous worldviews to reconceptualize what mathematics is and how it is practiced, I argue for a movement against objects, truths, and knowledge towards a way of being in the world that is guided by first principles—mathematx. This shift from thinking of mathematics as a noun to mathematx as a verb holds potential for honouring our connections with each other as human and other-than-human persons, for balancing problem solving with joy, and for maintaining critical bifocality at the local and global level.[26]

It is unclear how this could improve mathematics, but the political agenda here is obvious—and alarming. Similar curricula are under serious consideration for implementation in public schools at all levels in the Seattle area.[27]

HOW THIS AFFECTS THE BROADER WORLD

Unlike Vegas, what happens in the university doesn't stay in the university. Universities are cultural centers, research institutes, and halls of *education*. University culture leaks out into the broader culture almost by osmosis. Many people gravitate to the university's events, productions, and outreach programs, and are thereby influenced by its culture. Universities are among the best, and ideally the *least biased*, centers of knowledge production—just compare other research centers connected to corporations or politically motivated think tanks. As a society, we turn to universities to help identify which statements, ideas, and values we can trust. Universities then transmit both information and intellectual culture to students. In this way, these institutions produce the educational and cultural elite, who will later go into the professions, head industries, establish charities, produce media, and shape public policy. Done right, universities are invaluable. Done wrong, they are a means of harmful cultural indoctrination without equal.

The most visible manifestation of Social Justice scholarship is Social Justice activism. The most notorious example of this is seen in the actions of the self-proclaimed anti-fascist group Antifa,[28] but activism for Social Justice can take many forms: from protesting peacefully to stalking and harassment,[29] from throwing milkshakes[30] to objecting to "kimono try-ons" as "cultural appropriation,"[31] from telling people to "check their privilege" to doing "antiracism" work. Social Justice activism has a significant influence over many areas of society, especially through social media. As noted, prestigious companies such as Google, the BBC, and Asda have fired employees on the basis of complaints couched in Social Justice terms and brought to wider attention via social media. Although most people—including the owners of the companies themselves—probably do not subscribe to Social Justice ideas, these ideas are clearly influential, as demonstrated by the fact that tech, broadcasting, and retail giants are ready to placate their advocates.

Major companies are also increasingly called to account for their products. In 2019, Macy's found itself at the center of an outcry that began with *one offended person on Twitter*. They had to publicly apologize for producing a plate that showed portion sizes in terms of jeans sizes (which was considered "fat shaming").[32] They cancelled the line. The Japanese noodle giant "Nissin" apologized for and withdrew anime that depicted a Haitian-Japanese tennis player with pale skin and European features.[33] Gucci apologized and withdrew a sweater that some people believed produced the effect of "blackface."[34] The same accusation was levelled at some shoes produced by Katy Perry, now withdrawn.[35]

It is perhaps not surprising that large corporations have caved in so easily to Social Justice pressure. Their overriding goal is, after all, to make money, not to uphold liberal values. Since the majority of consumers and voters in Western countries support the general idea of social justice, and since most people fail to understand the difference between social justice and Social Justice, large corporations sometimes find that it is astute public relations to give in, at least on minor matters that do not much affect the bottom line, to the demands of Social Justice activists.

This may also go some way to explaining the wishy-washy stand of many university administrations. While universities in Western countries are supposed to be ardent defenders of liberal values such as freedom of debate, they are becoming increasingly bureaucratized, with power being taken away from professors and transferred to administrators—and increasingly being run like profit-oriented businesses. University administrators are as sensitive to public relations as corporate executives, though the political environment in which they navigate is quite different (especially for public universities, which are at the direct mercy of elected politicians). This produces a complex set of pressures on university administrators, in which the protection of academic freedom is frequently not the highest priority.

Online platforms currently seem to be tying themselves in knots with inconsistent and often seemingly inexplicable rules and codes of conduct. YouTube,[36] Patreon,[37] Facebook,[38] and Twitter[39] have been criticized for banning or demonetizing certain figures seen as problematic in Social Justice terms, but have also faced censure for having allowed the spread of "fake news," and enabled echo-chambers including far-right communities to form thus perpetuating polarisation and extremism. This is a complicated issue that cannot be properly addressed here but bears being mentioned.

Social Justice activists are very visible on social media and particularly keen to punish people who are influential within media and the arts. Calls for the punishment of celebrities, artists, athletes, and other prominent individuals who have spoken against Social Justice, often unwittingly, are often referred to as "cancel culture."[40] This chilling practice often involves the utter destruction of someone's career and reputation for something she might have said decades ago, or as a teenager. The black actor Kevin Hart was forced to step down as host of the Oscars, for example, when old tweets containing gay slurs were discovered,[41] and when he was later injured in a car accident, many Social Justice–oriented activists *celebrated* it. The lesbian presenter Ellen DeGeneres was also censured, for her qualified defense of him. Her crime: accepting his *mea culpa* on behalf of a community, some of whom didn't want it. She had already caused outrage by tweeting a humorous picture of herself appearing to ride on the back of Jamaican sprinter Usain Bolt, which some activists thought played into racist tropes.[42] Hollywood A-lister Matt Damon incurred online feminist wrath by saying that sexual assault occurred on a spectrum and describing a pat on the butt as different from rape,[43] and game-show host Mario Lopez was pressured to apologize by an online mob outraged by his view that parents shouldn't uncritically accept a three-year-old's self-defined gender identity.[44] Tennis superstar Martina Navratilova was attacked for arguing that it is not fair for trans women tennis players to compete against cis women.[45] John McEnroe also came under fire for saying Serena Williams would rank at about 700 against men. He later said he regretted the statement but that he did not consider it earth-shattering to say that there are physical differences between men and women.[46] The examples are nearly endless.

All of this comes from activists who have adopted Theory. Their underlying assumption, which is central to Theory, is that bigotry is everywhere, always, hiding just beneath the surface. The job of the Theorist as activist is to scrutinize texts, events, culture, activities, places, spaces, attitudes, mind-sets, phrasing, dress, and every other conceivable cultural artifact for hidden bigotry, then expose it and purge it and its sources from society—or at least access to the means of cultural production. Sometimes, as with DeGeneres' picture of herself on Usain Bolt's back, such bigotry is seen as an attempt to prop up an allegedly "white supremacist" culture (which is accused of seeing black men as "beasts of burden"). At other times, as when DeGeneres defended Hart, it is interpreted as speaking over a marginalized community and erasing its identity by negating its claim to offense or victimhood. At still other times—as with Damon, Lopez, Navratilova, and McEnroe—the problem is simply presenting a view that runs counter to Theory itself.

The Social Justice policing of language and thought also affects art itself. The objections usually fall into one of two sometimes contradictory categories—not representing minority groups on the one hand, and appropriating aspects of minority culture, on the other. Social Justice activism assumes that racist and supremacist attitudes are omnipresent and looks closely until it finds examples. It will calculate the proportion of women, people of color, trans people, gays or lesbians, disabled, or fat people in a book or film and object if any group is underrepresented, in its view. The absence, misrepresentation, or underrepresentation of such groups is understood to "erase" minorities and "deny their validity to exist," while upholding white supremacy, patriarchy, heteronormativity, cisnormativity, ableism, or fatphobia.

The opposite issue—*appropriation*—is also a significant source of complaints. This draws on the idea of standpoint theory, in which knowledge is rooted in "lived experience" and it is considered abhorrent for a character with a marginalized identity to be created or depicted by someone who is not a member of her group. Hence, we see demands that actors only play characters from their own identity groups—so a straight woman cannot be allowed to play a lesbian or trans woman in a film, nor can an able-bodied person take on the role of a disabled person. Similarly, we see demands that writers with particular marginalized identities be employed behind the scenes because it is forbidden for someone to "speak into" an experience of oppression. These situations become fruitful sites for importing Social Justice into media because the activists who demand these roles are building their careers by it.

Sometimes, concerns about representing minorities and concerns about appropriation are combined—as when trans activists pressured Scarlett Johansson out of playing a transmasculine character.[47] However, sometimes these demands are mutually contradictory, as when J. K. Rowling was condemned for not including people of color among her main protagonists and having no explicitly gay or trans characters in the

Harry Potter books,[48] yet was also criticized for including Native American wizarding lore.[49] Musicians and artists are particularly vulnerable to accusations of cultural appropriation. Madonna has been criticized for appropriating Indian and Hispanic culture and Gwen Stefani for appropriating Japanese and Native American aesthetics.[50] Even black artists are not immune: Rihanna has been accused of appropriating Chinese culture[51] and Beyoncé of appropriating Indian Bollywood styles.[52] This clearly obstructs the production of art. This is what Theory looks like when put into practice.

Media and art can also be negatively impacted when books, art, films, or video games are scrutinized as "discourse" and problematized on the grounds of the power dynamics which they "speak into." Of course, there genuinely are examples of negative stereotypes and legitimate criticisms and insightful analyses can be made of them. However, much of the recent analysis of "discourses" is both highly interpretive and unfalsifiable. Even Dr. Seuss books can be argued to be racist,[53] and the depictions of black people in film can be critiqued on the grounds of alleged stereotypes which include black women being presented as strong and tough characters.[54] It seems difficult to resolve this issue as it is likely that black women being weak and submissive would not go down well either. This uncharitable approach is particularly common in gender analysis. Feminist scholars and activists have measured the number of words spoken by women in comparison to men in certain films, for example,[55] and critiqued the sexualized portrayal of women.[56]

Not only is this tedious; it is costly, including to members of the groups it claims to help. As well as casting doubt on more rigorous and measured analyses, postmodern feminist analysis which assumes a gendered discourse to run through everything can limit the range of possible female characters. 20th Century Fox felt obliged to apologize after producing a billboard showing the *X-Men* supervillain Mystique being choked by Apocalypse after feminists like Rose McGowan complained about the "casual violence against women" portrayed in the image.[57] It would seem that female superheroes and villains can either not get into fights or must win them without ever getting hit themselves. Similarly, there has been criticism of the *Game of Thrones* character Sansa Stark for saying that having experienced rape and abuse made her stronger. Some feminists felt that this played into rape culture by somehow justifying rape.[58] If you are not a perpetual victim, in this view, you are complicit with the powers of evil. This analysis conveniently ignores the fact that a male character, Theon, also suffers sexual torture and even has his penis hacked off—and also becomes a stronger person as a result. How can female characters be depicted as powerful and resilient if they are not allowed to overcome abuse, violence, and adversity? These restrictions are likely to make female characters less interesting—an effect we are already starting to see. For example, while many people celebrated the introduction of a female "Doctor" in the series *Doctor Who*, some critics wondered why the producers had made her a less flawed and therefore less complex character than the male Doctors.[59] It seems likely that this was done to avoid arousing feminist ire.

Of potentially even greater concern is the impact Social Justice scholarship is having on medicine. Activism that holds that disability and obesity are socially constructed and that attempts to combat them are rooted in the hatred of disabled people and the obese can be positively dangerous. Some concrete examples of problems rooted in disability studies are to be found in activism around autism, deafness, and mental illness.

For example, a form of autism activism has grown fairly quickly in recent years. It is rooted in the premise that people on the autistic spectrum ought not to be considered disabled. There is much merit in this argument, since many high-functioning autistic individuals have pointed out that they are perfectly valuable and happy human beings, who are just wired somewhat atypically, and there is much evidence that, on average, autism is correlated with superior systemizing abilities.[60] However, other autistic people and their carers have pointed out that autism can often be profoundly disabling and distressing and autistic activism makes it harder for those more severely affected to receive support.[61] Others have pointed out that complicated Social Justice rules about language, bias, and social interactions are often particularly difficult for autistic people to follow and that the neurologically atypical, who tend to be overrepresented in careers like technology, engineering, and physics, are particularly vulnerable to running afoul of such rules.[62] James Damore, the autistic Google technician—who responded literally to a request for feedback on how to get more women into tech and was subsequently fired—is a good example. It is also worrying that autism activists have tended to respond to antiscientific claims that vaccines cause autism with accusations of ableism—why assume that being autistic is a bad thing?—rather than by pointing out that the claims are not true. This muddies already dangerously murky waters.

As deaf activists point out, cochlear implants sometimes work imperfectly and can be disorienting and stressful to use: deaf people should therefore not be pressured to tolerate them.[63] However, deaf activists have also bewilderingly claimed that offering the hearing parents of deaf children the option of having their children fitted with the implants is akin to genocide of the deaf. Some have advocated a deaf identity politics, which regards those who wish to try to restore their hearing as deserters. This is far from helpful.

Mental health activism also frequently regards mental illness as a marginalized identity. One problem with this approach is that people tend to get attached to their identities and this may discourage some from seeking treatment and trying to recover. Another problem is that patients may mistake symptoms of physical illness for imagined psychosomatic features of an identity-status-granting mental illness like stress, anxiety, or depression. While activists have done good work in addressing unkind, ignorant, and counterproductive stigmas attached to mental health problems, elevating mental illness to a victimhood-carrying identity status is profoundly unhelpful—especially for sufferers, since it tempts some to regard their illnesses not as treatable but as intrinsic aspects of their identity.

A similar problem arises in relation to fat activism, since being fat is also a marginalized identity, according to Social Justice scholarship. This is potentially even more dangerous. Central to fat activism is the belief that obesity is only considered unhealthy because of fat hatred and because we put too much trust in scientific discourses. This view is highly seductive to many dangerously obese people, particularly women, who have found it very difficult to lose weight. Rather than seek medical or psychological support, they can learn to love their bodies as they are. The body positivity movement promotes morbidly obese models as beautiful and healthy, despite the abundant evidence that obesity is linked to diabetes, heart disease, polycystic ovaries, joint and respiratory problems, and several forms of cancer.[64] Fat activists campaigned against the organization Cancer Research after the charity informed people of the risks on their billboards.[65] Others have campaigned against slim advertising models.[66] There are dozens of websites informing morbidly obese people how to find a doctor who won't tell them their weight is unhealthy. This attitude can kill.

CULTURES OF CODDLING AND VICTIMHOOD

These social changes exemplify the postmodern principles and themes in action. Though perhaps less than 10 percent of the population holds such ideas,[67] they exert considerable influence over how society understands itself. This tells us that postmodernism, now in an applicable and reified form, is not only alive and well but rapidly becoming increasingly dominant within our societies. Two important books, both published in 2018, address the causes, manifestations, and potential dangers of these social changes. They are *The Coddling of the American Mind: How Good Intentions and Bad Ideas Are Setting Up a Generation for Failure*[68] by Greg Lukianoff and Jonathan Haidt and *The Rise of Victimhood Culture: Microaggressions, Safe Spaces, and the New Culture Wars*[69] by Bradley Campbell and Jason Manning. Lukianoff and Haidt focus on psychology and Campbell and Manning on sociology, but their approaches are complementary. These are different aspects of the same phenomenon.

In *The Coddling of the American Mind*, Lukianoff and Haidt chart a dramatic decrease in young people's resilience and ability to cope with difficult ideas and hurt feelings. The authors do not belittle these struggles, but emphasize that they are a painful consequence of the acceptance of three "Great Untruths." These are the belief that people are fragile ("Anything that doesn't kill you makes you weaker"), the belief in emotional reasoning ("Always trust your feelings"), and the belief in Us versus Them ("Life is a battle between good people and evil people"). Their central thesis is that these untruths combine to produce a psychological approach to the world that functions as a kind of reverse cognitive behavioral therapy (CBT). CBT enables people to overcome habits of catastrophizing and encourages them to put things into perspective, think about events calmly and charitably, and act appropriately. The Great Untruths, on the other hand, encourage a negative, paranoid, and self-sabotaging mind-set.

These, we would argue, are some of the psychological problems that arise from Theory. The belief that people are fragile and that they are weakened by unpleasant or upsetting experiences is Theorized within Social Justice scholarship and activism as marginalized groups being harmed, erased, invalidated, or subjected to violence by dominant discourses. The commitment to always trusting one's feelings, rather than trying to be objective or charitable, reflects the Social Justice focus on experiential over objective knowledge. This is also tied to identity. Marginalized people's experiences and emotions are, for Theory, authoritative (when they support Theory, that is; they're false in one way or another when they don't). White people's experiences, emotions, and arguments—unless they agree with Social Justice tenets—can only be considered as signs of fragility, rather than as ethically and/or factually defensible positions. This is all underpinned by the belief that life is a battle between good people and bad people, as represented by dominant and marginalized discourses, in which some people try to maintain oppressive systems of power and privilege at the expense of others.

In *The Rise of Victimhood Culture*, Campbell and Manning describe the different modes of social conflict resolution in different times and cultures. They look at how people relate to each other, moralize those relationships, establish their place in the world, and seek status and justice. They identify the recent emergence of a culture of victimhood, which differs from both *dignity culture* and *honor culture*. In an honor culture, they explain, it is important to refuse to be dominated by anyone. Thus, people are highly sensitive to slights and respond to any indication of disrespect with immediate aggression, or even violence. Self-sufficiency is a core value in this kind of culture, which dominated the Western world for hundreds of years and is still prevalent in some non-Western cultures and in certain subcultures within the West, such as street gangs. It was superseded by dignity culture. Dignity culture also emphasizes self-sufficiency, but it encourages a different kind of resilience. In a dignity culture, people are encouraged to ignore most slights, be less sensitive to verbal insults, work most problems out between individuals, and resolve serious conflicts by legal means, rather than by taking matters into their own hands.

The new victimhood culture that Campbell and Manning see shares honor culture's sensitivity to slight, but responds with a show of weakness rather than strength. It maintains dignity culture's reliance on authorities to resolve conflict, rather than taking matters into one's own hands, but it dispenses with its commitment to trying to ignore slights or seeking a peaceful resolution first. In victimhood culture, status comes from being seen as victimized and therefore eliciting support from sympathetic third parties. Consequently, it works to generate sympathies in others and to make public cases for help along that axis. As a result, it tends to read power imbalances and victimization into many interactions—and even, occasionally, invents them—to exploit what Campbell and Manning refer to as "the natural moral currency of victimhood."[70] The rise of this culture has a great deal to do with the postmodern conception of the world as constructed in systems of power and privilege perpetuated in language and its newer reified manifestation, which assumes that oppression is omnipresent, seeks to make that oppression visible, and aims to dismantle it.

The valorization of victimhood and a Theoretical approach that fixates on how power oppresses and marginalizes go hand-in-hand. Victims vindicate the Theory, thus gaining status with those who subscribe to it. The moral imperative is to protect marginalized people from the nonobvious forms of harm contained in attitudes and discourses. In order to identify such problems, one has to read society through Lukianoff and Haidt's three Great Untruths. To address them, one has to dispense with honor culture's valorization of strength and dignity culture's resilience to slight and embrace what Campbell and Manning have called the culture of victimhood.

In many ways, the emergence of this culture of victimhood and coddling in much of the West suggests that activism for social justice (in the real sense) has become a victim of its own success. Accusations that people who focus on microaggressions and pronoun missteps don't have any *real* problems to worry about underestimate the extent to which these issues are genuinely experienced as painful (as Lukianoff and Haidt show, there has been an increase in suicide among young people, though the reasons for this uptick may be more complicated). However, a society that is free to worry about seemingly minor social faux pas or unwanted ideas and attitudes is one in which most of its members are probably not experiencing any directly life-threatening circumstances.

In their discussion of paranoid parenting and "safetyism," Lukianoff and Haidt argue that parents frequently fail to celebrate the eradication of fatal diseases like diphtheria and polio[71] and the decrease in dangerous products and practices, which have drastically reduced child mortality.[72] Instead they anxiously focus on smaller things that could still be potentially harmful. Furthermore, the focus has shifted from physical harm to psychological discomfort, creating an expectation of *emotional safety*.[73] Similarly, Campbell and Manning note that people seem most inclined to look for evidence of racism and bigotry where it is least evident, noting,

> We thought of Emile Durkheim, the nineteenth-century French sociologist, who famously asked his readers to imagine what would happen in a "society of saints." The answer is that there would still be sinners because "faults which appear venial to the layman" would there create scandal.[74]

We have made a similar argument that the development of postmodern ideas within the Social Justice context, with its focus on and catastrophizing of racist, sexist, and homophobic attitudes and discourses, has coincided with the radical reduction of such attitudes and discourses. It is not a coincidence that the applied postmodern turn began in the late 1980s, just as the Civil Rights Movement, liberal feminism, and Gay Pride began to see diminishing returns after twenty years of remarkably rapid progress towards racial, gender, and LGBT equality on a legal and political level. With Jim Crow laws dismantled, Empire fallen, male homosexuality legalized, and discrimination on the grounds of race and sex criminalized, Western society was newly aware and ashamed of its long history of oppression of marginalized groups and wanted to continue righting those wrongs. Since the most significant legal battles had been won, all that remained to tackle were sexist, racist, and homophobic attitudes and discourses. Postmodernism, with its focus on discourses of power and socially constructed knowledge, was perfectly placed to address these. As racism, sexism, and homophobia have continued to decline, however, deeper and deeper readings of situations and texts and increasingly complicated Theoretical arguments have been required to detect them. The increasingly interpretive, Theoretical analysis of discourses found within Social Justice approaches is a direct reflection of the radical reduction of social injustice.

SOCIAL JUSTICE INSTITUTIONALIZED—A CASE STUDY

There is a significant danger in Social Justice imposing its social constructivist beliefs on the institutions of society. A good case study of this is provided by the events at Evergreen State College, which got overtaken by the ideas of critical race Theory generally and of the Theorist and educator Robin DiAngelo specifically. When biology professor Bret Weinstein objected to white people being asked to absent themselves from campus for a day, a contingent of student-activists reacted angrily. The result was mayhem: student-activists began to protest and riot at events all over campus. Proceedings at the college were entirely disrupted, and graduation had to be held off campus. The student-activists besieged the college president, George Bridges, and repeatedly belittled him, insisting he lower his hands whenever he spoke and that he give in to all their demands.[75] The problem escalated to the point where student-activists were barricading doors against the police, holding faculty members as de facto hostages, and, armed with baseball bats, stopping cars to search for Weinstein. Meanwhile, they loudly lamented their own lack of safety on campus as "black and brown bodies," even as the university president told the campus police to stand down and let everything occur unhindered.

The campus descended into mob madness, and Evergreen has not yet recovered from it. Most chillingly and most tellingly, protesters were both unwilling to listen to and seemingly unable to comprehend the views they were protesting against. When Weinstein asked for evidence that the campus was racist, they shouted over him and told him that the request for evidence was itself racist. Had Weinstein any understanding of what it was like to be black, they insisted, he would know. Their evidence was that they lived the experience every day. So, instead of making any case for their incendiary claims about the college, which appear not to be supported by any data, the student-activists simply chanted Social Justice slogans like "white silence is violence" and demanded that the science department be monitored and its faculty brought in, retrained, and sanctioned for their inherently problematic views.

There is a one-word answer to how this could have happened: Theory. What happened at Evergreen is a demonstration at the microcosmic scale of what happens when Theory gets applied to an autonomous institution in a real-world setting. The Evergreen establishment set itself up for destruction by accepting enough of the "antiracism" views of critical race educators like Robin DiAngelo—not least the idea of white fragility—to have lost its ability to mount a defense against the protestors. Indeed, when some students of color expressed support for Weinstein and made similar statements to his, the mob shouted them down and dismissed their own lived experience, most probably because it didn't align with the "authentic" experience detailed by Theory. Thus, once enough people, most notably the faculty member Naima Lowe, who taught media studies at Evergreen at the time of the meltdown, accused the college of being a racist institution overrun by white supremacy, the faculty and administrators, who had taken on "antiracist" concepts from critical race Theory, had no recourse but to accept the accusation and start making the changes demanded.

What else could they do? The Theory of "white fragility," among others, tied their hands such that to do anything else was, in the eyes of the prevailing Theory, to confirm their complicity in the very problem they had every reason to deny. The very few who, like Bret Weinstein, argued back, expressed skepticism, asked for evidence, stood their ground, denied the charge, quietly voted against, or made consistent efforts to examine the proposed solution honestly were thereby accused of participation in the racist system and branded racist. Having accepted that "the question isn't 'did racism take place?' but rather 'how did racism manifest in that situation?',"[76] the only possible conclusion was that they were working for an intrinsically racist organization. Those were the charges.

Having accepted the Social Justice idea that the only possible way *not* to be complicit in racism is to accept the charge and take on an endless amount of antiracism work, as dictated by Theory, they were powerless against an extremist minority of faculty and students, particularly once administrators like the new president George Bridges got on board. It is extremely unlikely that the majority of the students and faculty at Evergreen who were sympathetic to the concerns voiced by Social Justice knew that this was what they were signing up for.

This dynamic is predictable once Theory is introduced into a closed system. The ideas begin to gain some currency with some of the population, who become sympathetic partisans and begin to take on the Theoretical worldview. In that state, they "know" that systemic bigotry is present in all institutions, including their own, and that it lurks beneath the surface in need of exposure and problematization through the "critical" methods. Eventually, a Theoretically relevant incident occurs or, as may have been the case at Evergreen, is manufactured, and the Theorists within that institution begin to focus intently on the revealed "problematics" at the bottom of the problem. This will be interpreted systemically, and the community fragments as every discussion and argument turns into a series of accusations and close readings of every utterance made by anyone who isn't being sufficiently Theoretical. To do anything but acquiesce and take up the fight on behalf of Theory is taken to "prove" one's complicity with the systemic problem at the institution's heart, and there is no recourse. If enough activists have adopted enough Theory in the institution by the time the incident occurs—and there will always be an incident eventually as even a misunderstanding or faux pas will qualify—Theory will consume the institution. If it folds, it deserved it because it was systemically bigoted in the first place. If it survives, even as a fragment of its former self, it will do so consistent with Theory or as a toxic battleground around Theory. This is not a bug of Theory; it's a feature. It is what the "critical" method at its heart was intended to do from the beginning. Indeed, this dynamic has played out in diverse settings beyond Evergreen, including online forums dedicated to hobbies like knitting,[77] the Atheism Movement of the early 2010s,[78] and even conservative churches.[79]

THEORY ALWAYS LOOKS GOOD ON PAPER

The ideas of Social Justice scholarship often look good on paper. That's almost always the way with bad theories. Take communism, for example. Communism presents the idea that an advanced and technological society can organize itself around cooperation and shared resources and minimize human exploitation. The injustices that spring from disparities between capitalism's winners and losers can be eliminated. With sufficient information—information that proves incredibly hard to get without markets, as we now know—surely we can redistribute goods and services in much fairer and more equitable ways, and surely the moral benefits are sufficient to inspire all good people to participate in such a system. We just have to get everyone on script. We just all have to co-operate. That's the theory. But, in practice, communism has generated some of the greatest atrocities of history and been responsible for the deaths of millions.

Communism is a great example of the human tendency to fail to appreciate how our best theories can fail catastrophically in practice, even if their adherents are motivated by an idealistic vision of "the greater good." Postmodernism began as a rejection of communism, along with all other grand theories belonging to the modern period, the Enlightenment, and the premodern faiths that came before them. The cynical Theorists whom we now recognize as the original postmodernists laid the groundwork for a new Theoretical approach to human hubris. Rather than following in the footsteps of their predecessors, who attempted grand, sweeping explanations and visions of how the world could and should work, they wanted to tear it all apart, right down to the foundations. They weren't just skeptical of specific visions of human progress: they were radically skeptical of the possibility of progress at all. This cynicism was effective. In becoming politically actionable, this cynicism was specifically applied to remake society—not just to complain about it—and thus evolved into Theories we face today, particularly in Social Justice scholarship and activism. On paper, those Theories seem to say good things. Let's get to the bottom of bigotry, oppression, marginalization, and injustice, and heal the world. If we could all just care a little more, and care in the right way, we could make our way to the right side of history. We just have to get everyone on script. We just have to get everyone to cooperate. We just have to ignore any problems and swear solidarity to the cause.

It isn't going to work. Social Justice is a nice-looking Theory that, once put into practice, will fail, and which could do tremendous damage in the process. Social Justice cannot succeed because it does not correspond with reality or with core human intuitions of fairness and reciprocity and because it is an idealistic metanarrative. Nevertheless, metanarratives can sound convincing and obtain sufficient support to significantly influence society and the way it thinks about knowledge, power and language. Why? Partly because we humans aren't as smart as we think we are, partly because most of us are idealists on at least some level, partly because we tend to lie to ourselves when we want something to work. But Theory is a metanarrative and metanarratives are, in fact, unreliable.

The postmodernists got that right. What they got disastrously wrong is mistaking effective and adaptive systems for metanarratives. Religions and many theoretical constructions are metanarratives, but liberalism and science are *not*. Liberalism and science are systems—not just neat little theories—because they are *self-skeptical* rather than *self-certain*, by design. This is a reasoned—not a radical—skepticism. They put the *empirical* first, rather than the *theoretical*. They are self-correcting. Liberal systems like regulated capitalism, republican democracy, and science resolve conflicts by subjecting human economies, societies, and knowledge-production to evolutionary processes that—over time, and with persistent effort—produce reliable societies, governments, and provisionally true statements about the world. The proof is that almost everything has changed over the last five hundred years, especially in the West. As Theory points out, that progress has sometimes been problematic, but it has still been *progress*. Things are better than they were five hundred years ago, for most people most of the time, and this is undeniable.

10 AN ALTERNATIVE TO THE IDEOLOGY OF SOCIAL JUSTICE

Liberalism Without Identity Politics

Postmodern Theory and liberalism do not merely exist in tension: they are almost directly at odds with one another. Liberalism sees knowledge as something we can learn about reality, more or less objectively; Theory sees knowledges as completely created by humans—stories we tell ourselves, largely in the unwitting service of maintaining our own social standing, privilege, and power. Liberalism embraces accurate categorization and clarity of understanding and exposition; Theory blurs boundaries and erases categories, while reveling in manufactured ambiguity. Liberalism values the individual and universal human values; Theory rejects both in favor of group identity and identity politics. Although left-leaning liberals tend to favor the underdog, liberalism across the board centers human dignity; Theory focuses on victimhood. Liberalism encourages disagreement and debate as means to getting at the truth; Theory rejects these as ways of reinforcing dominant discourses that suppress certain perspectives and insists that we *cannot* get to "the" truth, but only to "our" truths, which are rooted in our values. Liberalism accepts the correspondence theory of truth—that a statement is true if it accurately describes reality; Theory promotes the idea that truth is a "language game" and that words, ultimately, only point to other words and can never correspond concretely to reality—unless those words describe oppression. Liberalism accepts criticism, even of itself, and is therefore self-correcting; Theory cannot be criticized. Liberalism believes in progress; Theory is radically cynical about the possibility of progress. Liberalism is inherently constructive because of the evolutionary processes it engenders; Theory is inherently corrosive because of its cynicism and attachment to methods it calls "critical." This is no surprise since *critical* methods have always been explicitly and by design critical *of liberalism* as a means of social, political, and economic organization.

Liberalism also contains both the features and flaws that allowed postmodern Theory to undermine its public status. By tolerating differences of opinion and viewpoint diversity, liberalism allows for people not to support liberalism. By insisting on freedom of debate, liberalism explicitly permits and even welcomes criticism of its own tenets. By proclaiming universal human values, liberalism invites attention to the ways in which Western societies, both past and present, have failed to live up to those proclaimed values. By proclaiming the legal and political equality of all citizens, liberalism invites attention to the ways in which some citizens have acquired vastly more political influence than others. By being ever focused on progress, a liberal society shines the spotlight on its own imperfections, in the hope that they can be corrected or at least mitigated. Liberalism is not perfect. Nevertheless it is the antidote to Theory.

A liberal society can be dissatisfying because it is utterly impersonal. Under a liberal order, no individual or group is supposed to get special treatment. Not everyone likes this. Moreover, since liberalism aims to be perfectly unbiased on its front end, it creates inequities on its back end, some of which can be severe and need to be adjusted for. Capitalism, for example, is the purely liberal economic system. After having implemented this system, we learned that utterly unregulated capitalism is a catastrophe—this was what Karl Marx was reacting against. Paradoxical as it may seem, because of the power of monopolies and the influence of dishonest actors, a free market requires regulation—an infrastructure that prevents the system from getting out of hand. The ancient Greeks also recognized the tyranny inherent in the liberal political order, democracy, when it is not properly managed. The American experiment, in particular, recognized that a republican adjustment called *representative democracy*, involving divisions of power and limitations on the powers of government, is a necessary component of democratic systems and prevents them from descending into mob rule and the tyranny of the majority. These systems depend utterly on the liberal approach to knowledge production. Postmodern Theory views the failures of the liberal order and its knowledge-producing systems in a cynical way—as means by which the powerful obscure the limiting potential of oppression—and focuses on how unfair they can be, particularly to those who start out disadvantaged, since the system has no mechanisms to compensate for their bad luck. It would thus tear the systems down.

A further difficulty with liberalism is that it is difficult to define, which opens it up to Theoretical deconstruction. Liberalism is perhaps best understood as a desire to gradually make society fairer, freer, and less cruel, one practical goal after another. This is because liberalism is a system of conflict resolution, not a solution to human conflicts. In being a system that works through the inputs of its participants, it offers up no one in particular in whom to place our trust, which violates our deepest human intuitions. It is not revolutionary, but neither is it reactionary: its impulse is neither to turn society on its head nor to keep it from changing. Instead, liberalism is always a work in progress. This is because it actually works—it leads to progress—so, as it solves each problem, it moves on to new problems, continually finding new conflicts to resolve, and new goals to achieve. In this way, liberalism involves an evolutionary process, and processes of this kind are, by definition, always in progress and never complete. Such processes, therefore, invariably make mistakes and sometimes even go completely awry, before being subjected to the necessary criticisms and correction. Problematizing is Theory's way of exploiting these errors. When done right, this can be useful, as it highlights problems before they get out of control—the willingness of liberal systems to accept self-criticism is, in fact, the *feature* of liberalism that critical methods like postmodern Theory exploit to undermine it. When done cynically, as with Theory, it can destroy people's trust in the liberal system and obscure from them that it is this system that has made modernity possible.

Liberalism is also hard to place. It makes little sense to speak of when it began or how it developed, even though we can name philosophers who have articulated its essence, most of whom lived in the West in modern times. These thinkers include Mary Wollstonecraft, John Stuart Mill, John Locke, Thomas Jefferson, Francis Bacon, Thomas Paine, and many, many others. They drew inspiration from earlier thinkers in other traditions, reaching all the way back to Classical Greece two thousand years earlier, and provided concepts and arguments that continue to persuade and inspire liberals to this day. They did not, however, invent liberalism, which belongs neither to a historical period nor to a geographical location. The underlying impulse toward liberalism can be found in every time and place, whenever people want to modify an existing system in order to keep the good bits and eradicate the failures—especially when such failures constrain, oppress, or hurt people. It exists in tension with other impulses, particularly those that don't trust an impersonal *system* to solve any problems. This makes liberalism particularly susceptible to postmodern corruption, because the cynical Theorists can use those failures and harms as an excuse to condemn liberalism itself.

WHY FREEDOM OF DEBATE IS SO IMPORTANT

We are all accustomed to thinking of freedom of speech as a universal human right enshrined in democratic countries' constitutions and in the Universal Declaration of Human Rights. In looking at freedom of speech in this way, we tend naturally to focus on the right of the *speaker* to say what she believes, without censorship or punishment. But this focus leads us sometimes to forget the paramount importance of freedom of speech for the *listeners* or *potential listeners*—and especially for the listeners who *disagree* with the speaker (as well as those who are undecided).

This important aspect of the freedom of debate was emphasized by John Stuart Mill in his 1859 essay *On Liberty*:

But the peculiar evil of silencing the expression of an opinion is,

that it is robbing the human race; posterity as well as the existing generation; those who dissent from the opinion, still more than
those who hold it.[1]

There are two ways, Mill says, in which censorship harms the op-
ponents of the view being censored. Firstly,

If the opinion is right, they are deprived of the opportunity of ex-
changing error for truth.[2]

And secondly,

if wrong, they lose, what is almost as great a benefit, the clearer
perception and livelier impression of truth, produced by its colli-
sion with error.[3]

The first harm invoked by Mill is clear: suppression of a true idea—
like the Catholic Church's suppression, in the seventeenth century, of the
idea that the Earth travels around the Sun rather than vice versa—sets
back humanity in innumerable ways. But even if the majority view is in
most respects correct, and the view being censored mostly wrong, per-
mitting open debate is still crucial for allowing the majority view to be
refined and improved.

Mill's second harm is more subtle, but no less important, and to
illustrate it he takes an example from a sphere that is ordinarily less con-
tentious than politics or religion: namely, science. Isaac Newton founded
modern physics in 1687, writing the equations of what came to be called
Newtonian mechanics and which are nowadays taught in every fresh-
man physics course. Over the next century, scientists accumulated overwhelming evidence, from both terrestrial and astronomical observations,
that Newtonian physics was correct (even to the point of predicting
accurately, in 1846, the existence and precise location of the hitherto-
unknown planet Neptune). But suppose that, at some point in this history, the government (or even just the universities) had decided that, in
view of the overwhelming evidence of the correctness of Newtonian
mechanics, it would henceforth be forbidden to dispute it. In that case,

Mill observes, we would now have much less reason to believe in the correctness of Newtonian mechanics! It is precisely the fact that Newtonian mechanics has held up in the face of free and open debate that gives us such justified confidence in its validity:

> If even the Newtonian philosophy were not permitted to be questioned, mankind could not feel as complete assurance of its truth as they now do. The beliefs which we have most warrant for, have no safeguard to rest on, but a standing invitation to the whole world to prove them unfounded. If the challenge is not accepted, or is accepted and the attempt fails, we are far enough from certainty still; but we have done the best that the existing state of human reason admits of; we have neglected nothing that could give the truth a chance of reaching us.[4]

In fact this story has an interesting twist, which Mill could not have foreseen, and which illustrates his first harm. It turns out that Newtonian mechanics is not correct! It is an amazingly good approximation for nearly all practical purposes, but not exactly correct. This was discovered by Albert Einstein in 1905–1915, more than 30 years after Mill's death: Newtonian mechanics is replaced and superseded by Einstein's special and general relativity. But this important advance in science might never have occurred if criticism of Newton's theory had been forbidden. (And with it, the technological applications—from radiotherapy for cancer to the Global Positioning System (GPS)—that rely, in one way or another, on Einstein's relativity.)[5]

Mill was primarily concerned with censorship by governments or ecclesiastical authorities, but the arguments in favor of freedom of debate apply equally well to censorship carried out by corporations or universities, or even by groups of private citizens—self-appointed guardians of public virtue—wielding the power of social ostracism.

Thus, even if Theory were 99 percent correct, and its critics (like ourselves) 99 percent wrong, freedom of debate would still be advantageous to Theorists: firstly by allowing them to improve their Theory further, and secondly by giving them—and us—more *rational confidence* in the correctness of Theory by virtue of its successful confrontation with opposing ideas. However, if what Theorists are seeking is not rational confidence in the truth of their ideas—and it often isn't, as both reason and objective truth are often understood as oppressive manifestations of white, Western, male power—but merely the subjective feeling of certainty, then freedom of debate may, alas, become, from their point of view, optional or even counterproductive. Sadly, this attitude is amply demonstrated by their rather conspicuous unwillingness to engage in debate and tendency to regard attempts of others to engage with them as *fragility* or *wilful ignorance* or *privilege preserving epistemic pushback*.

THEORY DOESN'T UNDERSTAND LIBERALISM

Liberalism has firm tenets of individual liberty, equality of opportunity, free and open inquiry, free speech and debate, and humanism, and, although these are expansive ideals, they are also strong and consistent. This is why they have slowly but surely won out over the last five hundred years and produced the freest, most equal societies, with the least suffering and oppression, the world has ever known. Liberalism's success can be put down to a few key points. It is intrinsically goal-oriented, problem-solving, self-correcting, and—despite what postmodernists think—genuinely *progressive*. While some on the far right might want to halt progress or even consider it to have gone too far already, and some on the far left consider progress a myth and insist that life in liberal democracies is still as oppressive as it ever has been (thanks, Foucault), liberalism both appreciates progress and is optimistic that it will continue. Within the liberal spectrum, which encompasses people on both the political right and left, everyone agrees that liberalism implies progress, though the speed and means of that progress are up for debate.

For cognitive psychologist Steven Pinker, it is vital that we appreciate how much progress we have made in liberal democracies—and that we owe that progress to Enlightenment humanism—if we wish it to continue:

A liberal democracy is a precious achievement. Until the messiah comes, it will always have problems, but it's better to solve those problems than to start a conflagration and hope that something better arises from the ashes and bones. By failing to take note of the gifts of modernity, social critics poison voters against responsible custodians and incremental reformers who can consolidate the tremendous progress we have enjoyed and strengthen the conditions that will bring us more.[6]

The journalist Edmund Fawcett, in a preface to the paperback edition of his book *Liberalism: The Life of an Idea* (2015), addresses the criticism that liberalism is too broad and ill-defined to have a productive locus to organize around. For Fawcett, "Liberalism is bound to be capacious. Among its remarkable achievements was to create a kind of politics in which profound ethical discord and sharp conflicts of material interest might be brokered, assuaged, or held at bay rather than fought out with a view to total victory."[7] With reference to a review of the earlier hardcover edition of the book, he adds, in beautifully testy tones,

> Samuel Brittan objected in the *Financial Times* that after 1945 my liberalism included everybody but "authoritarians and totalitarians." Had he added "populists and theocrats" to those I excluded, I would have taken his complaint as praise. Liberal democracy is not the only attractive-looking path for present-day capitalism. Non-liberal paths beckon as well. They include authoritarianism, popular nationalism, and religious totalitarianism. An understanding of liberalism that excluded such alternatives was, I would say, doing its definitional job well.[8]

This is a good way to understand liberalism—as opposition to illiberalism. While liberalism might be hard to define, illiberalism is easily recognizable in totalitarian, hierarchical, censorious, feudal, patriarchal, colonial, or theocratic states and in people who want to bring about such states, limit freedoms, or justify inequalities. Liberals oppose this, not because they want to establish their own authoritarian regime, but because they are opposed to all such regimes. Therefore, liberalism is expansive, but it is not weak. For Fawcett, the four themes of liberalism are "acceptance of conflict, resistance to power, faith in progress, and respect for persons."[9] Liberalism accepts that it will always be fighting unjust and oppressive powers and mediating between different ideas. It is opposed not to conservatism in general but to the kind of conservatism that seeks to conserve hierarchies of class, race, or gender. Postmodern movements fight oppressive power systems too, but they have no faith in progress—and neither do they believe that we can continue to make progress by persisting in those things we do well and reforming what we do badly. Furthermore, liberalism respects people both as individuals and as members of the human race. It does not respect identity groups or collectives per se: it values the individual and the universal; the human and humanity.

For journalist and essayist Adam Gopnik, liberalism is inseparable from humanism. He observes:

> Liberalism has many mouths, but the liberalism that those of us who think of ourselves as liberal humanists want to defend— opposed both to the leftists with whom we sometimes make common cause and the right wing with which we sometimes share common premises—has one true point, equally potent, equally plain. *Liberalism is an evolving political practice that makes the case for the necessity and possibility of (imperfectly) egalitarian social reform and ever greater (if not absolute) tolerance of human difference through reasoned and (mostly) unimpeded conversation, demonstration, and debate.*[10] (emphasis in original)

This is pluralism, but not relativism; it welcomes viewpoint diversity, but is not committed to respecting all views on principle. Gopnik stresses the need for conversation and *debate*. This is the marketplace of ideas, in which better ideas eventually win out, allowing society to advance. This stands against the conservative position that some ideas are sacred (literally or otherwise) and must not be challenged and against the postmodern position that some ideas are dangerous and must not be spoken. Liberalism is optimistic and humanism has confidence in humans. If we are able to get all our ideas together, with no holds barred, and encourage free expression and civil debate, we can make the world better. This is not a Utopian fantasy. It's messy, imperfect, and slow. Also, the last five hundred years have showed that it works. Writes Gopnik, "What liberalism has in its favor are the facts. Liberals get nothing accomplished—except everything, eventually."[11] Liberals, he tells us,

> believe in reform rather than revolution because the results are in: it works better. More permanent positive social change is made incrementally rather than by revolutionary transformation. This was, originally, something like a temperamental instinct, a preference for social peace bought at a reasonable price, but by now it is a rational preference. The nameable goals of the socialist and even Marxist manifestos of the nineteenth century—public education, free health care, a government role in the economy, votes for women—have all been achieved, mostly peacefully and mostly successfully, by acts of reform in liberal countries. The attempt to achieve them by fiat and command, in the Soviet Union and China and elsewhere, created catastrophes, moral and practical, on a scale still almost impossible to grasp.[12]

When Gopnik argues that liberalism is the *rational* preference, it is hard to disagree with him given the evidence that liberal methods work and—despite their incremental approach—they work remarkably fast. It is no coincidence that liberalism, rationalism, and empiricism go together under the banner of the "Enlightenment" or that, together, they have decreased human suffering so much through technological improvements, effective infrastructure, and medical and other scientific advances, as well as by upholding human rights. These concepts are mutually supportive and reinforcing. Despite the postmodern claim that Enlightenment thinking was and is too confident that it has all the answers, it is, in fact, characterized by doubt and humility about humanity's capabilities. For Pinker,

> It begins with skepticism. The history of human folly, and our own susceptibility to illusions and fallacies, tell us that men and women are fallible. One therefore ought to seek good reasons for believing something. Faith, revelation, tradition, dogma, authority, the ecstatic glow of subjective certainty—all are recipes for error, and should be dismissed as sources of knowledge.[13]

Does this sound like skepticism towards metanarratives? That's because it is. That skepticism—treated responsibly under liberal thought— has helped us advance so far and so fast that some people have the luxury of dedicating their lives to obscure anti-Enlightenment theories, instead of eking out a living as subsistence farmers, before dying in childbirth or of smallpox. Postmodernism didn't invent skepticism: it perverted it into a corrosive cynicism. Although postmodern Theorists frequently tell us that liberals and humanists are regressive and want to take us backwards, it is they who advocate returning to satisfying local narratives, revelation, and the "ecstatic glow of subjective certainty," rather than pursuing progress in the way that has worked so well.

Some might argue that an appreciation of the Enlightenment and of the advance of science and reason implies support for atrocities like slavery, genocide, and colonialism, which accompanied our "progress." This might seem like a good argument if it weren't for the fact that slavery, invasions, and brutal occupations have happened throughout history. What was special about the modern period is that emerging liberalism showed that those activities were wrong. Others might say that progress is a myth because Nazism, the Holocaust, and genocidal communism all occurred less than a century ago—and *after* the Enlightenment. This would be reasonable if the argument were that everything that came after the Enlightenment was liberal. In fact, these phenomena show what happens when totalitarianism is allowed to dominate over liberalism. Liberalism has not always been victorious, nor will it always prevail. But life is much better when it does and we should take steps to ensure that.

Liberalism, despite its shortcomings, is simply better for humans. As Pinker argues in *Enlightenment Now*, "The data show that more liberal countries are also, on average, better educated, more urban, less fecund, less inbred (with fewer marriages among cousins), more peaceful, more democratic, less corrupt, and less crime- and coup-ridden."[14] It is simply astonishing that over the same twenty year period (1960–1980) during which women gained access to contraception and equal pay for equal work, racial and sexual discrimination in employment and other areas became illegal, and homosexuality was decriminalized, the postmodernists emerged and declared that it was time to stop believing in liberalism, science, reason, and the myth of progress. The only charitable explanation for this is that, in their nihilism and despair (not least at the failure of communism), they failed to understand what progress is and how it is achieved. Let's not follow in their footsteps. Don't stop believing in liberalism, science, reason, and progress. Instead, make a concerted effort to defend evidence-based knowledge, reason, and consistent ethical principles. The way to do this has been best described by Jonathan Rauch, under the label of "liberal science."

LIBERAL SCIENCE

In 1992, journalist Jonathan Rauch wrote an impassioned defense of liberalism in a book called *Kindly Inquisitors: The New Attacks on Free Thought*. There, he explains the virtues of the knowledge production method that liberalism relies on, which he calls "liberal science." This idea is described as the "liberal intellectual system"[15] and billed as the liberal contribution to "the reality industry," "charged with producing true statements about the external world."[16] Liberal science, to Rauch, is a system that applies two consistent rules: the "skeptical rule" and the "empirical rule."[17] These he summarizes as *"no one gets the final say"* and *"no one has personal authority,"*[18] respectively, arguing that "these peculiar rules are two of the most successful social conventions the human species has ever evolved."[19] Why? Because "those two rules define a decision-making system that people can agree to use to figure out whose opinions are worth believing,"[20] and it works because the system "may not fix the outcome in advance or for good (no final say)" and "may not distinguish between participants (no personal authority)."[21]

Rauch contrasts "the liberal principle" with four others, each of which is shown to be fatally inadequate to its task: looking for statements that are reliable enough to be called *knowledge* and resolving conflicts in the disagreements that inevitably come up around those claims. These principles are the fundamentalist principle, the simple egalitarian principle, the radical egalitarian principle, and the humanitarian principle.

"The Fundamentalist Principle: Those who know the truth should decide who is right."[22]

The fundamentalist principle is the bedrock of theocracies and secular totalitarian regimes; but we also see this fundamentalist impulse in the increasingly authoritarian nature of Social Justice scholarship and activism and in its attempts to shut down criticism. This way lies totalitarianism, if fundamentalists can get themselves in power.

> "*The Simple Egalitarian Principle:* All sincere persons' beliefs have equal claim to respect."[23]

This implies that something doesn't need to be true to be respected. This is the kind of epistemological and moral relativism that underlies Social Justice scholarship and activism.

> "*The Radical Egalitarian Principle:* Like the simple egalitarian principle, but the beliefs of persons in historically oppressed classes or groups get special consideration."[24]

This is at the core of "epistemic injustice" scholarship, which has characterized much of Theory since 2010. It relies on standpoint theory and the belief that all ideas are equally valid, although some have been devalued due to prejudice and now need to be foregrounded.

> "*The Humanitarian Principle:* Any of the above, but with the condition that the first priority be to cause no hurt."[25]

This is the justification for censoring certain ideas that are believed to cause psychological pain, "epistemic violence," or the erasure of certain groups of human beings—an argument found throughout Social Justice scholarship and activism.

> "*The Liberal Principle:* Checking of each by each through public criticism is the only legitimate way to decide who is right."[26]

Unlike the other four, this last principle cannot be accepted by postmodern Social Justice thought. Theory insists that it isn't acceptable to criticize some ideas. It also holds that whether a person is right or wrong cannot be established by evaluating the soundness of her ideas, but is dependent on her identity ("positionality") and willingness to employ the right discourses. The "checking of each by each" is effectively impossible in Theory, as people from different identity groups can never fully understand each other. This is the essence of the postmodern knowledge principle. It is clear that postmodernism contains a rejection of liberalism at its very core.

If we reject the liberal approach to generating knowledge, we are only left with illiberal alternatives, and, as these gain in moral status and their underlying assumptions are increasingly adopted, they become ever more fundamentalist. This is the essence of the postmodern political principle. Rauch expresses the fundamental difference between liberal science and the two postmodern principles, especially as seen in applied and reified postmodernism, concisely: "liberal science insists absolutely on freedom of belief and speech, but *freedom of knowledge it rejects absolutely*" (emphasis in original).[27] People in liberal systems are free to believe anything they wish, and they're free to argue for anything they want, but to claim that such beliefs are *knowledge* and demand they be respected as such is another matter.

Within Social Justice scholarship and activism and, increasingly, within a society infected by it, freedom of "knowledge" is the coin of the realm—so long as the "knowledge" speaks from "oppression" and is consistent with Theory. To say otherwise, according to Theory, is to participate in bigotry. The results are not good. They include an erosion of the system by which we generate reliable statements about reality and a concomitant loss of the conflict-resolution system that liberal science evolved to provide. This leads to social divisions, as people lose the ability to speak to one another on shared terms and have no objective means by which to settle differences of opinion. You have "your truth," and I have "my truth," and, when those diverge, there is no means of resolution. All we can do is each turn to our sect, the people who share our subjective experiences, attempt to claim victimhood, and hope what is on the table isn't using either "truth" to build a bridge or implement medical care—and that no one tries to settle the dispute through violence. This effectively denominationalizes "knowledge," which in turn generates a crisis of confidence in all knowledge claims. Such is the result in any system that has bent itself to the postmodern knowledge principle and the Theorizing that follows from it. This helps no one, and—as Social Justice scholars love to point out—the biggest losers in such a situation are those who are already marginalized and oppressed. It has been rightly said: the truth will set us free. So much for Social Justice.

THE PRINCIPLES AND THEMES IN LIGHT OF LIBERALISM

We can do much better than establishing denominations of "truth." Each of the postmodern principles and themes has a kernel of truth and points to a problem that needs to be dealt with, but none of these problems are effectively addressed by postmodernism. There is an alternative to Social Justice for liberals and supporters of modernity who are concerned about issues of social justice. It involves the near-total rejection of the two postmodern principles as well as the four postmodern themes, in favor of an older paradigm—universal liberalism, fueled by liberal-scientific knowledge production. This, then, is a call to remember the value of reason and evidence-based approaches to knowledge acquisition, characterized by their freedom from predetermined political assumptions and by their consistently liberal ethics. We must also recognize that, although very little of what the postmodernists and their academic and activist descendants put forth is original, the liberal project should accept the criticisms they have raised and respond as it always does: by self-correcting, adapting, and progressing.

There is nothing that postmodern Theory can do that liberalism cannot do better, and it's high time we regained the confidence to argue for this, applied liberalism to correct its past shortcomings and orient it towards future challenges, and got on with things. How, then, do we counter the postmodern principles and themes simply and confidently and show any waverers that liberal ideas should win out in the intellectual marketplace? We can start by acknowledging what Theory gets right, in order to reject its wayward approach to the problems it highlights.

The Postmodern Knowledge Principle

The postmodern knowledge principle assumes that knowledge is a socially constructed cultural artifact. This is true in a banal sense, but false in the profound sense that postmodernism intends. Knowledge is certainly part of the realm of ideas, and whether or not an idea is considered "true" in a certain culture says something about that culture. Nevertheless, there are better and worse ways to obtain (provisional) knowledge about what is going on in the world. The better methods—reason and evidence—are cultural artifacts too, but they are undeniably effective at winnowing out statements that accurately describe and predict what is occurring out there, both physically and socially. We need to reject the postmodern knowledge principle by seeing it for what it is—a language game—and reinstate the general understanding that knowledge is difficult to find, yet can be obtained through the processes of liberal science. Confidence in science is not naive—we have evidence that science works—and it is certainly neither racist, sexist, nor imperialistic. Science and reason are not white, Western, masculine ideas, and it is racist and sexist to suggest that they are. Science and reason belong to everybody. Indeed, they would be useless if they didn't.

The postmodern knowledge principle nevertheless provides us with a larger kernel of value. From Foucault's complaints about the misapplication of scientific claims about madness and sexuality to the critical race Theorists' insistence that the problems of minorities aren't being taken seriously, postmodernism is full of calls to be less brash and to *listen*. The postmodern knowledge principle exhorts us to do a better job of *listening and considering* and *listening and investigating*. However, we are under no obligation to "listen and believe" or to "shut up and listen." Demands that we circumvent or discard epistemological rigor even for the best of causes cannot be complied with in a liberal society because causes simply aren't best served this way. People's insights about the world are usually accurate in certain ways, but they also tend to interpret those insights incorrectly because getting to the bottom of things can be hard. For example, the worth of a law cannot best be gauged by the lived experience of those whom it has helped or harmed. The former are likely to ask for it to be preserved and the latter to want it repealed—and both these perspectives are valuable, but incomplete. The liberal approach would be to listen to both parties, consider their points carefully, and make arguments about what needs to be conserved and what reformed. *Listen and consider* asks us to take seriously some important information that we might otherwise ignore, and then evaluate fairly and rationally the totality of the evidence and arguments; *listen and believe* encourages confirmation bias, depending on who we feel morally obliged to listen to. If we follow that rule, we will get a lot of consequential things wrong, and as a result, the rule will undermine itself, resulting in listening even less than we already do and should.

The Postmodern Political Principle

The postmodern political principle holds that the social construction of knowledge is intimately tied to power, and that the more powerful culture creates the discourses that are granted legitimacy, and determines what we consider to be truth and knowledge, in ways that maintain its dominance. It sees the world as a zero-sum power game and a conspiracy theory without individual conspirators. This is a dismal and stultifying view that, drawing on Michel Foucault, arises from the most cynical reading possible of the history of progress, modernity, and the Enlightenment project. It cannot accept that human progress is always incremental and fraught with errors—some of which have had horrifying consequences, but from which we have learned and continue to learn. It seems to feel personally injured by our scientists' lack of omniscience (while the scientific method itself is based on that precise recognition of human fallibility).

The postmodern political principle needs to go. Yes, harmful discourses can gain undue power, masquerade as legitimate knowledge, and thus damage society and harm people, and we should remain aware of this. Postmodernism itself is one such discourse. We are speaking back. We are arguing against it. The postmodern idea that people are born into certain discourses that shape their understanding is worth considering; the idea that they learn to parrot these discourses from their positions within a power structure, without even realizing what they are doing, is prejudicial and absurd. The claim that, say, women of color who uphold Social Justice ideas are "woke" and that all other women of color who do not accept such ideas have been brainwashed into employing discourses of power that oppress them is a self-serving, arrogant, and presumptuous narrative—but that's what happens when you tie knowledge to identity and Theorize away variations in experience and interpretation as inauthentic or confused.

We, as liberals, don't have to do that. We can support the arguments of liberals from every identity group, and we can evaluate whether they conform to evidence and reason, without claiming that any single argument is representative of "women" or "people of color." We know exactly which ideas we hold and why, and we can pay Social Justice activists the respect of assuming they do too.

The Blurring of Boundaries

It is wise to be skeptical of rigid categories and boundaries. They should be constantly tested, prodded, pushed, and moved where warranted. Radical skepticism, which has no method of improving the accuracy of the categories, but simply distrusts categories on principle, is profoundly unhelpful—and reality remains unaffected by it. We can use reason to come to provisional conclusions and form hypothetical models and test them. There are valid and invalid categories and there are arguments for and against using specific categories to label people. Science and reason can provide information that we can use to strengthen *liberal* arguments and debunk both socially conservative and postmodern ones.

The simplistic postmodern view, so dominant in queer Theory, which sees categories as inherently oppressive, is simply not justified. If one wishes to argue that men and women do not fit neatly into boxes—and therefore should not be limited by the traits, abilities, and roles traditionally assigned to their sex—one can use science to show that they do not and liberalism to argue that they should not, and reason will employ the former in the service of the latter. An understanding of science and mathematics—in particular, basic statistics—reveals just how mistaken the call to obliterate categories really is. Biological reality

is such that, cognitively and psychologically, men and women are massively overlapping populations with somewhat different distributions of
average traits—a fact that allows us to predict trends, but can tell us
very little about any specific individual. To queer Theorists, who fear
that a reliance on biology will restrict men and women to distinct roles,
we say, "Look at the data." The data are pretty queer already. Science
already knows that human variation exists and that nature tends to be
messy.

The Focus on the Power of Language

The postmodern focus on the power of language also has some justification, given that it is language that allowed humans to develop science,
reason, and liberalism in the first place. Language has the power to convince and persuade, to change minds, and to change society. This is why
we advocate a marketplace of ideas, informed by Rauch's liberal principle—so that humans can use this power to bring all their ideas together
and see which ones are best, using the methods we know can work. Even
the smartest humans often reason poorly when alone or in ideologically
homogenous groups, because we use reason mostly to justify our existing
beliefs, desires, and underlying intuitions.[28] We are at our best in a group
of people with different intuitions and different reasoning, in which no
one can get away with a self-serving assertion unchallenged. Under such
circumstances, we can achieve great things.

The idea that social justice is best served by restricting what can be
said, and by banning some ideas and terminologies and enforcing others,
is unsupported by history, evidence, or reason. The power to designate
some ideas virtuous and thus utterable and others appalling and thus
forbidden is always in the hands of those who hold the majority view (or
who hold political power). Historically, censorship has not worked out
well for atheists, or for religious, racial, or sexual minorities—and there's
no reason to believe that Theory contains a magic ingredient that might
make censorship work differently. We urge Social Justice advocates to
see that the more they achieve their goal of controlling discourse, the
clearer it will become that theirs is a hegemonic ideology: an oppressive

dominant discourse that acts in pursuit of power and therefore needs to be deconstructed and countered. We will gladly help out with that.

Cultural Relativism

The only salvageable kernel of cultural relativism is something nobody denies: some cultures do some things differently and, in many cases, the differences don't matter much and are interesting to learn about and share. Knowledge production, however, transcends specific cultures—as does *moral* knowledge production. We all live in the same world and are all humans first and humans from particular cultures second, thus most of what is true about the world has nothing to do with us and most of what is true *about us* is true about us *as humans* and not as members of any particular culture. It is as dangerous as it is absurd to pretend that we cannot make any judgments about the practices of a culture other than our own. Despite the relatively minor cultural differences between different countries and sects, we all share a single human culture, grounded in a universal human nature. The range of human variation may be great, but it isn't *that* great. (The distance between any of us is immeasurably smaller than the distance between any of us and our nearest primate neighbors, the chimpanzees and bonobos.) The societal structures that are conducive to the flourishing, freedom, and security of its citizens are almost certainly bound by the nature of humanity, and any attempts to work to an ideal outside of this are doomed to failure.[29]

Social justice—the principle, not the ideology—can only be served if we have consistent principles. Women's rights, LGBT rights, and racial or caste equality must either be the right of all people or of none. Claims that only the women, LGBT, and members of a minority group within a specific culture or subculture may critique the oppression of their own group are a failure of both empathy and ethical consistency. We hinder the cause of human rights if we chastise anyone who points out humanitarian abuses as imperialist or racist. Liberals rightly do not do that. Believing in individual freedom and universal human rights, we can support those who advocate for those things—fellow liberals—wherever they are and whatever their dominant cultural norms may be. We need feel no hesitation in supporting the equal rights, opportunities, and freedoms of all women, all LGBT people, and all racial and religious minorities because these values don't belong to the West but to all liberals everywhere—and they are *everywhere*.

The Loss of the Individual and the Universal

There is some truth in the observation that individualism and universalism cannot describe the whole of human experience. People exist within communities, which impact how they experience the world and the opportunities available to them. Different people process information differently and hold different core values.[30] Understanding the experience of oppression, on some level, requires either having been oppressed or a lot of listening and a vivid imagination. A liberalism that focuses solely on the individual and on humanity as a whole may fail to see how certain identity groups are disadvantaged. Greater attention to this aspect of identity is warranted, though not to the exclusion of all other concerns.

Social Justice approaches that focus *solely* on group identity and neglect individuality and universality are doomed to fail for the simple reasons that people are individuals and share a common human nature. Identity politics is not a path to empowerment. There is no "unique voice of color" or of women or of trans, gay, disabled, or fat people. Even a relatively small random sample drawn from any of those groups will reveal widely varying individual views. This does not negate the likelihood that prejudice still exists and that the people who experience it are the most likely to be aware of it. We still need to "listen and consider," but we need to listen to and consider a variety of experiences and views from members of oppressed groups, not just a single one that has been arbitrarily labeled "authentic" because it represents the view essentialized by Theory.

Social Justice scholarship and activism is also constrained by its social constructivist views, often called "blank slatism."[31] This leads scholars and activists to deny the possibility of a universal human nature, a denial that makes empathy between groups very difficult. This denial does not bode well for minority groups, and this view was not shared by

Martin Luther King, Jr., or by the liberal feminists and Gay Pride activists of the 1960s and 1970s. Their overall message was strongly (if imperfectly) liberal, individual, and universal, and it succeeded by appealing to empathy and fairness. "I have a dream that my four little children will one day live in a nation where they will not be judged by the color of their skin, but by the content of their character," said Dr. King,[32] appealing to white Americans' pride in their country as the Land of Opportunity and their sense of fairness, and making common cause with them in their hopes for the next generation.[33] He called upon their empathy and stressed their shared humanity. Had he, like Robin DiAngelo, asked white Americans to be "a little less white, which means a little less oppressive, oblivious, defensive, ignorant, and arrogant,"[34] would this have had the same effect? We think not. An understanding of human nature is essential to any attempt to improve society.

Humans are capable of great empathy and of horrifying callousness and violence. We have evolved this way because it has been in our interest to both cooperate within our own groups and compete with others. Our empathy is therefore largely limited to those whom we see as members of our own tribe and our callous disregard and violence is reserved for those seen as competitors or traitors. By seeking to expand our circle of empathy ever wider, liberal humanism has achieved unprecedented human equality. It did so by exploiting the better part of our nature—our empathy and sense of fairness.[35] By seeking to divide humans into marginalized identity groups and their oppressors, Social Justice risks fuelling our worst tendencies—our tribalism and vengefulness. This cannot work out well for women, or for minority groups, or for society as a whole.

What is, perhaps, most frustrating about Theory is that it tends to get literally every issue it's primarily concerned with backwards, largely due to its rejection of human nature, science, and liberalism. It allots social significance to racial categories, which inflames racism. It attempts to depict categories of sex, gender, and sexuality as mere social constructions, which undermines the fact that people often accept sexual minorities because they recognize that sexual expression varies *naturally*. It depicts the East as the opposite of the West and thus perpetuates the very Orientalism it seeks to unmake. Theory is highly likely to spontaneously combust at some point, but it could cause a lot of human suffering and societal damage before it does. The institutions it attacks before it collapses will lose much of their prestige and influence, and they may not survive. It could also leave us at the mercy of nationalists and right-wing populists, who pose an even greater potential threat to liberalism.

FUEL FOR THE IDENTITY POLITICS OF THE EXTREME RIGHT

One of the biggest problems with the identity politics of the identitarian left is that it validates and emboldens identity politics on the identitarian right. Right-wing identity politics have long held that white people should hold all the power in a society, that Western culture should dominate the world, and that men should take a dominant role in the public sphere and women a passive one in the home. Heterosexuality was regarded as normal and morally good (within certain gendered frameworks) while homosexuality was a perversion and morally bad. When the liberal left explicitly challenged all of this and advocated the view that people should not be evaluated by their race, sex or sexuality, it held a convincing moral highground over right-wing elements who argued that they should.

Liberals, spearheaded by the Civil Rights Movement, liberal feminism and Gay Pride, overwhelmingly won this battle of ideas in the second half of the twentieth century and attained legal equality on the grounds of race, gender and sexuality. So successful were they that by the end of the first decade of the twenty-first century, mainstream conservatives had largely accepted this too. Those socially or religiously conservative elements who still believed that women, black people or gay people should be restricted to certain roles in life or denied equal rights became recognized as holding an extremist, "far-right" position, and could expect reputational damage in a liberal society.

This dramatic and rapid change in society's conception of gender roles, race relations and sexual freedom is still very fragile and new, however. Liberal feminists had to put a lot of work into convincing society that women are as intellectually rigorous and psychologically tough as men. It took time to defeat stereotypes about women being prone to hysteria and emotional thinking, being too sensitive to cope in the public sphere and in need of protecting from difficult ideas or people. Nor did racial minorities find they were immediately recognized by a majority white society as equally intelligent and ethical citizens. The narratives of colonialism and Jim Crow, which held that non-white people were unintelligent, irrational, emotionally volatile, and unscrupulous, didn't go away overnight. Indeed, they took decades. Similarly, lesbian, gay, bisexual, and transgender people did not find immediate acceptance from mainstream society once having had their sex lives decriminalized, their gender identities legally supported, or their committed relationships recognized in marriage. Instead, they faced a lengthy cultural battle trying to convince anxious social conservatives that they had no "agenda" to destroy the family, heterosexuality, masculinity, or femininity.

However, these battles were being won. It became normal for women to have careers and be assumed to be competent adults who are able to cope with the harsh realities of public life. It became unremarkable for people of racial minority to be professors, doctors, judges, scientists, politicians, and accountants. Increasing numbers of homosexuals felt comfortable to speak of their partners socially and at work and to be affectionate to each other in public. The acceptance of trans people was taking longer, as they are such a tiny minority, have uniquely complicated issues to work out, and contradict many people's understanding of sex and gender, but the situation was improving—at least until recently. Now, Critical Social Justice threatens to reverse—and seems to be reversing—much of this progress, and it does so in two ways.

Firstly, Social Justice approaches re-inscribe negative stereotypes against women and racial and sexual minorities by the kind of Theories it develops. Much of its feminism infantalizes women by suggesting that they are fragile, timid, lack agency, and require much of the public sphere softened for them. Arguments for "research justice" based on traditional and religious beliefs, emotions, and lived experiences mostly orientalizes non-white people by suggesting science and reason are not for them—against all historical and current evidence. Identity-first approaches to politics like we see across the intersectional pantheon aim not just to put social significance back into categories of identity, but also to make them central—the one-directional nature of which won't be something that remains under the control of Theory. Authoritarian attempts to dictate what people must believe about gender and sexuality and the language they must express those beliefs in in the name of Social Justice are rapidly creating a hostile resistance to mainstream acceptance of trans people in particular.

Secondly, the critical approach to Social Justice encourages tribalism and hostility by its aggressively divisive approach. Whereas the civil rights movements worked so well because they used a universalist approach—everybody should have equal rights—that appealed to human intuitions of fairness and empathy, Social Justice uses a simplistic identity politics approach which ascribes collective blame to dominant groups—white people are racist, men are sexist, and straight people are homophobic. This explicitly goes against the established liberal value of not judging people by their race, gender, or sexuality, and it is incredibly naive to expect it not to produce a counter-revival of old right-wing identity politics. Arguments that it is acceptable to be prejudiced against white people, men, straight, or cisgender people because of historical power imbalances do not work well with human intuitions of reciprocity.

If a majority feels threatened by a vocal minority with institutional power, it is likely to try to change those institutions, and not merely because of paranoid fears about losing dominance and privilege once had. If it becomes socially acceptable to speak disparagingly of "whiteness" and call for punishment of anyone who can be interpreted as expressing "anti-blackness," this will be experienced as unfair by white people. If it becomes acceptable to pathologize masculinity and speak hatefully of men while being hypersensitive to anything that can be called "misogyny," almost half of the population (as well as much of the other half who loves them) is likely to take this badly. If cisgender people, who are 99.5 percent of the population, are accused of transphobia for simply existing, failing to use the correct terminology, allowing genitals to influence their dating preferences, or even having non-queer Theory beliefs about gender, this is likely to result in much unfair antagonism against trans people (most of whom do not believe in this either).

There are certainly a number of causes for the current surge to the right and these include things that have nothing to do with Social Justice scholarship or activism, but it certainly isn't helping. Of the greatest importance, however, is that since Social Justice has taken such pains to establish absolute hegemony over the discourses relevant to these issues—especially on the left and in the center—other reasonable and moderate voices are the least likely to enter the conversation with reasonable and moderate alternatives to Social Justice's pronouncements on these issues. This leaves only those with the most extreme voices to speak up against Social Justice, and to the degree they can be perceived as speaking an obvious truth that no one else will say, they will gain support they would not otherwise have been able to garner. In this way, through the systematic and near-total silencing of reasonable and moderate voices from the left, center, and center-right, Social Justice opens itself and our society up most precariously and certainly to an authoritarian far-right backlash. (This, it will then uselessly interpret, of course, as more proof that our society is as degenerate and bigoted as they've always insisted it is—a self-fulfilling prophecy none of us has to suffer, if we're willing to speak up while we can.)

A BRIEF DISCUSSION OF SOLUTIONS

Some people have suggested fairly drastic solutions to the problem of postmodernism. Some, including Prime Minister Viktor Orbán in Hungary,[36] have argued that we should ban gender studies and other courses rooted in postmodern Theory. They regard them as so socially harmful that they merit being forbidden. We oppose that stance strongly. We cannot fight illiberalism with illiberalism or counter threats to freedom of speech by banning the speech of the censorious. We must not become what we hate. If we do, we cannot expect to be supported by those who hate what we hate; that is, liberals of all stripes—from left, right, and center.

Others have argued that Social Justice courses should not be publicly funded. They make a not-unreasonable argument that the taxpayer should not be expected to pay for scholarship that is neither rigorous nor ethical. We disagree with this too. Governments should not be given control over what universities teach—such a move would amount to establishing a kind of Ministry of Truth. Although we also want universities to uphold rigorous scholarship and do not believe that postmodernism qualifies as such, it would set a terrible precedent if governments—rather than universities—were to make that call. If a theocratic government came to power, or a government influenced by the postmodern left, for example, it could decide that science or anything else it didn't like was socially harmful and proscribe it. It is important to defend people's right to hold postmodern ideas and to express them to whoever wants to hear. However, it is also important to keep them from gaining institutional power—something which, as chapter 9 shows, is already happening.

In liberal societies, we already have the answer to the problem of how to deal with reified philosophical systems that threaten to impose themselves on society: this answer is called *secularism*. Secularism is best known as a legal principle: the "separation of church and state." But this principle is based on a more profound philosophical idea—that no matter how certain you may be that you are in possession of the truth, you have no right to impose your belief on society as a whole. Construed broadly, this means that you can hold whatever moral beliefs you want and require people to follow them (within legal bounds) within a voluntary community, whose members adopt those beliefs as matters of private conscience, but you cannot enforce them on outsiders. Believe what you will, but, in exchange, you must allow others to believe what they will—or won't, as the case may be.

This is accompanied by the inalienable right to reject the moral injunctions and prescriptions of any particular ideology *without blame*. In a secular society, for example, no one is legally or morally compelled to feel guilty for rejecting the tenets of any faith, including those of the majority religion. That is up to each individual, and no ideological or moral group can decide for that person. No one is subject to the *oughts* of any particular moral group, no matter how strong the conviction of its members.

The postmodernist project, especially following the applied turn—and even more so after its reification—is overwhelmingly prescriptive, rather than descriptive. An academic theory that prioritizes what it believes *ought* to be true over the aim of describing what *is*—that is, one that sees personal belief as a political obligation—has ceased to search for knowledge because it believes it has The Truth. That is, it has become a system of faith, and its scholarship has become a sort of theology. This is what we see in Social Justice scholarship. Declarations of *ought* have replaced the search for what *is*.

It is one thing to believe that knowledge is a cultural construct that is used to enforce power, and that this can occur in unjust ways. This is an argument that can be submitted to the marketplace of ideas. It is quite another thing to take this belief as a given and assert that to disagree is, in itself, an act of dominance and oppression. It is even worse to insist that everything short of constant spiritual submission to your belief system and calls for a puritanical social revolution is complicity in moral evil. In other faiths, this is the remedy to a problem called *depravity*, the corrupt desire to sin. Secularism relegates these matters to the individual's *private conscience*, and absolves anyone of the requirement to accept or play lip service to a belief they do not share, to avoid social stigma.

With this attitude in mind, we advocate two approaches to the problem of reified postmodernism. First, we must oppose the institutionalization of its belief system. Because the Social Justice movement is not officially a religion and because genuine social justice aims are in keeping with antidiscrimination legislation, it has been allowed to bypass the usual barriers to imposing one's belief system on others. As liberals, we must object to this imposition and defend people's right to disbelieve in Social Justice, without incurring any form of punishment. While all public institutions and organizations have a right to require their students, employees, or users to refrain from discrimination and uphold equality, they should not be able to require an affirmation of the Creed of Social Justice. We must object to any requirement of an orthodox Social Justice statement of diversity, equity, and inclusion, or mandatory diversity or equity training, just as we would object to public institutions that required a statement of Christian or Muslim belief or attendance of church or mosque.

Second, we must do fair battle with the ideas in Social Justice. We do not believe that bad ideas can be defeated by being repressed, especially when they are as socially powerful as postmodern ideas are right now. Instead, they need to be engaged and defeated within the marketplace of ideas, so that they may die a natural death and be rightly recognized as defunct. Defeating postmodern Theory in the marketplace of ideas is entirely possible—in fact, inevitable—if we engage it head-on and arm ourselves with stronger reasoning. This takes exposing its attempts to avoid fair scrutiny for what they are and holding the ideas to a higher standard that might, in time, refine what is useful within them. As they are, the ideas are demonstrably bad and ethically incoherent and cannot withstand rigorous scrutiny without imploding and disappearing in a puff of contradictions. The academic disciplines involved need to be reformed, to make them more rigorous and ethical. This is the kind of problem that the academic system knows how to deal with and will be able to deal with effectively, once the taboo against criticizing Social Justice scholarship evaporates.

A CONCLUSION AND A STATEMENT

Maintaining our commitment to and belief in liberalism in the face of Theory is possible, and it is to our benefit. It can be difficult, however. For one thing, new, radical answers have a certain appeal. They get people excited, especially when things seem bad. Problems that feel big and pressing seem to invite revolutionary new solutions. Incremental improvements feel desperately slow when there are people suffering *right now*. As ever, the perfect is the enemy of the good—including the unrealistic expectation that a good system should have been able to produce better results by now. This is an invitation to radicalism, authoritarianism, fundamentalism, and cynicism. This is what makes Theory seductive—or populism, or Marxism, or any other form of Utopianism that looks good on paper and is ruinous in practice. It seems like the necessary solution to the world's myriad problems, some of which feel like (or are) emergencies.

The answer to these problems isn't new, though, and perhaps that's why it isn't immediately gratifying. The solution is liberalism, both political (universal liberalism is an antidote to the postmodern political principle) and in terms of knowledge production (Jonathan Rauch's "liberal science" is the remedy for the postmodern knowledge principle). You don't need to become an expert on Jonathan Rauch's work, or on John Stuart Mill, or on any of the great liberal thinkers. Nor do you need to become well versed in Theory and Social Justice scholarship, so that you can confidently refute it. But you do need to have a little bit of courage to stand up to something with a lot of power. You need to recognize Theory when you see it, and side with the liberal responses to it—which might be no more complicated than saying, "No, that's your ideological belief, and I don't have to go along with it."

To make this easier, we'd like to close with a few examples of how you can recognize social injustice, while rejecting the solutions the ideology of Social Justice proposes. We hope to show that social justice issues are serious and important, but that illiberal means of addressing them are, at best, inadequate and, at worst, wrongheaded, dangerous, and harmful to both people and worthy causes. You can, of course, create your own variations of principled opposition to Social Justice ideas.

Principled Opposition: Example 1

We affirm that racism remains a problem in society and needs to be addressed.

We deny that critical race Theory and intersectionality provide the most useful tools to do so, since we believe that racial issues are best solved through the most rigorous analyses possible.

We contend that racism is defined as prejudiced attitudes and discriminatory behavior against individuals or groups on the grounds of race and can be successfully addressed as such.

We deny that racism is hard-baked into society via discourses, that it is unavoidable and present in every interaction to be discovered and called out, and that this is part of a ubiquitous systemic problem that is everywhere, always, and all-pervasive.

We deny that the best way to deal with racism is by restoring social significance to racial categories and radically heightening their salience.

We contend that each individual can choose not to hold racist views and should be expected to do so, that racism is declining over time and becoming rarer, that we can and should see one another as humans first and members of certain races second, that issues of race are best dealt with by being honest about racialized experiences, while still working towards shared goals and a common vision, and that the principle of not discriminating by race should be universally upheld.

We affirm that sexism remains a problem in society and needs to be addressed.

We deny that Theoretical approaches to gender issues, including queer Theory and intersectional feminism, which work on blank slatist theories of sex and gender, are useful to address it as we believe it is necessary to acknowledge biological realities to address such issues.

We contend that sexism is defined as prejudiced attitudes and discriminatory behaviors against individuals or a whole sex on the grounds of sex and can be successfully addressed as such.

We deny that sexism and misogyny are systemic forces that operate throughout society through socialization, expectations, and linguistic enforcement, even in the absence of sexist or misogynistic people or intentions.

We deny that there are no psychological or cognitive biological differences on average between men and women and that gender and sex are therefore merely social constructs.

We contend that men and women are human beings of equal value who are equally capable of being discriminated against on the basis of their sex, that sexist acts are intentional acts, undertaken by individuals, who should be expected to do otherwise, and that gender and sex have both biological and social origins, which need to be acknowledged in order to optimize human flourishing.

Principled Opposition: Example 3

We affirm that discrimination and bigotry against sexual minorities remains a problem in society and requires addressing.

We deny that this problem can be solved by queer Theory, which attempts to render all categories relevant to sex, gender, and sexuality meaningless.

We contend that homophobia and transphobia are defined as prejudiced attitudes and discriminatory acts against homosexual and transgen-
dered people on the grounds of their sexuality or gender identity.

We deny that dismantling categories of sex, gender, or sexuality or that
forwarding concepts of an oppressive "heteronormativity" and "cisnormativity"—recognizing heterosexuality and a gender identity consistent
with biological sex as normal—is the best way to make society more
welcoming to sexual minorities.

We contend that sexual minorities are also "normal" and represent a
naturally occurring variation on sexuality and gender identity and can
easily be accepted as such in the same way that other variations (like red
hair and left-handedness) are currently recognized as traits found in a
minority of humans who are regarded as completely normal human individuals and valued members of society. Homophobia and transphobia
are intentional acts, undertaken by individuals who should be expected
to do otherwise.

We could give examples for more issues currently dominated by
Theory—colonialism, disability, obesity, and so on—but you get the
idea. One final, more general, example, then, concerns Theory as it has
evolved into Social Justice scholarship.

Principled Opposition: Example 4

We affirm that social injustice still exists and that scholarship on issues
of social justice is necessary and important.

We affirm the value of interdisciplinary theoretical approaches, including the study of race, gender, sexuality, culture, and identity within the
humanities.

We affirm that many of the ideas generated even by the reified postmodernism of Social Justice scholarship—including the basic idea of
intersectionality, that unique injustices can lie in "intersected" identities
that require special consideration—are insightful and worthy of submission to the marketplace of ideas for evaluation, adaptation, further study,
refinement, and potentially eventual application.

We deny that any ideas, ideologies, or political movements can be identified as the authoritative position of any identity group, since such groups are comprised of individuals with diverse ideas and a common humanity.

We deny the worth of any scholarship that dismisses the possibility of objective knowledge or the importance of consistent principles and contend that that is ideological bias, rather than scholarship.

We deny the worth of any theoretical approach that refuses to submit itself to criticism or refutation and contend that that is sophistry, rather than scholarship.

We deny that any approach that assumes a problem to exist (say, in a systemic way) and then searches "critically" to find proofs of it is of any significant worth, especially as a form of scholarship.

We contend that, if these methods are reformed and made rigorous, they could be of tremendous scholarly value and significantly advance the cause of humanity—not least the cause of social justice.

NOTES

Introduction

1. James Lindsay and Helen Pluckrose, "A Manifesto against the Enemies of Modernity," *Areo Magazine*, August 22, 2017, areomagazine. com/2017/08/22/a-manifesto-against-the-enemies-of-modernity/.

2. John Rawls, *A Theory of Justice.* (Oxford: Oxford University Press, 1999).

3. Audre Lorde, *Sister Outsider: Essays and Speeches* (Berkeley, CA: Crossing Press, 2007), 110–114.

1 *Postmodernism*

1. Critical Theory is often attributed to the famous Frankfurt School, which arose as a vehicle for Marxist critiques of modernity. It is mostly distinct from postmodern critical theory, which is often referred to simply as "Theory" or, more specific critical Theoretic lines like "critical race Theory" or "critical dietetics." In fact, the members of the Frankfurt School, especially Jürgen Habermas, were largely critical of postmodernism. Contemporary approaches that are typically referred to as "critical theory" tend to refer to postmodern variants because they currently hold sway over much of academia. An accessible explanation of the different meanings of "critical theory" is to be found in James Bohman, "Critical Theory," in *Stanford Encyclopedia of Philosophy*, ed. Edward N. Zalta (Winter 2019 Edition), plato. stanford.edu/archives/win2019/entries/critical-theory/.

From its original conception, a Critical Theory was to be set aside from a traditional theory, which seeks to understand and explain phenomena in terms of what it is and how it works, including social phenomena. A critical theory, by contrast, must satisfy all of three criteria. First, it must arise from a "normative" vision, which is to say a set of moral views about how society ought to be, and this moral vision should both inform the theory and serve as a goal for a new society. Second, it must explain what is wrong with society or its current systems, usually in terms of "problematics," which are shortcomings in the system or ways in which it fails to accord with or generate the normative moral view of the theory. Third, it must be actionable by social activists who wish to use it to change society.

The postmodern Theorists adopted the critical method, or at least the critical *mood*, of the Frankfurt School and adapted it into the structuralist context, particularly its view of power. The "critical" goal remained the same, however: to make the problems inherent in "the system" more visible to the people allegedly oppressed by it—however happily they might be living their lives within it—until they come to detest it and seek a revolution against it. The Frankfurt School developed the Critical Theoretic approach specifically to expand beyond critiques of capitalism, as the Marxists had been doing, and to target the assumptions of Western civilization as a whole, particularly liberalism as a sociopolitical philosophy and Enlightenment thought in general. It was this approach to critique that the postmodernists turned upon the entire social order and its institutions, insisting that hegemonic power structures (a concept adopted from Antonio Gramsci) exist across all facets of difference and require exposing and eventually overturning.

2. We have written about the need to defend modernity against both the premodernists (those who would take us back to preindustrial and secular times) and the postmodernists in James Lindsay and Helen Pluckrose. "A Manifesto against the Enemies of Modernity," *Areo Magazine*, August 22, 2017, areomagazine.com/2017/08/22/a-manifesto-against-the-enemies-of-modernity/.

3. Brian McHale, *The Cambridge Introduction to Postmodernism* (Cambridge University Press, 2015), 1.

4. Although Jacques Lacan and French feminists such as Luce Irigaray and Julia Kristeva were extremely influential participants in the postmodern turn, psychoanalysis will not be discussed much in this book. Their ideas are rooted in the development of the psyche, rather than in cultural constructivism, and therefore have not been as influential on current cultural studies as those of other thinkers. They have also been criticized as "essentialist" for this reason.

5. A comprehensive account of every postmodern thinker and his or her sources of inspiration is beyond the scope of this book.

6. Jean François Lyotard, *The Postmodern Condition: A Report on Knowledge* (Manchester: Manchester UP, 1991).

7. Jean Baudrillard, *Simulacra and Simulation*, trans. Sheila Faria Glaser (Ann Arbor: University of Michigan Press, 1994).

8. Baudrillard takes this odd view to a macabre and nihilistic extreme, calling for drastic measures to return us to a more productive, pretechnological time. Jean Baudrillard, *Symbolic Exchange and Death*, trans. Iain Hamilton Gran (London: SAGE Publications, 2017).

9. Gilles Deleuze and Felix Guattari, *Anti-Oedipus: Capitalism and Schizophrenia*, trans. Robert J. Hurley (London: Bloomsbury Academic, 2016).

10. Fredric Jameson, *Postmodernism: Or, the Cultural Logic of Late Capitalism* (New York: Verso Books, 2019).

11. David Harvey, *The Condition of Postmodernity* (Cambridge, MA: Blackwell, 2000).

12. It is unclear whether the general population shared either this perception of society or the skepticism about Enlightenment values it induced in certain thinkers, but something significant was changing, particularly within the academy.

13. Brian Duignan, "Postmodernism," *Encyclopædia Britannica*, July 19, 2019, britannica.com/topic/postmodernism-philosophy (accessed August 15, 2019).

14. Paraphrased from Walter Truett Anderson, *The Fontana Postmodernism Reader* (London: Fontana Press, 1996), 10–11.

15. Steinar Kvale, "Themes of Postmodernity," in *The Fontana Postmodernism Reader*, ed. Walter Truett Anderson (London: Fontana Press, 1996), 18.

16. Kvale, "Themes," 18.

17. Ibid., 20.

18. For Richard Rorty, the crucial factor was the change from "found" to "made"—by which he meant that the truth was not out there to be discovered, but rather to be constructed by people. This clearly expresses the underlying postmodern anxiety about the artificiality of modernity (and, ironically, postmodernity) and helps us characterize it as a kind of crisis of authenticity. For Brian McHale, the most important shift was a change in philosophical focus from the epistemological to the ontological—that is, from concerns about how we produce knowledge to attempts to characterize the nature of being. Modernism, he writes, is "preoccupied with *what we*

know and *how we know it*, with the accessibility and reliability of knowledge," and, as a result, "it pursued epistemological questions." Postmodernism "privileged questions of *world-making* and *modes of being* over questions of *perception* and *knowing*: It was *ontological* in its orientation" (emphasis in original). Richard Rorty, *Contingency, Irony, and Solidarity* (Cambridge: Cambridge University Press, 2009), 3; McHale, *The Cambridge Introduction to Postmodernism*, 14–15.

19. Steven Seidman, *The Postmodern Turn: New Perspectives on Social Theory* (Cambridge University Press, 1998), 1.

20. Anderson, *Reader,* 2.

21. The following three thinkers, for example, view the rise of postmodernism as a result of the failures of the Enlightenment. For Walter Anderson,

> The postmodern verdict on the Enlightenment project is that it was a brilliant, ambitious effort, but that its field of vision was limited. Its leaders thought the task of building a universal human culture upon a foundation of rational thought would be easier than it has turned out to be. The universe now seems, if not infinite, at least infinitely complex and mysterious. Our eternal truths now seem to be inseparable from the cultures that created them and the languages in which they are stated. (*Reader,* 216)

David Harvey contends that the Enlightenment thinkers

> took it as axiomatic that there was only one possible answer to any question. From this it followed that the world could be controlled and rationally ordered if we could only picture and represent it correctly. But this presumed that there existed a single, correct mode of representation which, if we could uncover it (and this was what scientific and mathematical endeavors were all about) would provide the means to Enlightenment ends.

Harvey therefore characterises the Enlightenment as a belief in "linear progress, absolute truths, and rational planning of ideal social orders" (*Condition,* 27).

Steven Seidman also describes the Enlightenment in very simple, dogmatic terms,

> At the heart of the modern west is the culture of the Enlightenment. Assumptions regarding the unity of humanity, the individual as the creative force of society and history, the superiority of the west, the idea of science as Truth, and the belief in social progress, have been fundamental to Europe and the United States. This culture is now is a state of crisis. (*Turn,* 1)

22. None of these ideas are new. In fact, as Stephen R. C. Hicks details in his book, *Understanding Postmodernism:Skepticism and Socialism from Rousseau to Foucault* (Tempe, AZ: Scholargy Publishing, 2004) they are a relatively recent manifestation of a continuum of anti-Enlightenment thought that stretches as far back as the Enlightenment itself. Our reliance on our faculties to mediate knowledge was a primary concern for Kant and Hegel roughly two centuries ago, for instance, and much has been written about Kantian and Hegelian philosophy in relation to postmodern thought. Of even greater and more direct significance to the development of postmodern ideas were Nietzsche's and Heidegger's ideas about the subject and the nature of reality. For those interested in the philosophical precursors to postmodernism, both Hicks' book and David Detmer's earlier *Challenging Postmodernism Philosophy and the Politics of Truth* (Amherst, NY: Humanity Books, 2003) will be valuable.

23. Incidentally, this is a case in which the postmodernists have made a valid observation and used it to justify very poor philosophy. It is accurate to say that what we know about reality depends upon the models of reality that we put forward to explain it. Where the postmodern view goes wrong is assuming that this is a catastrophe for scientific knowledge production. The truth is, this fact isn't alarming to any serious scientist or philosopher of science. Indeed, in their book *The Grand Design* (2012), Stephen Hawking and Leonard Mlodinow explain this way of interpreting the world, which they call "model-dependent realism" (New York: Bantam Books, 2010). In this approach, we formulate mostly linguistic constructs called *models* that explain phenomena, and we examine the evidence we can gather about the world to determine how consistent it is with those models. When a model has been shown to do the best currently possible job of explaining the available data and predicting new results (and, in the "hard" sciences like physics, the standards used are extremely exacting), we accept its facts as *provisionally true* within the context of the model. If a better model is devised, scientists can change their understanding accordingly, but this seeming flexibility is, in fact, quite rigorous and not at all like cultural constructivism. (This point was well understood by the philosophers of science Thomas Kuhn and Willard Van Orman Quine.)

24. Richard Rorty, *Contingency, Irony, and Solidarity* (Cambridge: Cambridge University Press, 2009), 3.

25. Rorty makes this case ten years earlier in *Philosophy and the Mirror of Nature* (Princeton, NJ: Princeton University Press, 1979).

26. Michel Foucault, *The Order of Things: An Archaeology of the Human Sciences* (London: Routledge, 2002), 168. Although at other times, Foucault seems to have accepted that there can be more than one episteme in play in society, he consistently conceived of knowledge as the product of a powerful apparatus which determined what could be known.

27. Michel Foucault, *Madness and Civilization: A History of Insanity in the Age of Reason*, trans. Richard Howard and Jean Kafka (New York: Routledge, 2001); Michel Foucault, *Birth of the Clinic: An Archaeology of Medical Perception*, trans. A. M. Sheridan Smith (London: Tavistock, 1975); Michel Foucault, *The Archaeology of Knowledge: And the Discourse on Language*, trans. A. M. Sheridan Smith (London: Tavistock, 1972).

28. This is formally known as *anti-foundationalism*.

29. Alan Sokal and Jean Bricmont distinguish these two types of skepticism in *Fashionable Nonsense*:

> Specific skepticism should not be confused with radical skepticism. It is important to distinguish carefully between two different types of critiques of the sciences: those that are opposed to a particular theory and are based on specific arguments, and those that repeat in one form or another the traditional arguments of radical skepticism. The former critiques can be interesting but can also be refuted, while the latter are irrefutable but uninteresting (because of their universality). . . . If one wants to contribute to science, be it natural or social, one must abandon radical doubts concerning the viability of logic or the possibility of knowing the world through observation and/or experiment. Of course, one can always have doubts about a specific theory. But general skeptical arguments put forward to support those doubts are irrelevant, precisely because of their generality.

Alan Sokal and Jean Bricmont, *Fashionable Nonsense: Postmodern Intellectuals Abuse of Science* (New York: St. Martin's Press, 1999), 189.

30. Lyotard, *Postmodern Condition*.

31. Lyotard describes a "strict interlinkage" between the language of science and that of politics and ethics (ibid, 8).

32. Michel Foucault, "On the Genealogy of Ethics: An Overview of Work in Progress," afterword to *Michel Foucault: Beyond Structuralism and Hermeneutics*, 2nd ed., by Hubert L. Dreyfus and Paul Rabinow (Chicago: University of Chicago Press, 1983).

33. Lyotard, *Postmodern Condition*, 7.

34. Specifically, Derrida rejected the idea that the "signifier" (the written or spoken word) directly refers to the "signified" (the meaning, idea, or object about which it aims to communicate) and instead saw words as relational. For instance, he argued that "house" is to be understood in relation to "hut" (smaller) and "mansion" (larger) and lacks clear meaning outside of these relations.

35. Jacques Derrida, *Of Grammatology*, trans. Gayatri Chakravorty Spivak (Baltimore: John Hopkins University Press, 1976).

36. Roland Barthes, "The Death of the Author," Aspen no. 5–6, ubu.com/aspen/aspen5and6/threeEssays.html.

2 Postmodernism's Applied Turn

1. The first rule is, above all else, never be boring.

2. One common position taken by academics today is that postmodernism is dead and that the kind of Theory we see today is not postmodernism. This argument is reliant on a purist approach, which identifies postmodernism with its high deconstructive phase and distinguishes it from the subsequent Theories that adapted its concepts. This distinction is mostly insisted upon by those who wish to defend postmodernism from the identity-based Social Justice scholarship of today or, alternatively, to defend Social Justice scholarship from the taint of postmodernism. Scholars who value postmodernism point out that identity politics, which relies on consistent identity categories and objectively real systems of power and privilege, simply doesn't work within a postmodern conception of the world. Those who value Social Justice scholarship assert that the deconstructive aimlessness of postmodernism and the white maleness of its originators are antithetical to current Theory, which seeks to construct a better world.

    In fairness to these objections, there are many misconceptions about what is and isn't postmodernism. The most common one conflates postmodernism with Marxism, referring to "cultural Marxism" or "Postmodern Neo-Marxism." Although there are complicated connections between Marxism and the postmodernism that deconstructed it, this claim is frequently a simplistic one that insists that "applied postmodernism" takes the Marxist ideas of oppressed and oppressor classes and applies them to other identity categories, such as race, gender, and sexuality. This is specious. As the previous chapter shows, Marxism was one of the "metanarratives" that postmodernism rejected, but the *critical* methods that arose in service to Marxist activism were retained and expanded. As the following chapters will show, the descendants of the Marxists—the materialist scholars—continue to work in very different ways from and are usually very critical of the descendants of the postmodernists.

    See Matthew McManus, "On Marxism, Post-Modernism, and 'Cultural Marxism,'" *Merion West*, May 18, 2018, merionwest.com/2018/05/18/on-marxism-post-modernism-and-cultural-marxism/.

3. See, for example, Patricia Hill Collins, *Black Feminist Thought: Knowledge, Consciousness, and the Politics of Empowerment* (New York: Routledge, 2015).

4. Recall that Critical Theory was organized by design to explain what is wrong with (Western) society in moral terms and to enact societal change through dedicated activism. In this sense, what we see in applied postmodernism is a fusion of postmodernism with the derivatives of Critical Theory as they had come down through the decades in the forms of "New Left" activism, which, in contrast to postmodernist theorizing, was often direct and militant through the 1960s and 1970s.

5. McHale. *The Cambridge Introduction to Postmodernism*, 48.

6. McHale, *Introduction*, 97.

7. Mark Horowitz, Anthony Haynor, and Kenneth Kickham. "Sociology's Sacred Victims and the Politics of Knowledge: Moral Foundations Theory and Disciplinary Controversies." *The American Sociologist* 49, no. 4 (2018): 459–95.

8. Jonathan Gottschall, *Literature, Science and a New Humanities* (New York: Palgrave Macmillan, 2008), 5.

9. Brian Boyd, Joseph Carroll, and Jonathan Gottschall, eds., *Evolution, Literature, and Film: A Reader* (New York: Columbia University Press, 2010), 2.

10. McHale, *Introduction*, 172.

11. René Descartes, *Discourse on the Method: The Original Text with English Translation* (Erebus Society, 2017).

12. Although Said later became quite critical of Foucault, his groundbreaking text, *Orientalism*, which draws explicitly on Foucauldian concepts of knowledge construction through discourse, remains a key text in postcolonial studies and continues to influence work in the field today.

13. Edward Said, *Orientalism* (London: Penguin, 2003), xiii.

14. Linda Hutcheon, "'Circling the Downspout of Empire'." In *Past the Last Post: Theorizing Post-Colonialism and Post-Modernism,* eds. Ian Adam and Helen Tiffin, (London: Harvester/ Wheatsheaf, 1991), 171.

15. This schism is primarily between gender critical (radical) feminists and trans activist (intersectional and queer) feminists, whose theoretical disagreements are as profound as they are divisive.

16. As Poovey wrote in 1988,

> To take deconstruction to its logical conclusion would be to argue that "woman" is only a social construct that has no basis in nature, that "woman," in other words, is a term whose definition depends upon the context in which it is being discussed and not

upon some set of sexual organs or social experiences. This renders the experience women have of themselves and the meaning of their social relations problematic, to say the least. It also calls into question the experiential basis upon which U.S. feminism has historically grounded its political programs. The challenge for those of us who are convinced both that real historical women do exist and share certain experiences and that deconstruction's demystification of presence makes theoretical sense is to work out some way to think both women and "woman." It isn't an easy task.

Mary Poovey, "Feminism and Deconstruction," *Feminist Studies* 14, no. 1 (1988): 51.

17. Judith Butler, *Gender Trouble* (London: Routledge, 2006).

18. Butler defends postmodernism against its detractors in her essay titled "Contingent Foundations: Feminism and the Question of 'Postmodernism'" :

I don't know about the term "postmodern," but if there is a point, and a fine point, to what I perhaps better understand as poststructuralism, it is that power pervades the very conceptual apparatus that seeks to negotiate its terms, including the subject position of the critic; and further, that this implication of the terms of criticism in the field of power is *not* the advent of a nihilistic relativism incapable of furnishing norms, but, rather, the very precondition of a politically engaged critique. To establish a set of norms that are beyond power or force is itself a powerful and forceful conceptual practice that sublimates, disguises and extends its own power play through recourse to tropes of normative universality. (p. 158)

Her essay appears in *The Postmodern Turn: New Perspectives on Social Theory*, ed. Steven Seidman (Cambridge: Cambridge University Press, 1994).

19. Seidman, *Postmodern Turn*, 159.

20. bell hooks, "Postmodern Blackness," in *The Fontana Postmodernism Reader*, ed. Walter Truett Anderson (London: Fontana Press, 1996).

21. Ibid., 117.

22. Ibid., 115.

23. Ibid., 120.

24. Kimberlé Crenshaw, "Mapping the Margins: Intersectionality, Identity Politics, and Violence against Women of Color," *Stanford Law Review* 43, no. 6 (1991).

25. Crenshaw, "Mapping the Margins," 1244n9.

26. Intersectionality proved to be effective at providing a framework—which Crenshaw's contemporary, Patricia Hill Collins, dubbed the "matrix of domination"—that allowed disparate minority groups to unite under a single banner. It also provided the tools for defining a hierarchical structure within this loose coalition and for bullying more recognized and effective movements, such as feminism, into taking up the charges of smaller factions under a euphemistic rubric of "allyship" and "solidarity."

27. Crenshaw, "Mapping the Margins," 1297.

28. Ibid., 1297.

29. Ibid., 1297.

30. See, for example, Fiona Kumari Campbell, *Contours of Ableism: The Production of Disability and Abledness* (New York: Palgrave Macmillan, 2012).

31. Esther D. Rothblum and Sondra Solovay, eds., *The Fat Studies Reader* (New York: New York University Press, 2009).

32. One paradigmatic example of this is the critical treatment the stop-motion animated television special *Rudolph the Red-Nosed Reindeer* (1964) has received in recent years. Despite the film's clear portrayal of an inclusive, antibullying theme—don't discriminate unfairly against those who are different— current theorists and activists have taken issue with the film for portraying potentially offensive language and attitudes on the part of the bullies, despite the fact that these details are crucial to the overall theme.

33. Andrew Jolivétte, *Research Justice: Methodologies for Social Change* (Bristol, UK: Policy Press, 2015).

34. Miranda Fricker, *Epistemic Injustice: Power and the Ethics of Knowing* (Oxford: Oxford University Press, 2007).

35. Kristie Dotson, "Conceptualizing Epistemic Oppression," *Social Epistemology* 28, no. 2 (2014).

36. Nora Berenstain, "Epistemic Exploitation," *Ergo, an Open Access Journal of Philosophy* 3, no. 22 (2016).

37. Gayatri Chakravorty Spivak, "Can the Subaltern Speak?" in *Marxism and the Interpretation of Culture*, ed. Cary Nelson and Lawrence Grossberg (Chicago: University of Illinois Press, 1988).

38. Perhaps the most egregious example of this is a case investigated by FIRE (the Foundation for Individual Rights in Education) at the University of South Carolina at Columbia, in which class rules required students "to acknowledge that racism, classism, sexism, heterosexism, and other institutionalized forms of oppression exist" and to agree to combat them and the myths and stereotypes that perpetuate them. A student objected to being told she must share her teacher's ideological beliefs and FIRE issued an objection to this academic requirement. (As described in Barbara Applebaum, *Being White, Being Good: White Complicity, White Moral Responsibility, and Social Justice Pedagogy* [Lanham: Lexington Books, 2010], 103.) While prejudices do exist and countering them is a good thing, these class rules are worrying for two reasons. Firstly, it is disturbing that students were being required to subscribe to a belief and become activists in its service, and, secondly, the requirement to combat myths and stereotypes probably relies on a subjective (and ideological) definition of what is mythical and stereotypical.

39. Breanne Fahs and Michael Karger, "Women's Studies as Virus: Institutional Feminism, Affect, and the Projection of Danger," *Multidisciplinary Journal of Gender Studies* 5, no. 1 (2016).

40. Sandra J. Grey, "Activist Academics: What Future?" *Policy Futures in Education* 11, no. 6 (2013).

41. Laura W. Perna, *Taking It to the Streets: The Role of Scholarship in Advocacy and Advocacy in Scholarship* (Baltimore: Johns Hopkins University Press, 2018).

42. This characterization comes from evolutionary biologist Heather Heying (personal communication).

43. Sean Stevens, "The Google Memo: What Does the Research Say About Gender Differences?" *Heterodox Academy*, February 2, 2019, heterodoxacademy.org/the-google-memo-what-does-the-research-say-about-gender-differences/.

44. Emma Powell and Patrick Grafton-Green, "Danny Baker Fired by BBC Radio 5 Live over Racist Royal Baby Tweet," *Evening Standard*, May 9, 2019, www.standard.co.uk/news/uk/danny-baker-fired-broadcaster-sacked-by-bbc-radio-5-live-over-racist-tweet-a4137951.html.

3 *Postcolonial Theory*

1. Some postcolonial scholars are materialists (often Marxists) and look at colonialism and its aftermath in terms of economics and politics. They are often very critical of the postmodern postcolonialists. See particularly Meera Nanda, Aijaz Ahmad, Benita Parry, Neil Lazarus, and Pal Ahluwalia.

2. Decoloniality and indigeneity constitute two related but separate fields of study, which share many of the features of postcolonial Theory. They both focus on the ways in which the powerful inheritors of colonialism maintain their social and political dominance, especially by othering through language. Decoloniality focused originally on Latin America. Walter Mignolo, in particular, works on epistemology and challenges the knowledge production methods of Enlightenment thinking. However, decolonial scholars frequently reject postmodernism as a Western phenomenon. Indigenous scholars have taken a similar tack in relation to knowledge and systems of power. Linda Tuhiwai Smith, professor of indigenous education at the University of Waikato in New Zealand, is influential in this area. Her book *Decolonizing Methodologies: Research and Indigenous Peoples* (1999) describes itself as "drawing on Foucault" to argue that Western scholarship is central to the colonization of indigenous people. See Linda Tuhiwai Smith, *Decolonizing Methodologies: Research and Indigenous Peoples* (London: Zed Books, 1999).

3. Frantz Fanon, *Black Skin, White Masks*, trans. Richard Philcox (New York: Penguin Books, 2019).

4. Frantz Fanon, *A Dying Colonialism*, trans. Haakon Chevalier (Harmondsworth (Middlesex: Penguin Books, 1970).

5. Frantz Fanon, *The Wretched of the Earth*, trans. Constance Farrington (Harmondsworth: Penguin, 1967).

6. Said, *Orientalism*.

7. Mathieu E. Courville, "Genealogies of Postcolonialism: A Slight Return from Said and Foucault Back to Fanon and Sartre," *Studies in Religion/Sciences Religieuses* 36, no. 2 (2007): Said's approach was broadly Foucauldian, though he rejects some aspects of Foucault's work in favor of Fanon's. His approach can therefore be seen as a synthesis of the work of those two thinkers.

8. Said, *Orientalism*, 3.

9. Joseph Conrad, *Heart of Darkness: and Other Stories* (New York: Barnes & Noble, 2019).

10. Said, *Orientalism*, xviii.

11. Linda Hutcheon, "'Circling the Downspout of Empire,'" in *Past the Last Post: Theorizing Post-Colonialism and Post-Modernism*, ed. Ian Adam and Helen Tiffin (London: Harvester/Wheatsheaf, 1991).

12. Ibid., 168.

13. Gayatri Chakravorty Spivak, "Can the Subaltern Speak?" in *Marxism and the Interpretation of Culture*, ed. Cary Nelson and Lawrence Grossberg (Chicago: University of Illinois Press, 1988).

14. Gayatri Chakravorty Spivak, "Subaltern Studies: Deconstructing Historiography," in *Selected Subaltern Studies*, ed. Ranajit Guha and Gayatri Chakravorty Spivak (New York: Oxford University Press, 1988), 13.

15. Spivak, "Can the Subaltern Speak?" 308.

16. Lecturer in Anglophone literatures and cultures, Stephen Morton describes him thus: "Bhabha's work often exposes the ambivalence and uncertainty at the heart of seemingly robust, powerful forms of knowledge. His critique of the discourses of colonialism uncovers a perpetual process of fracturing and splitting at their heart as they anxiously seek (but always fail) to secure knowledge about the colonized." Stephen Morton, "Poststructuralist Formulations," in *The Routledge Companion to Postcolonial Studies*, ed. John McCleod (London: Routledge, 2007), 205.

17. The Bad Writing Contest, www.denisdutton.com/bad_writing.htm (accessed August 22, 2019).

18. Homi Bhabha is best known for the idea of *hybridity*, introduced in his 1994 book, *The Location of Culture*, and for related concepts, such as *mimicry, ambivalence,* and *third space*. These pertain to notions of duality, doubling, appropriation, and ambiguity. Such terms come up frequently in postmodern Theory. These concepts are best understood as the rejection of stable categories. The terms refer to people who operate in multiple realms at the same time, while feeling part of both, but also divided, either in their own perception of themselves and their position or in someone else's. They can feel "hybrid"—for instance, Asian-American—or they can feel that they are mimicking or conforming to a dominant culture or having theirs mimicked or appropriated by that culture. Bhabha's concept of hybridity describes the mixing of cultures and languages to create a new form, containing elements of both. *Ambivalence* describes the divided individual and *mimicry* is a practice of communication within the (third) space where the two parts meet. However, within postcolonial Theory, this mixing of cultures is characterized by a power imbalance that results in the imposition of one culture and language over another. See Homi K. Bhabha, *The Location of Culture* (London: Routledge, 1994).

19. This method of postcolonial analysis is very much about interpreting and reinterpreting, deconstructing, and reconstructing culture, narratives, perceptions, and identity and very little about looking empirically at material reality. As Simon Gikandi, a professor of English language and literature, argues, "It was as a method of cultural analysis and as a mode of reading that poststructuralism became central to the postcolonial project" (Simon Gikandi, "Poststructuralism and Postcolonial Discourse," *Cambridge Companion to Postcolonial Studies*, ed. Neil Lazarus [Cambridge: Cambridge University Press, 2004], 113). Morton goes further, arguing that to "read" culture in this highly theoretical and removed way actually silences the colonized.

By framing political resistance in the abstract terms of signs, codes and discursive strategies, in other words, materialist critics of a postcolonial Theory informed by the work of Jacques Derrida and Michel Foucault argue that postcolonial Theory—either wittingly or unwittingly—denies the agency and voice of the colonized (Morton, "Formations," 161).

In short, the focus on language and interpretation, viewed through a narrow postcolonial lens, reduces previously colonized people to foils of the West again. They can only be understood in terms of their collective relationship with the West and are denied both individuality and universality. This politically motivated approach to "reading" through power structures that we have called *applied postmodernism* therefore recreates the stereotypes that it claims were created by the West, though, unlike previous Orientalists, it valorizes, rather than denigrates them.

20. Bhabha, *Location*, 20–21.

21. The most consistent critics of postmodern postcolonial scholars are Marxist postcolonial scholars, of whom the most prominent is arguably Vivek Chibber. Of most concern to Chibber is the essentializing nature of postcolonial studies. By this, he means that universal or shared human goals are devalued in postcolonial studies, in favor of stark cultural differences that recreate Orientalism. By making science, reason, liberalism, and the whole Enlightenment tradition Western, Chibber fears that

> [t]he lasting contribution of postcolonial theory—what it will be known for, in my view, if it is remembered fifty years from now—will be its revival of cultural essentialism and its acting as an endorsement of orientalism, rather than being an antidote to it.

Vivek Chibber, "How Does the Subaltern Speak?" Interview by Jonah Birch, *Jacobin*, April 21, 2013, www.jacobinmag.com/2013/04/how-does-the-subaltern-speak/.

22. Joseph-Ernest Renan, *La Réforme intellectuelle et morale (1871),* as quoted in Ahdaf Soueif, "The Function of Narrative in the War on Terror," in *War on Terror*, ed. Chris Miller (Manchester: Manchester University Press, 2009), 30.

23. Mariya Hussain, "Why Is My Curriculum White?" *National Union of Students*, March 11, 2015, www.nus.org.uk/en/news/why-is-my-curriculum-white/; Malia Bouattia and Sorana Vieru, "#LiberateMyDegree @ NUS Connect," *NUS Connect*, www.nusconnect.org.uk/campaigns/liberate-mydegree.

24. Dalia Gebrial, "Rhodes Must Fall: Oxford and Movements for Change," in *Decolonising the University*, ed. Gurminder K. Bhambra, Dalia Gebrial, and Kerem Nişancıoğlu (London: Pluto Press, 2018).

25. Bhambra and colleagues explain it like this,

> "Decolonising" involves a multitude of definitions, interpreta-

tions, aims and strategies. . . . First, it is a way of thinking about
the world which takes colonialism, empire and racism as its empirical and discursive objects of study; it re-situates these phenomena as key shaping forces of the contemporary world, in a
context where their role has been systematically effaced from
view. Second, it purports to offer alternative ways of thinking
about the world and alternative forms of political praxis.

Gurminder K. Bhambra, Dalia Gebrial, and Kerem Nişancıoğlu, eds., *Decolonising the University* (London: Pluto Press, 2018), 1–2.

26. We see this when Bhambra and colleagues say, "one of the key challenges that decolonising approaches have presented to Eurocentric forms of
knowledge is an insistence on positionality and plurality and, perhaps more
importantly, the impact that taking 'difference' seriously would make to
standard understandings" (ibid., 2–3).

27. Ibid., 3.

28. Ibid., 2–3.

29. The idea that the Western elite effectively promotes "whiteness" over all
other ways of knowing appears in the introduction to the 2018 book *Rhodes Must Fall: The Struggle to Decolonise the Racist Heart of Empire* by Kehinde
Andrews, the United Kingdom's first professor of black studies. Andrews
writes, "Oxford's prestige is founded on its elite status, which is a code word
for its whiteness" (p. 1). The evidence of this is experiential: "It is easy to
underestimate the symbolic violence that is committed on a daily basis in
spaces like Oxford. But you only need to walk on the campus to feel the oppression in the environment." Kehinde Andrews, "Introduction," in *Rhodes
Must Fall: The Struggle to Decolonise the Racist Heart of Empire*, ed. Roseanne
Chantiluke, Brian Kwoba, and Athinangamso Nkopo (London: Zed Books,
2018), 2.

30. Bhambra et al., *Decolonising*, 5 .

31. Andrews, "Introduction," 4.

32. "Our Aim." *#RHODESMUSTFALL*, December 24, 2015. rmfoxford.word-
press.com/about/.

33. This belief is expressed perhaps most explicitly by branding and rejecting
Western concepts of knowledge as *positivist*. "Positivist" means that knowledge is defined as that which can be shown and seen, tested scientifically or
proved mathematically. A positivist understanding of knowledge involves
accepting that which is evidenced, rather than that which has only been
theorized, experienced subjectively, or is a question of faith. Such an attitude, rather than being seen as *rigorous*, is understood within postcolonial
and decolonial movements to be merely Western and colonial.

34. Gebrial, "Movements for Change," 24.

35. Nelson Maldonado-Torres, Rafael Vizcaíno, Jasmine Wallace, and Jeong Eun Annabel, "Decolonizing Philosophy," in *Decolonising the University*, eds Gurminder K. Bhambra, Dalia Gebrial, and Kerem Nişancıoğlu (London: Pluto Press, 2018), 64.

36. Maldonado-Torres et al., "Decolonising Philosophy," 66.

37. Ibid., 66–67.

38. Andrew Jolivétte, *Research Justice: Methodologies for Social Change* (Bristol, UK: Policy Press, 2015), 5.

39. Kagendo Mutua and Beth Blue Swadener, *Decolonizing Research in Cross-cultural Contexts: Critical Personal Narratives* (Albany, NY: SUNY Press, 2011).

40. Mutua and Swadener, *Cross-Cultural Contexts*, 1.

41. Ibid., 2.

42. Meera Nanda, "We Are All Hybrids Now: The Dangerous Epistemology of Post-colonial Populism," *Journal of Peasant Studies* 28, no. 2 (2001): 165.

43. Ibid., 164.

44. Nanda writes,

> Postmodern/post-colonial theory's animus against the Enlightenment values and its indulgence towards contradictions make it eminently compatible with a typically right-wing resolution of the asynchronicity (or the time-lag) between advanced technology and a backward social context that developing societies typically experience in the process of modernization. (Ibid., 165)

45. To this effect, Nanda writes,

> If we grant the very foundations of objectivity to the West, are we not back to the old stereotypes of irrational emotional natives? Ironically for a intellectual genre that is founded on a denial of essential ahistorical, permanent features, these critics fail to see that these characteristically modern features are not sanctioned by Western religion and culture, but they have had to be struggled for even in the West. (Ibid., 171)

46. Carolette R. Norwood, "Decolonizing My Hair, Unshackling My Curls: An Autoethnography on What Makes My Natural Hair Journey a Black Feminist Statement," *International Feminist Journal of Politics* 20, no. 1 (2017).

47. Meera Sabaratnam, "Decolonising the Curriculum: What's All the Fuss About?" *SOAS Blog*, June 25, 2018, www.soas.ac.uk/blogs/study/decolonising-curriculum-whats-the-fuss/.

48. Alan J. Bishop, "Western Mathematics: The Secret Weapon of Cultural Imperialism," *Race & Class* 32, no. 2 (1990).

49. Laura E. Donaldson, "Writing the Talking Stick: Alphabetic Literacy as Colonial Technology and Postcolonial Appropriation," *American Indian Quarterly* 22, no. 1/2 (1998).

50. Mutua and Swadener, *Cross-Cultural Contexts.*

51. Lucille Toth, "Praising Twerk: Why Aren't We All Shaking Our Butt?" *French Cultural Studies* 28, no. 3 (2017).

4 *Queer Theory*

1. Sherry B. Ortner, "Is Female to Male as Nature Is to Culture?" in *Woman, Culture, and Society*, ed. Michelle Zimbalist Rosaldo and Louise Lamphere (Palo Alto, CA: Stanford University Press, 1974).

2. There are cultures that have perceived a third sex or a multitude of genders. These largely seem to be ways to think about people who don't fit into the expected categories of "masculine man attracted to women" and "feminine woman attracted to men," and have generally been regarded as outliers from a prevailing norm, with roots deeply embedded in the biological realities of a sexually reproducing species.

3. The name "queer Theory" is believed to have been coined in a collection of essays edited by Teresa de Lauretis in 1991. Teresa De Lauretis, *Queer Theory: Lesbian and Gay Sexualities* (Providence, RI: Brown University Press, 1991).

4. Mikael and Sune Innala, "The Effect of a Biological Explanation on Attitudes towards Homosexual Persons: A Swedish National Sample Study," *Nordic Journal of Psychiatry* 56, no. 3 (2002).

5. The "Q" here seems to be co-opting the L, G, B, and T status for its own political project, to which the others may not (and often do not) subscribe.

6. Judith Halberstam, *In a Queer Time and Place: Transgender Bodies, Subcultural Lives* (New York: New York University Press, 2005).

7. David M. Halperin, "The Normalization of Queer Theory," *Journal of Homosexuality* 45, no. 2–4 (2003).

8. David M. Halperin, *Saint Foucault: Towards a Gay Hagiography* (New York: Oxford University Press, 1997), 62.

9. The authors hasten to note that "genderfucking" is a technical academic term in queer Theory, which means, roughly, "to fuck about with the meaning of 'gender' so as to queer it."

10. Annamarie Jagose, *Queer Theory: An Introduction* (New York: New York University Press, 2010), 1. Jagose also attempts the following definition of queer Theory:

> While there is no critical consensus on the definitional limits of queer—determinacy being one of its widely promoted charms—its general outlines are frequently sketched and debated. Broadly speaking, queer describes those gestures or analytical models which dramatise incoherencies in the allegedly stable relations between chromosomal sex, gender and sexual desire. Resisting that model of stability—which claims heterosexuality as its origin, when it is more properly its effect—queer focuses on mismatches between sex, gender and desire. Institutionally, queer has been associated most prominently with lesbian and gay subjects, but its analytic framework also includes such topics as cross-dressing, hermaphroditism, gender ambiguity and gender-corrective surgery. Whether as transvestite performance or academic deconstruction, queer locates and exploits the incoherencies in those three terms which stabilise heterosexuality. Demonstrating the impossibility of any "natural" sexuality, it calls into question even such apparently unproblematic terms as "man" and "woman." (p. 3)

11. "Many psychological traits relevant to the public sphere, such as general intelligence, are the same on average for men and women. . . . [G]eneralizations about a sex will always be untrue of many individuals. And notions like 'proper role' and 'natural place' are scientifically meaningless and give no grounds for restricting freedom." Steven Pinker, *The Blank Slate: The Modern Denial of Human Nature* (London: Penguin, 2002), 340.

12. E. O. Wilson, "From Sociobiology to Sociology," in *Evolution, Literature, and Film: A Reader*, ed. Brian, Joseph Carroll, and Jonathan Gottschall, (New York: Columbia University Press, 2010), 98.

13. Some trans scholars and activists have recently begun to call upon science, as neuroscience has increasingly provided evidence that trans people's experience of their gender as different from their sex is biologically based. This has not made significant inroads into queer Theory.

14. Michel Foucault, *The History of Sexuality: Volume 1, an Introduction*, trans. Robert J. Hurley (New York: Penguin, 1990).

15. Ibid., 69.

16. Ibid., 54.

17. Ibid., 93.

18. Louise Amoore, *The Global Resistance Reader* (London: Routledge, 2005), 86.

19. Another influential and power-obsessed French sociological theorist, Pierre Bourdieu, who was strongly at odds with Foucault and the orthodox postmodern view, saw things similarly and described this using his concept of social *habitus*.

20. While society's views on the moral status of various aspects of human sexuality have changed dramatically over the last fifty years—extra-marital sex and homosexual sex have increasingly been seen as morally neutral—Rubin alarmingly includes pedophilia in her list of merely socially constructed taboos, saying, "It is harder for most people to sympathize with actual boy-lovers. Like communists and homosexuals in the 1950s, boy-lovers are so stigmatized that it is difficult to find defenders for their civil liberties, let alone for their erotic orientation." Gayle Rubin, "Thinking Sex: Notes for a Radical Theory of the Politics of Sexuality," in *The Lesbian and Gay Studies Reader*, ed. Henry Abelove, Michèle Aina Barale, and David M. Halperin (Abingdon: Taylor & Francis, 1993), 7.

21. Ibid., 9.

22. Ibid., 10.

23. Ibid., 11.

24. Rubin explicitly describes this hierarchy:

> Modern Western societies appraise sex acts according to a hierarchical system of sexual value. Marital, reproductive heterosexuals are alone at the top erotic pyramid. Clamouring below are unmarried monogamous heterosexuals in couples, followed by most other heterosexuals. . . . The most despised sexual castes currently include transsexuals, transvestites, fetishists, sadomasochists, sex workers such as prostitutes and porn models, and the lowliest of all, those whose eroticism transgresses generational boundaries. (Ibid., 12)

25. Ibid., 15.

26. Ibid., 22.

27. Judith Butler, *Bodies that Matter: On the Discursive Limits of "Sex"* (New York: Routledge, 1993), xii.

28. Judith Butler, *Gender Trouble* (London: Routledge, 2006), 192.

29. Ibid., 192.

30. Ibid., 192.

31. Ibid., 192–3.

32. Adrienne Rich, *Compulsory Heterosexuality and Lesbian Existence* (Denver, CO: Antelope Publications, 1982).

33. Butler, *Gender Trouble*, 169.

34. Ibid., 44.

35. Ibid., 44.

36. Ibid., 9–10.

37. Ibid., 7.

38. Eve Kosofsky Sedgwick, *Epistemology of the Closet* (Berkeley, CA: University of California Press, 2008), 13.

39. Ibid., 1.

40. Ibid., 3.

41. Ibid., 9.

42. Elizabeth Freeman, *Time Binds: Queer Temporalities, Queer Histories* (Durham, NC: Duke University Press, 2010).

43. Mel Y. Chen, *Animacies: Biopolitics, Racial Mattering, and Queer Affect* (Durham, NC: Duke University Press, 2012).

44. Butler, *Gender Trouble*, 4.

45. Queer Theorists might respond to this by saying that it is a radical over-simplification of their position, which they claim does not deny biological realities but merely argues that such realities are mediated through historical discourses, which in turn determine the categories in which we think. This is yet another distinction without a difference. Because of queer Theory's moral imperative to reject, disrupt, and subvert scientific claims and "common sense" about gender, sexuality, and even sex, queer Theorists spend almost no time acknowledging that biological realities exist and almost all their time rejecting them and asserting the social construction of those categories.

5 Critical Race Theory and Intersectionality

1. Michael Neill, "'Mulattos,' 'Blacks,' and 'Indian Moors': Othello and Early Modern Constructions of Human Difference," *Shakespeare Quarterly* 49, no. 4 (1998).

2. Some third-century Han Chinese people described barbarians with blond hair and green eyes, commenting it was obvious that—unlike the Han— they had clearly descended from monkeys. Thomas F. Gossett, *Race: The History of an Idea in America* (Oxford: Oxford University Press, 1997).

3. Sojourner Truth, "The Narrative of Sojourner Truth," ed. Olive Gilbert, in *A Celebration of Women Writers*, www.digital.library.upenn.edu/women/truth/1850/1850.html.

4. Frederick Douglass, *Narrative of the Life Frederick Douglass* (Lexington, KY: CreateSpace, 2013).

5. W. E. B. Du Bois, *The Souls of Black Folk: The Unabridged Classic* (New York: Clydesdale, 2019).

6. Winthrop D. Jordan, *White over Black American Attitudes toward the Negro, 1550–1812* (Chapel Hill, NC: University of North Carolina Press, 2012).

7. Richard Delgado and Jean Stefancic, *Critical Race Theory: An Introduction* (New York: New York University Press, 2017), 3.

8. Ibid., *Introduction*, 26.

9. Derrick A. Bell, *Race, Racism, and American Law* (Boston: Little, Brown, and Co., 1984).

10. Derrick Bell, *And We Are Not Saved: The Elusive Quest for Racial Justice* (New York: Basic Books, 2008).

11. Ibid., 159.

12. Derrick A. Bell, Jr., "*Brown v. Board of Education* and the Interest-Convergence Dilemma," *Harvard Law Review* 93, No. 3 (1980).

13. Bell writes,

> Black people will never gain full equality in this country. Even those herculean efforts we hail as successful will produce no more than temporary "peaks of progress," short-lived victories that slide into irrelevance as racial patterns adapt in ways that maintain white dominance. This is a hard-to-accept fact that all history verifies. We must acknowledge it and move on to adopt policies based on what I call: "Racial Realism." This mind-set or philosophy requires us to acknowledge the permanence of our subordinate status. That acknowledgement enables us to avoid despair, and frees us to imagine and implement racial strategies that can bring fulfillment and even triumph.

Derrick A. Bell, Jr., "Racial Realism," *Connecticut Law Review* 24, no. 2 (1992).

14. Bell, *Brown v. Board*, esp. pp. 530–533.

15. Alan David Freeman, "Legitimizing Racial Discrimination Through Antidiscrimination Law: A Critical Review of Supreme Court Doctrine," *Minnesota Law Review* 62, no. 1049 (1978), scholarship.law.umn.edu/mlr/804.

16. Mark Stern and Khuram Hussain, "On the Charter Question: Black Marxism and Black Nationalism," *Race Ethnicity and Education* 18, no. 1 (2014).

17. As Delgado and Stefancic put it:

A persistent internal critique accuses the movement of straying from its materialist roots and dwelling overly on matters of concern to middle-class minorities—microaggressions, racial insults, unconscious discrimination, and affirmative action in higher education. If racial oppression has material and cultural roots, attacking only its ideational or linguistic expression is apt to do little for the underlying structures of inequality, much less the plight of the deeply poor. (*Introduction*, 106)

18. Patricia J. Williams, *The Alchemy of Race and Rights* (Cambridge, MA: Harvard University Press, 1991).

19. See "About This Book" on the page for *The Alchemy of Race and Rights* by Patricia J. Williams in Harvard University Press's online catalog, www.hup.harvard.edu/catalog.php?isbn=9780674014718.

20. Harvard University Press, "Honoring the Work of Patricia Williams." Harvard University Press Blog, February 2013, harvardpress.typepad.com/hup_publicity/2013/02/honoring-the-work-of-patricia-williams.html.

21. Angela P. Harris, "Race and Essentialism in Feminist Legal Theory," *Stanford Law Review* 42, no. 3 (1990): 584.

22. Delgado and Stefancic, *Introduction*, 8–11.

23. Although critical race Theory arose in the United States in response to a very specific historical racial context, it has not remained in the United States. The British Educational Research Association has formed its own list of tenets of critical race Theory.

1. Centrality of racism
2. White supremacy
3. Voices of people of color
4. Interest convergence
5. Intersectionality

It concludes,

CRT has developed rapidly into a major branch of social theory and has been taken up beyond the United States to include work in Europe, South America, Australia and Africa. It is often denigrated by people working with alternative perspectives who view the emphasis on race and racism as misguided or even threatening. Despite such attacks, which frequently rest on a lack of understanding and oversimplification of the approach, CRT continues to grow and is becoming one of the most important perspectives on the policy and practice of race inequality in the UK.

Nicola Rollock and David Gillborn, "Critical Race Theory (CRT)," *BERA*, 2011, www.bera.ac.uk/publication/critical-race-theory-crt.

24. For example, Payne Hiraldo, of the University of Vermont, set out five tenets of critical race Theory for use in higher education. These are:

> *Counter-storytelling*—"A framework that legitimizes the racial and subordinate experiences of marginalized groups." Because society is believed to be constructed of the ideological narratives—discourses—of dominant groups, counternarratives are believed to represent the previously neglected knowledges of marginalized identity groups. This is standpoint theory, which assumes that people of certain identities have perspectives, experiences, and values in common, that these constitute alternative forms of knowledge, and that belonging to a marginalized identity group confers access to a richer knowledge set than can be accessed by members of relatively privileged groups.
>
> *The permanence of racism*—The idea that racism is prevalent and pervasive in all spheres of American society: political, social, and economic. Therefore it cannot be defeated by antidiscrimination legislation, but must be detected in all kinds of systems and interactions and acted against.
>
> *Whiteness as property*—A complicated argument that "whiteness"—the social constructions associated with a white identity—confers property rights, due to ingrained prejudices and assumptions with their roots in slavery. Closely akin to white privilege, it posits that covert systematic discrimination continues to uphold white people's superiority and greater rights of access and property and that this can only be addressed by affirmative action or other equity initiatives.
>
> *Interest conversion*—The belief that white people and societies that are understood to be white supremacist only allow advances in rights for people of color when it serves their own interests.
>
> *The critique of liberalism*—Liberalism is criticized for universalist ideas, such as "color blindness," equal opportunities, equal rights, and meritocracy. It is believed to overlook systemic racism by assuming an already "level playing field."

Payne Hiraldo, "The Role of Critical Race Theory in Higher Education," *Vermont Connection* 31, no. 7 (2010): Article 7, scholarworks.uvm.edu/tvc/vol31/iss1/7.

Underlying all of these tenets is the postmodern conception of society as constructed by discourses into systems of power and privilege—the postmodern knowledge and political principles. These tenets also clearly advocate the application of interpretation and theoretical constructs rather than the presentation of observable evidence.

25. *The Encyclopedia of Diversity in Education* presents yet another variation on these core tenets but stresses the political aims of critical race Theory more strongly. Under the subheading "Centrality of Racism," Christine E. Sleeter writes, "Critical race theorists assume that racism is not an aberration, but rather a fundamental, endemic, and normalized way of organizing society." Christine E. Sleeter, "Critical Race Theory and Education," in *Encyclopedia of Diversity in Education*, ed. James A. Banks (Thousand Oaks, CA: SAGE, 2012), 491.

Sleeter continues to identify the following tenets of critical race Theory:

1. Challenges to claims of neutrality, color blindness, and meritocracy;
2. Whites as beneficiaries of racial remedies (interest convergence thesis);
3. Centrality of experiential knowledge (telling counterstories; standpoint theory);
4. Commitment to working towards social justice ("Ultimately, critical race theorists are committed to working for social justice. Although some theorists see racism as intractable, most hope that deep analyses of it, coupled with the development of rich counter-stories about how people have worked against racism, will ultimately result in its elimination").

26. Delgado and Stefancic, *Introduction*, 7.

27. Ibid., 7–8.

28. Ibid., 7–8.

29. Ibid., 127.

30. bell hooks, "Postmodern Blackness," in *The Fontana Postmodernism Reader*, ed. Walter Truett Anderson (London: Fontana Press, 1996), 117.

31. Kimberlé Crenshaw, "Demarginalizing the Intersection of Race and Sex: A Black Feminist Critique of Antidiscrimination Doctrine, Feminist Theory, and Antiracist Politics," *University of Chicago Legal Forum* 1, no. 8 (1989), chicagounbound.uchicago.edu/uclf/vol1989/iss1/8.

32. Kimberlé Crenshaw, "Mapping the Margins: Intersectionality, Identity Politics, and Violence against Women of Color," *Stanford Law Review* 43, no. 6 (1991): 1224n9.

33. Collins, *Black Feminist Thought*.

34. Crenshaw, "Mapping the Margins," 1297.

35. Ibid., 1242.

36. Ibid., 1296.

37. While much critical race Theory was the work of African American scholars, the field has broadened in the last few decades, to include Latino, Asian, Muslim, and Arab branches. These groups are all seen as having different subordinated relationships to white people and even to each other. For more, see Helen Pluckrose and James A. Lindsay, "Identity Politics Does Not Continue the Work of the Civil Rights Movements," *Areo*, September 26, 2018, areomagazine.com/2018/09/25/identity-politics-does-not-continue-the-work-of-the-civil-rights-movements/.

38. Patricia Hill Collins and Sirma Bilge, *Intersectionality* (Cambridge: Polity Press, 2018).

39. Adam Fitzgerald, "Opinion: Time for Cis-Gender White Men to Recognise Their Privilege," *news.trust.org*, May 2, 2019, news.trust.org/item/20190502130719-tpcky/.

40. Jezzika Chung, "How Asian Immigrants Learn Anti-Blackness from White Culture, and How to Stop It," *Huffington Post*, September 7, 2017, www.huffpost.com/entry/how-asian-americans-can-stop-contributing-to-anti-blackness_b_599f0757e4b0cb7715bfd3d4.

41. Kristel Tracey, "We Need to Talk about Light-skinned Privilege," *Media Diversified*, February 7, 2019, mediadiversified.org/2018/04/26/we-need-to-talk-about-light-skinned-privilege/.

42. Damon Young, "Straight Black Men Are the White People of Black People," *Root*, September 19, 2017, verysmartbrothas.theroot.com/straight-black-men-are-the-white-people-of-black-people-1814157214.

43. Miriam J. Abelson, "Dangerous Privilege: Trans Men, Masculinities, and Changing Perceptions of Safety," *Sociological Forum* 29, no. 3 (2014).

44. Sara C., "When You Say 'I Would Never Date A Trans Person,' It's Transphobic. Here's Why," *Medium*, November 11, 2018, medium.com/@QSE/when-you-say-i-would-never-date-a-trans-person-its-transphobic-here-s-why-aa6fdcf59aca.

45. Iris Kuo, "The 'Whitening' of Asian Americans," *Atlantic*, September 13, 2018, www.theatlantic.com/education/archive/2018/08/the-whitening-of-asian-americans/563336/; Paul Lungen, "Check Your Jewish Privilege," *Canadian Jewish News*, December 21, 2018, www.cjnews.com/living-jewish/check-your-jewish-privilege.

46. Zachary Small, "Joseph Pierce on Why Academics Must Decolonize Queerness," *Hyperallergic*, August 10, 2019, hyperallergic.com/512789/joseph-pierce-on-why-academics-must-decolonize-queerness/.

47. Peter Tatchell, "Tag: Stop Murder Music," *Peter Tatchell Foundation*, May 13, 2016, www.petertatchellfoundation.org/tag/stop-murder-music/.

48. Arwa Mahdawi, "It's Not a Hate Crime for a Woman to Feel Uncomfortable Waxing Male Genitalia," *Guardian*, July 27, 2019, www.theguardian.com/commentisfree/2019/jul/27/male-genitalia-week-in-patriarchy-women.

49. Pluckrose and Lindsay, "Identity Politics Does Not Continue the Work of the Civil Rights Movements."

50. Collins and Bilge, *Intersectionality*, 30.

51. Rebecca Ann Lind, "A Note From the Guest Editor," *Journal of Broadcasting & Electronic Media* 54 (2010): 3.

52. Cho, Crenshaw, and McCall identify three overlapping "sets of engagements": "the first consisting of applications of an intersectional framework or investigations of intersectional dynamics, the second consisting of discursive debates about the scope and content of intersectionality as a theoretical and methodological paradigm, and the third consisting of political interventions employing an intersectional lens." Sumi Cho, Kimberlé Williams Crenshaw, and Leslie McCall, "Toward a Field of Intersectionality Studies: Theory, Applications, and Praxis," *Signs: Journal of Women in Culture and Society* 38, no. 4 (2013): 785.

53. Ange-Marie Hancock, *Intersectionality: An Intellectual History* (New York: Oxford University Press, 2016), 5.

54. Ibid., 5.

55. Ibid., 6.

56. These Hancock names as Crenshaw and Collins; "the original" is the white Frenchman Michel Foucault (*Intellectual History*, 9).

57. Hancock remarks,

> How do intersectionality scholars find a middle ground between an impossible conceptualization of intersectionality as intellectual property, and a destructive conceptualization of intersectionality as meme, which shape-shifts so much as to no longer be recognizable as anything other than a meme gone viral? (*Intellectual History*, 17)

58. Crenshaw says,

> Some people look to intersectionality as a grand theory of everything, but that's not my intention. If someone is trying to think about how to explain to the courts why they should not dismiss a case made by black women, just because the employer did hire blacks who were men and women who were white, well, that's what the tool was designed to do. If it works, great. If it doesn't

work, it's not like you have to use this concept. The other issue is that intersectionality can get used as a blanket term to mean, "Well, it's complicated." Sometimes, "It's complicated" is an excuse not to do anything.

Kimberlé Crenshaw, "Kimberlé Crenshaw on Intersectionality, More than Two Decades Later," *Columbia Law School*, June 2017, www.law.columbia. edu/pt-br/news/2017/06/kimberle-crenshaw-intersectionality.

59. See Robin J. DiAngelo, "White Fragility," *International Journal of Critical Pedagogy* 3, no. 3 (2011) and Robin J. DiAngelo, *White Fragility: Why It's so Hard for White People to Talk about Racism* (London: Allen Lane, 2019).

60. Greg Lukianoff and Jonathan Haidt, *The Coddling of the American Mind: How Good Intentions and Bad Ideas Are Setting Up a Generation for Failure* (New York: Penguin Books, 2019).

61. See Heather Bruce, Robin DiAngelo, Gyda Swaney (Salish), and Amie Thurber, "Between Principles and Practice: Tensions in Anti-Racist Education" (panel, 2014 Race & Pedagogy National Conference, University of Puget Sound), video posted by Collins Memorial Library, vimeo. com/116986053.

62. Bruce et al, *Tensions*, 2014.

63. Ibid., 2014.

64. James Lindsay, "Postmodern Religion and the Faith of Social Justice," *Areo Magazine*, December 26, 2018, areomagazine.com/2018/12/18/postmodern-religion-and-the-faith-of-social-justice/.

65. David Rock and Heidi Grant, "Is Your Company's Diversity Training Making You More Biased?" *Psychology Today*, June 7, 2017, www.psychologytoday.com/intl/blog/your-brain-work/201706/is-your-company-s-diversity-training-making-you-more-biased.

6 *Feminisms and Gender Studies*

1. Stevi Jackson, "Why a Materialist Feminism Is (Still) Possible—and Necessary," *Women's Studies International Forum* 24, no. 3–4 (2001).

2. In the United States: Barbara J. Risman, "Good News! Attitudes Moving Toward Gender Equality," *Psychology Today*, December 17, 2018, www. psychologytoday.com/gb/blog/gender-questions/201812/good-news-attitudes-moving-toward-gender-equality; in the United Kingdom: Radhika Sanghani, "Only 7 per Cent of Britons Consider Themselves Feminists," *Telegraph*, January 15, 2016, www.telegraph.co.uk/women/life/only-7-per-cent-of-britons-consider-themselves-feminists/.

3. It is virtually certain that we have left out at least one feminist camp here and equally likely that we'll hear about it as a result.

4. To avoid drawing intersectional feminist ire ourselves—as though this is possible—here we note that many of the branches of feminism reject the "linear wave model" that sees a first-wave feminism that fought for women's suffrage followed by a second-wave liberal model that expanded women's rights legally, in the home, in the workplace, and in society, followed by a third wave that is intersectional (and, sometimes, a fourth wave that focuses primarily upon applying a radically expanded view of sexual assault through concepts like rape culture). The rejection of the linear wave model is especially true of many branches of black and intersectional feminist thought.

5. Paraphrased from Judith Lorber, "Shifting Paradigms and Challenging Categories," *Social Problems* 53, no. 4 (2006): 448.

6. Simone de Beauvoir, *The Second Sex*, trans. H. M. Parshley (New York: Vintage Books, 1974).

7. Betty Friedan, *The Feminine Mystique* (New York: W. W. Norton & Company, 2013).

8. Kate Millett, Catharine A. MacKinnon, and Rebecca Mead, *Sexual Politics* (New York: Columbia University Press, 2016).

9. Germaine Greer, *The Female Eunuch* (London: Fourth Estate, 2012).

10. Lorber writes, "On the hegemony of dominant men, as an adaptation of Gramsci's (1971) idea of dominant elites and Marxist class consciousness, it was easy to view women as a subordinated class in the domestic division of labor" ("Shifting Paradigms," 448).

11. Ibid., 449.

12. Jane Pilcher and Imelda Whelehan, *Key Concepts in Gender Studies* (Los Angeles: Sage, 2017), xiii.

13. Pilcher and Whelehan, *Key Concepts*.

14. Ibid., xiii.

15. In the words of Pilcher and Whelehan, gender studies "have been a key driver of the increased recognition of diversity and difference. Inequalities and differences, not just between genders but within genders, based on class, sexuality, ethnicity, age, nationality and religion, and citizenship status, for example, are now attended to" (ibid., xiii).

16. Ibid., xiii.

17. Lorber, "Shifting Paradigms," 449.

18. Ibid., 448.

19. Ibid., 448.

20. Ibid., 448.

21. Ibid., 448.

22. We should not misunderstand this to mean that every feminist became an applied postmodernist, intersectional feminist by the early 2000s or that every feminist is one now. In fact, it is unlikely that even a majority are—except in certain enclaves, like the academy. Feminists of dozens of stripes still exist, are active, and fight with one another, but the intersectional branch dominates both activism and scholarship.

   Radical feminists, liberal feminists, and material feminists—among many other types—still exist and are quite active. Radicals and materialists are interested in the material realities of economics, law, and government and accept that objective truths exist, while the postmodernists—and their descendants, the intersectionalists—are interested in how discourses construct knowledge and enforce power (the postmodern knowledge and political principles). Both kinds of feminist ultimately believe that gender is a cultural construct, but, while the radical materialist feminists believe it has been constructed by men to oppress women (a typically Marxist understanding of power as operating from above), the intersectionalists believe that the power to enforce gender permeates all of society in the form of discourses—how we talk about things—and that liberation can only come from disrupting the stability and relevance of categories of sex, gender, and sexuality—including those relied upon by radical feminists. This puts them at considerable odds.

   The most recognizable conflict between radical and intersectional feminists occurs on the incredibly hostile battleground between postmodern trans activists—who believe in self-identification of gender, which necessitates the acceptance of trans women as women, for example—and the gender-critical radical feminists (often disparagingly called Trans-Exclusionary Radical Feminists, or TERFs)—who believe that gender is an oppressive imposition and trans women are men who are complicit in that oppression. There is a similar conflict, often involving the same feminists, between those who are positive about sex work done by women and those radical feminists (often disparagingly called Sex-Worker-Exclusionary Radical Feminists, or SWERFs), who believe sex work to be exploitation of women.

   During the 1970s and into the 1980s, the radical and materialist feminist viewpoint held sway in the universities, but—following the turn to applied postmodernism and the creation of intersectional feminism, queer Theory, and postcolonial feminism—the intersectional feminists, queer

Theorists, and trans activists have gained dominance. This has led to the deplatforming of once-popular feminist figures like Germaine Greer and Julie Burchill for their views on trans identity and sex work. Radical feminists also face fierce criticism from postcolonial and intersectional feminists because they see women as one class and are therefore frequently opposed to cultural relativism. They are critical of the oppression of women under Islam, for example, and postcolonial and intersectional scholars sometimes see this as imperialist universalizing.

23. Another example of this phenomenon can be found among those Christian sects who reinterpret Jesus' promises to return within a generation to establish the Kingdom of God (Matthew 24:34, and elsewhere) spiritually, as having happened in various ways, such as in Heaven or through the establishment of the Christian religion itself.

24. Leon Festinger, Henry W. Riecken, and Stanley Schachter, *When Prophecy Fails: A Social and Psychological Study of a Modern Group That Predicted the Destruction of the World* (New York: Harper Torchbooks, 1956).

25. A fitting example of this new line of feminist thought is the award-winning and influential book *Down Girl: The Logic of Misogyny*, by Cornell philosophy professor Kate Manne, who argues that misogyny is best understood as a systemic feature of society, by which women's inferiority is enforced socially, even if actual misogynists are rare or nonexistent. See Kate Manne, *Down Girl: The Logic of Misogyny* (New York: Oxford University Press, 2018).

26. Candace West and Don H. Zimmerman, "Doing Gender," *Gender and Society* 1, no. 2 (1987).

27. Ibid., 126.

28. Ibid., 137.

29. Ibid., 142.

30. They write, "If we do gender appropriately, we simultaneously sustain, reproduce, and render legitimate the institutional arrangements that are based on sex category. If we fail to do gender appropriately, we as individuals—not the institutional arrangements—may be called to account (for our character, motives, and predispositions)" (ibid., 146).

31. Catherine Connell, "Doing, Undoing, or Redoing Gender?" *Gender & Society* 24, no. 1 (2010): 31–55.

32. Pilcher and Whelehan, *Key Concepts*, 54.

33. Crenshaw, "Mapping the Margins," 1297.

34. Pilcher and Whelehan, *Key Concepts*, 42.

35. Ibid., 43.

36. Nancy J. Hirschmann, "Choosing Betrayal," *Perspectives on Politics* 8, no. 1 (2010).

37. bell hooks, "Racism and Feminism: The Issue of Accountability," in *Making Sense of Women's Lives: An Introduction to Women's Studies*, ed. Lauri Umansky, Paul K. Longmore, and Michele Plott (Lanham, MD: Rowman & Littlefield).

38. Collins, *Black Feminist Thought*.

39. Patricia Hill Collins, "Toward a New Vision: Race, Class, and Gender as Categories of Analysis and Connection," *Race, Sex & Class* 1, no. 1 (1993): 38–39.

40. The socialist feminist Linda Gordon writes,

> The intersectionality concept also began to focus on some social positions more than others. Of particular concern in reducing the potential of intersectionality as a concept is the neglect of class inequality. One example: a SUNY–Albany School of Social Work syllabus contains a "module" on intersectionality that lists gender, age, ethnic group or race and career identities as the influences to be considered. Neglecting class or economic inequality—and I am aware that these two are by no means identical—is a common and over-determined phenomenon. (p. 348)

She continues,

> Few of the core activist/intersectionality websites that I have discovered—whether predominantly black or predominantly female or both—discuss the problems of low-income people, such as the prohibition on federal funding for abortion, the high cost of decent child care, the lack of paid family and sick leave, unemployment, prison conditions, school defunding, prescription medicine costs, low minimum wages and wage theft. (p. 353)

Linda Gordon, "'Intersectionality,' Socialist Feminism and Contemporary Activism: Musings by a Second-Wave Socialist Feminist," *Gender & History* 28, no. 2 (2016).

41. Peggy McIntosh, *On Privilege, Fraudulence, and Teaching As Learning: Selected Essays 1981–2019* (New York: Taylor & Francis, 2019), 29–34.

42. See journalistic analyses: Janet Daley, "The Bourgeois Left Has Abandoned the Working Class to the Neo-fascists," *Telegraph*, January 14, 2018, www.telegraph.co.uk/news/2018/01/14/bourgeois-left-has-abandoned-working-class-neo-fascists/; Michael Savage, "'Cities Are Now Labour Heartland, with Working-class Turning Away'," *Guardian*, September 22, 2018, www.theguardian.com/politics/2018/sep/22/cities-are-now-labour-heartland-as-traditional-working-class-desert; Paul Embery, "Why

Does the Left Sneer at the Traditional Working Class?" *UnHerd*, April 5, 2019, unherd.com/2019/04/why-does-the-left-sneer-at-the-traditional-working-class/; Sheri Berman, "Why Identity Politics Benefits the Right More than the Left," *Guardian*, July 14, 2018, www.theguardian.com/com-mentisfree/2018/jul/14/identity-politics-right-left-trump-racism.

43. Gordon, "Musings," 351.

44. Suzanna Danuta Walters, "Why Can't We Hate Men?" *Washington Post*, June 8, 2018, www.washingtonpost.com/opinions/why-cant-we-hate-men/2018/06/08/f1a3a8e0-6451-11e8-a69c-b944de66d9e7_story.html?noredirect=on.

45. Michael S. Kimmel, *The Politics of Manhood: Profeminist Men Respond to the Mythopoetic Men's Movement (and the Mythopoetic Leaders Answer)* (Philadelphia: Temple University Press, 1995).

46. Raewyn Connell, *Masculinities* (Vancouver: Langara College, 2018).

47. Terry A. Kupers, "Toxic Masculinity as a Barrier to Mental Health Treat-ment in Prison," *Journal of Clinical Psychology* 61, no. 6 (2005).

48. It should be noted that the election of Donald Trump to the office of Presi-dent of the United States is treated from within Theory as the best possible confirmation of Theory's insistences that society is secretly inherently rac-ist, sexist, and all other manners of bigoted and that the need to expose this through more Theory is more important and pressing than ever. (See Lisa Wade, "The Big Picture: Confronting Manhood after Trump," *Public Books*, January 4, 2019, www.publicbooks.org/big-picture-confronting-manhood-trump/.)

49. American Psychological Association, "APA Guidelines to Psychological Practice with Boys and Men," 2018, www.apa.org/about/policy/boys-men-practice-guidelines.pdf.

50. Nancy E. Dowd, *The Man Question: Male Subordination and Privilege* (New York University Press, 2016).

51. Eric Anderson, *Inclusive Masculinity: The Changing Nature of Masculinities* (Lon-don: Routledge, 2012).

52. This idea is often attributed to the feminist and postcolonial scholar Sandra Harding's book *Feminism and Methodology: Social Science Issues* (Bloomington, IN: Indiana University Press, 1996). Harding was perhaps most influential for developing the idea of "strong objectivity" in standpoint theory and is perhaps most famous for referring to Isaac Newton's *Principia Mathematica* as a "rape manual" in her 1986 book, *The Science Question in Feminism*, which she later claimed to have regretted writing. Sandra G. Harding, *The Science Question in Feminism* (Ithaca, NY: Cornell University Press, 1993).

53. Steven Pinker, *Enlightenment Now: The Case for Reason, Science, Humanism and Progress* (Penguin Books, 2019).

54. Armin Falk and Johannes Hermle, "Relationship of Gender Differences in Preferences to Economic Development and Gender Equality," *Science* 362, no. 6412 (2018): eaas9899.

7 Disability and Fat Studies

1. This strange notation is relatively common in disciplines that use postmodern methods and means. Here it means the study both of the disabled and the abled at the same time.

2. Oliver et al write,

> The "individual model" of disability presupposes that the problems disabled people experience are a direct consequence of their impairment, which leads professionals to attempt to adjust the individual to their particular disabling condition. There is likely to be a programme of re-ablement designed to return the individual to as near normal a state as possible.

Michael Oliver, Bob Sapey, and Pam Thomas, *Social Work with Disabled People* (Basingstoke: Palgrave Macmillan, 2012), 12.

3. Ibid., 16.

4. Ibid., 19.

5. Brown, in Jennifer Scuro, *Addressing Ableism: Philosophical Questions via Disability Studies* (Lanham, MD: Lexington Books, 2019), 48.

6. "Crip" in "crip theory" is a contraction of "cripple." Taking this term upon themselves and their Theory is an act of "strategic essentialism," as described by Spivak.

7. Robert McRuer and Michael Bérubé, *Crip Theory: Cultural Signs of Queerness and Disability* (New York University Press, 2006), 8.

8. See the transcription of Jennifer Scuro's conversation with Devonya N. Havis, in which Havis remarks,

> I guess I come at this with a Foucauldian lens. It is not specifically disability as such but also the systemic and structural power dynamics that determine what will count as the "norm" and the processes by which those things that lie outside what is deemed "normal" will be managed and subjected to forms of "correction" designed to enforce performance of the established norms. These power dynamics and their deployment can be explored historically through institutions and

in terms of conceptual battles. Crucial for Foucault is the necessity of examining the processes by which certain practices get established as rational, normal, and desirable. It is certainly the case that histories of racialization, attributions of sex and sex differences, as well as what is considered "abnormal" have such histories and relationships to deployments of power that privilege certain races, sexes, and a certain sense of what counts as able. In this respect, I think Foucault is useful in pointing out the power operative in how particular conceptions of what counts as normal have been naturalized. Foucault clearly sees the construction of the norm and those categories that fall outside of established norms as mechanisms that influence how people are categorized. He goes as far as developing a conception of "racism" against the abnormal. This, for me, has been an instructive way to interrogate categories that we often consider basic or given. Under what conditions and with whose interests in mind do such categories emerge? (Havis, in Scuro, *Addressing Ableism*, 72)

9. Dan Goodley, *Dis/ability Studies: Theorising Disablism and Ableism* (New York: Routledge, 2014), 3.

10. Goodley writes, "Discourses, strategies and modes work on the population and the individual. Biopower has micro and macro targets" (ibid., 32).

11. Ibid., 26.

12. Ibid., 36.

13. Ibid., 35.

14. Ibid., 8.

15. Fiona Kumari Campbell, *Contours of Ableism: The Production of Disability and Abledness.* (New York: Palgrave Macmillan, 2012).

16. Ibid., 5.

17. Ibid., 6.

18. Ibid., 17.

19. Ibid., 28.

20. Brown, in Scuro, *Addressing Ableism*, 70.

21. "It became part of my identity to be suicidal," as documented here by Andrew Sullivan. "Andrew Sullivan: The Hard Questions about Young People and Gender Transitions," *Intelligencer*, November 1, 2019, nymag.com/intelligencer/2019/11/andrew-sullivan-hard-questions-gender-transitions-for-young.html.

22. Joseph P. Shapiro, *No Pity: People with Disabilities Forging a New Civil Rights Movement* (New York: Times Books, 1994), 3.

23. Shapiro, *No Pity,* 20.

24. Brown and Scuro, in Scuro, *Addressing Ableism,* 92–94.

25. Sometimes hearing aids do not restore hearing straightforwardly but result in some improvement in hearing at the cost of having to endure unpleasant and intrusive noises leading deaf people to find the "cure" worse than the problem.

26. See Bradley Campbell and Jason Manning, *The Rise of Victimhood Culture: Microaggressions, Safe Spaces, and the New Culture Wars* (New York: Palgrave Macmillan, 2018).

27. "Naafa—We Come in All Sizes," National Association to Advance Fat Acceptance, www.naafaonline.com/dev2/ (accessed August 21, 2019).

28. Micaela Foreman, "The Fat Underground and the Fat Liberation Manifesto," *Feminist Poetry Movement,* December 20, 2018, sites.williams.edu/engl113-f18/foreman/the-fat-underground-and-the-fat-liberation-manifesto/.

29. Association for Size Diversity and Health ASDAH, www.sizediversityandhealth.org/index.asp (accessed August 21, 2019).

30. Linda Bacon, *Health at Every Size: The Surprising Truth about Your Weight* (Dallas, TX: BenBella Books, 2010).

31. The manifesto based on Bacon's book seems to be most in keeping with the liberal body positivity movement, which has a celebratory ethos.

> Refuse to fight in an unjust war. Join the new peace movement: "Health at Every Size" (HAES). HAES acknowledges that well-being and healthy habits are more important than any number on the scale. Participating is simple:
>
> 1. Accept your size. Love and appreciate the body you have. Self-acceptance empowers you to move on and make positive changes.
> 2. Trust yourself. We all have internal systems designed to keep us healthy—and at a healthy weight. Support your body in naturally finding its appropriate weight by honoring its signals of hunger, fullness, and appetite.

Linda Bacon, "Health at Every Size: Excerpts and Downloads," LindaBacon.org, n.d., lindabacon.org/health-at-every-size-book/haes-excerpts-and-downloads/.

32. See these metastudies addressing the claims of HAES: Caroline K. Kramer, Bernard Zinman, and Ravi Retnakaran, "Are Metabolically Healthy Overweight and Obesity Benign Conditions?: A Systematic Review and Meta-analysis," *Annals of Internal Medicine* 159, no. 11 (December 3,

2013), annals.org/aim/article-abstract/1784291/metabolically-healthy-overweight-obesity-benign-conditions-systematic-review-meta-analysis? doi=10.7326/0003-4819-159-11-201312030-00008; Lara L. Roberson et al., "Beyond BMI: The 'Metabolically Healthy Obese' Phenotype and Its Association with Clinical/Subclinical Cardiovascular Disease and All-Cause Mortality—A Systematic Review," *BMC Public Health* 14, no. 1 (2014): article 14.

33. The ASDAH website states that its commitment to inclusion

> encompasses diversity based on ethnicity, race, nationality, immigration status, gender identity, sexual orientation, age, spirituality, abilities, education, economic class, social class, body shape and size, and others. Systems of oppression do not occur in isolation. Because they have a cumulative impact, we cannot dismantle weight/size oppression without addressing the intersectionality of all oppressions. Therefore, we at ASDAH believe that working in an inclusive and intersectional way is the only way to create a world where all bodies are safe and valued.

34. *Fat Studies*, Taylor and Francis Online.

35. Charlotte Cooper, *Fat Activism: A Radical Social Movement* (Bristol, England: HammerOn Press, 2016), 145. Cooper notes, "Radical lesbian feminist separatism is commonly constructed in opposition to third wave queer feminism" (p145). Recall that we have also seen this shift in gender studies in the distinction between the radical feminists considered trans-exclusionary and the intersectional feminists who are trans activists. Remember too that divides between materialists and postmodernists are prominent in both postcolonial Theory and critical race Theory.

36. This new alignment can be seen in the foreword to *The Fat Studies Reader*, which focuses on Theoretical developments:

> Like feminist studies, queer studies, and disability studies, which consider gender, sexuality, or functional difference, fat studies can show us who we are via the lens of weight. Fat studies can offer an analysis that is in solidarity with resistance to other forms of oppression by offering a new and unique view of alienation.

Marilyn Wann, "Foreword," in *The Fat Studies Reader*, ed. Esther D. Rothblum and Sondra Solovay (New York Unviersity Press, 2009), xxii.

It also appears in the more accessible text *Fat Shame*, which begins:

> The way fat denigration overlaps with racial, ethnic, and national discrimination; the connections between both of these (fat and ethnic denigration) and class privilege; and, finally, the ways that all these elements (fat denigration, ethnic discrimination, and class privilege)

intersect with gender and the construction of what it means to be a "popular girl," a properly constituted gendered subject.

Amy Erdman Farrell, *Fat Shame: Stigma and the Fat Body in American Culture* (New York University Press, 2011), 3. This book focuses on race and gender, claiming that "fat denigration is intricately related to gender as well as racial hierarchies, in particular the historical development of 'whiteness'" (Farrell, *Fat Shame*, 5).

This intersectional approach is also taken up by the book *You Have the Right to Remain Fat,*

> A fat woman who is cisgender is likely to be treated differently than a fat woman who is trans. . . . Fat trans women experience the violence that exists at the nexus of sexism, fatphobia, and transphobia. Race is another mitigating factor. The lighter you are the more culturally valued you are. So, whiteness or light skin can soften fat negative bias, whereas dark-skinned women may experience increased hostility due to the combined effects of colorism and fatphobia.

Virgie Tovar, *You Have the Right to Remain Fat* (New York: Feminist Press, 2018), 67–68.

37. Cooper, *Fat Activism*, 4.

38. Ibid., 36.

39. Ibid., 35.

40. She writes, "Michel Foucault's work (1980) has shown us that placing bodies under the microscope of science, in the name of liberal projects of self-improvement, in fact reinscribes their deviance and increases their oppression" (in Rothblum and Solovay, *Reader*, 70).

41. In their essay "Disappeared Feminist Discourses on Fat in Dietetic Theory and Practice," Lucy Aphramor and Jacqui Gringas write, "Butler reminds us that as we continue to try to change the world, we remain deeply tied to the world as it is by desire and the need for recognition. What's more, we are not held to give an account of ourselves in our misuse and misunderstandings of power, discourse, and knowledge" (in Rothblum and Solovay, *Reader*, 102).

42. Cooper, *Fat Activism*, 24.

43. Wann, in Rothblum and Solovay, *Reader*, xi.

44. Tovar, *Remain Fat*, 371.

45. Cooper, *Fat Activism*, 169.

46. Ibid., 175.

47. Ibid., 175.

48. Wann, in Rothblum and Solovay, *Reader*, xiii.

49. Ibid., xiii.

50. LeBesco, in Rothblum and Solovay, *Reader*, 70.

51. Allyson Mitchell, "Sedentary Lifestyle: Fat Queer Craft," *Fat Studies* 7, no. 2 (2017): 11.

52. LeBesco, in Rothblum and Solovay, *Reader*, 83.

53. Aphramor and Gringas, in Solovay, *Reader*, 97.

54. Ibid., 97.

55. Ibid., 100.

56. Ibid., 100.

57. John Coveney and Sue Booth, *Critical Dietetics and Critical Nutrition Studies* (Cham, Switzerland: Springer, 2019), 18.

58. Cooper, *Fat Activism*, 7.

59. Ibid., 2.

8 Social Justice Scholarship and Thought

1. Alan Sokal and Jean Bricmont, *Fashionable Nonsense: Postmodern Intellectuals Abuse of Science* (New York: St. Martin's Press, 1999).

2. See, for example: Ruth Bleier, *Science and Gender: A Critique of Biology and Its Theories on Women* (New York: Pergamon Press, 1984); Donna Haraway, "Situated Knowledges: The Science Question in Feminism and the Privilege of Partial Perspective," *Feminist Studies* 14, no. 3 (1988).

3. Kristie Dotson, "Tracking Epistemic Violence: Tracking Practices of Silencing," *Hypatia* 26, no. 2 (2011).

4. Hancock, *Intersectionality*, 1.

5. The "science wars" refer to a series of heated debates between natural scientists and postmodern scholars about the objective or socially constructed nature of knowledge that took place in the 1990s, primarily in the United States.

6. Fricker, *Epistemic Injustice*. Although the term "epistemic injustice" has been ascribed to Fricker, arguments that people can be disadvantaged in their relationship to knowledge are much older. As Amy Allen argues, "Michel Foucault could well be considered a theorist of epistemic injustice *avant la lettre*." Amy Allen, "Power/Knowledge/Resistance: Foucault and Epistemic Injustice," *The Routledge Handbook of Epistemic Injustice*, ed. Ian James

Kid, José Medina, and Gaile Pohlhaus, Jr. (London: Routledge, 2017), 187.

7. See, for example: Rae Langton, "*Epistemic Injustice: Power and the Ethics of Knowing* by Miranda Fricker," book review, *Hypatia* 25 no. 2 (2010); Elizabeth Anderson, "Epistemic Justice as a Virtue of Social Institutions," *Social Epistemology* 26, no. 2 (2012).

8. What is "epistemic injustice"? It is a kind of Social Justice philosophy. As Kid, Medina, and Polhaus argue, it functions

> as both a phenomenon and a topic of study, [it] obviously connects to and interpenetrates with major social and intellectual movements, such as feminism, hermeneutics, critical race theory, disability studies, and decolonialising, queer, and trans epistemologies.

Ian James Kid, José Medina, and Gaile Polhaus, "Introduction," in *The Routledge Handbook of Epistemic Injustice*, ed. Ian James Kid, José Medina, and Gaile Pohlhaus, Jr. (London: Routledge, 2017), 1.

9. Kristie Dotson, "Conceptualizing Epistemic Oppression," *Social Epistemology* 28, no. 2 (2014).

10. Spivak's description of epistemic violence draws on Foucault's thoughts about oppression under a prevailing episteme, and these parallel the concept of *symbolic violence* put forth in the 1970s by the French sociologist Pierre Bourdieu. For Bourdieu, symbolic violence occurs whenever a person is led to believe that she should accept her oppression. These two similar concepts help explain why Social Justice scholarship and activism so readily identifies disagreeable speech as a form of violence.

11. Nora Berenstain, "Epistemic Exploitation," *Ergo* 3, no. 22 (2016).

12. José Medina, "Varieties of Hermeneutical Injustice," in *The Routledge Handbook of Epistemic Injustice*, ed. Ian James Kid, José Medina, and Gaile Pohlhaus, Jr. (London: Routledge, 2017).

13. Jeremy Wanderer, "Varieties of Testimonial Injustice," in *The Routledge Handbook of Epistemic Injustice*, ed. Ian James Kid, José Medina, and Gaile Pohlhaus, Jr. (London: Routledge, 2017).

14. Susan E. Babbit, "Epistemic and Political Freedom," in *The Routledge Handbook of Epistemic Injustice*, ed. Ian James Kid, José Medina, and Gaile Pohlhaus, Jr. (London: Routledge, 2017).

15. Lorraine Code, "Epistemic Responsibility," in *The Routledge Handbook of Epistemic Injustice*, ed. Ian James Kid, José Medina, and Gaile Pohlhaus, Jr. (London: Routledge, 2017).

16. Heidi Grasswick argues, "Given their epistemic strength and political influence, scientific institutions and their practices need to be investigated as possible sites and sources of epistemic injustice." Thus, simply because they have earned such a high prestige, science and reason must be suspected of having some kind of unjust epistemic advantage. Grasswick continues,

> That racism and sexism, among other forms of oppression, have significantly shaped the practices and results of science is by now well documented by postcolonial science and technology studies scholars, feminist theorists and philosophers of science, and critical race theorists alike.

Heidi Grasswick, "Epistemic Injustice in Science," in *The Routledge Handbook of Epistemic Injustice*, ed. Ian James Kid, José Medina, and Gaile Pohlhaus, Jr. (London: Routledge, 2017), 313.

17. Ibid., 313.

18. Kristie Dotson, "How Is This Paper Philosophy?" *Comparative Philosophy* 3, no. 1 (2012).

19. Code, "Epistemic Responsibility."

20. Allison B. Wolf, "'Tell Me How That Makes You Feel': Philosophys Reason/Emotion Divide and Epistemic Pushback in Philosophy Classrooms," *Hypatia* 32, no. 4 (2017): 893–910, doi.org/10.1111/hypa.12378.

21. Alexis Shotwell, "Forms of Knowing and Epistemic Resources," in *The Routledge Handbook of Epistemic Injustice*, ed. Ian James Kid, José Medina, and Gaile Pohlhaus, Jr. (London: Routledge, 2017), 79.

22. Ibid., 81.

23. Alison Bailey, "The Unlevel Knowing Field: An Engagement with Dotson's Third-Order Epistemic Oppression," *Social Epistemology Review and Reply Collective* 3, no. 10 (2014), ssrn.com/abstract=2798934.

24. Nancy Tuana, "Feminist Epistemology: The Subject of Knowledge," in *The Routledge Handbook of Epistemic Injustice*, ed. Ian James Kid, José Medina, and Gaile Pohlhaus, Jr. (London: Routledge, 2017), 125.

25. José Medina, *The Epistemology of Resistance: Gender and Racial Oppression, Epistemic Injustice, and Resistant Imaginations* (New York: Oxford University Press, 2013), 44.

26. Feminist theorist Sandra Harding, writing in the late 1980s and early 1990s, called this extra sight "strong objectivity." Sandra Harding, "Rethinking Standpoint Epistemology: What Is 'Strong Objectivity'?" *Centennial Review* 36, no. 3 (1992).

27. Standpoint theory is most closely associated with the work of feminist scholar Sandra Harding in the 1980s, but, unlike contemporary Theorists, Harding did not think that one had to be a member of a certain group to

imagine oneself in their position. Thus, her work, like Fricker's, retains a certain confidence in people's ability to empathize with members of other groups. Sandra Harding, *Whose Science/Whose Knowledge?* (Ithaca, NY: Cornell University Press, 1991); Harding, *The Science Question in Feminism*; Harding, *Feminism and Methodology*; Sandra Harding, "Gender, Development, and Post-Enlightenment Philosophies of Science," *Hypatia* 13, no. 3 (1998).

28. Collins writes,

> Identity politics and standpoint epistemology constitute two important forms of authorization for people of color, women, poor people and new immigrant populations that constitute sources of epistemic authority. Identity politics claims the authority of one's own experiences and social location as a source of epistemic agency. Standpoint epistemology asserts the right to be an equal epistemic agent in interpreting one's own realities within interpretive communities.

Furthermore:

> Painting identity politics as an inferior form of politics and standpoint epistemology as a limited and potentially biased form of knowing illustrates this general practice of discrediting the epistemic agency of oppressed subjects.

Patricia Hill Collins, "Intersectionality and Epistemic Injustice," in *The Routledge Handbook of Epistemic Injustice*, ed. Ian James Kid, José Medina, and Gaile Pohlhaus, Jr. (London: Routledge, 2017), 119.

29. Dotson argues, "It is like experiencing the impossible as possible and, correspondingly, viewing the limits of one's epistemological systems that designate the possible as impossible. Being able to make this step is difficult enough. Being able to change those limitations may be impossible for many" ("Epistemic Oppression," 32).

30. Dotson writes, "It is imperative that those perpetrating third order epistemic oppression take a step back and become aware of their overall epistemological systems that are preserving and legitimating inadequate epistemic resources. This kind of recognition, which can be seen as akin to a broad recognition of one's 'cultural traditions systems,' is extraordinarily difficult" (ibid., 32).

31. Medina, *Epistemology of Resistance*, 32.

32. Ibid., 30–35.

33. Georg W. F. Hegel, *The Phenomenology of Spirit* (1807).

34. Charles Mills, "Ideology," in *The Routledge Handbook of Epistemic Injustice*, ed. Ian James Kid, José Medina, and Gaile Pohlhaus, Jr. (London: Routledge, 2017), 108.

35. James Lindsay, "Postmodern Religion and the Faith of Social Justice," *Areo Magazine*, December 26, 2018, areomagazine.com/2018/12/18/postmodern-religion-and-the-faith-of-social-justice/.

36. Barbara Applebaum, *Being White, Being Good: White Complicity, White Moral Responsibility, and Social Justice Pedagogy* (Lanham, MD: Lexington Books, 2010), 31.

37. Ibid., 100.

38. Ibid., 99.

39. Ibid., 43.

40. Ibid., 43.

41. Ibid., 102.

42. Ibid., 108.

43. Ibid., 96.

44. Ibid., 97.

45. Ibid., 112.

46. Alison Bailey, "Tracking Privilege-Preserving Epistemic Pushback in Feminist and Critical Race Philosophy Classes," *Hypatia* 32, no. 4 (2017): 877.

47. Ibid., 877.

48. Ibid., 881.

49. Ibid., 882.

50. Of course, we cannot assume that the *Hypatia* editors agreed with Bailey's argument. They could have published it in order to generate debate. However, they also published Alison Wolf's paper drawing on it to argue against privileging reason in philosophy and they accepted our "hoax" paper drawing on it to argue that satirical criticism of Social Justice scholarship is invalid and unethical with one editor saying: "The topic is an excellent one and would make an excellent contribution to feminist philosophy and be of interest to Hypatia readers." Wolf, "'Tell Me How That Makes You Feel'"; James Lindsay, Peter Boghossian, and Helen Pluckrose, "Academic Grievance Studies and the Corruption of Scholarship," *Areo Magazine*, October 2, 2018, areomagazine.com/2018/10/02/academic-grievance-studies-and-the-corruption-of-scholarship/.

51. Bailey, "Tracking Privilege-Preserving Epistemic Pushback," 886.

52. Ibid., 878.

53. Ibid., 886.

54. Ibid., 887.

55. Ibid., 887.

56. Ibid., 887.

57. DiAngelo, Robin J. DiAngelo, "White Fragility," *International Journal of Critical Pedagogy* 3, no. 3 (2011).

58. Ibid., 54.

59. Ibid., 57.

60. This is not to accuse her of hypocrisy, of course. DiAngelo has been quite clear that as a result of her Theorizing, she wishes that she could be "less white." She also points out repeatedly that she is only speaking to white people. See Michael Lee, "'Whiteness Studies' Professor to White People: You're Racist If You Don't Judge by Skin Color," *Pluralist*, May 29, 2019, pluralist.com/robin-diangelo-colorblindness-dangerous/.

61. Robin J. DiAngelo, *White Fragility: Why It's So Hard for White People to Talk about Racism* (London: Allen Lane, 2019), 142.

62. Ibid., 158.

63. Ibid., 105.

64. Ibid., 89.

65. Jonathan Church first identified DiAngelo's concept of "white fragility" as falling prey to the fallacy of reification. Jonathan Church, "Whiteness Studies and the Theory of White Fragility Are Based on a Logical Fallacy," *Areo Magazine*, April 25, 2019, areomagazine.com/2019/04/25/whiteness-studies-and-the-theory-of-white-fragility-are-based-on-a-logical-fallacy/. Church has produced an enlightening series of essays on the epistemological problems with DiAngelo's work accessible through his website www.jonathandavidchurch.com.

66. In particular the Critical Theory of Max Horkheimer and the Frankfurt School.

67. See, in particular, Breanne Fahs and Michael Karger, "Women's Studies as Virus: Institutional Feminism, Affect, and the Projection of Danger," *Multidisciplinary Journal of Gender Studies* 5, no. 1 (2016) and John Coveney and Sue Booth, *Critical Dietetics and Critical Nutrition Studies* (Cham, Switzerland: Springer, 2019).

68. Lindsay, "Postmodern Religion."

9 Social Justice in Action

1. Hardeep Singh, "Why Was a Disabled Grandad Sacked by Asda for

Sharing a Billy Connolly Clip?" *Spectator*, June 27, 2019, blogs.spectator.
co.uk/2019/06/why-was-a-disabled-grandad-sacked-by-asda-for-sharing-
a-billy-connolly-clip/.

2. Sean Stevens, "The Google Memo: What Does the Research Say about
Gender Differences?" *Heterodox Academy*, February 2, 2019, heterodoxacad-
emy.org/the-google-memo-what-does-the-research-say-about-gender-dif-
ferences/.

3. Emma Powell and Patrick Grafton-Green, "Danny Baker Fired by BBC
Radio 5 Live over Racist Royal Baby Tweet," *Evening Standard*, May 9, 2019,
www.standard.co.uk/news/uk/danny-baker-fired-broadcaster-sacked-by-
bbc-radio-5-live-over-racist-tweet-a4137951.html.

4. Charlotte Zoller, "How I Found a Fat-Positive Doctor Who Didn't Just
Tell Me to Lose Weight," *Vice*, August 15, 2018, www.vice.com/en_us/
article/43ppwj/how-to-find-a-fat-positive-doctor.

5. Lukianoff and Haidt, *The Coddling of the American Mind*.

6. Jonathan W. Wilson, "'I've Never Had a Student Ask for a Safe Space.
Here's What They Have Asked for,'" *Vox*, December 12, 2018, www.vox.
com/first-person/2018/12/12/18131186/college-campus-safe-spaces-
trigger-warnings; Judith Shulevitz, "In College and Hiding From Scary
Ideas," *New York Times*. March 21, 2015.

7. Daniel Koehler, "Violence and Terrorism from the Far-Right: Policy Options to Counter an Elusive Threat," *Terrorism and Counter-Terrorism Studies*
(February 2019), doi.org/10.19165/2019.2.02.

8. Julia Ebner, "The Far Right Have a Safe Haven Online. We Cannot Let
Their Lies Take Root," *Guardian*, November 14, 2018, www.theguardian.
com/commentisfree/2018/nov/14/far-right-safe-haven-online-white-su-
premacist-groups.

9. Natalie Gil, "'Inside The Secret World Of Incels'—The Men Who Want
to Punish Women," *BBC Three Review*, July 2019, www.refinery29.com/en-
gb/2019/07/237264/inside-the-secret-world-of-incels-bbc-three.

10. Timothy Egan, "How the Insufferably Woke Help Trump," *New York Times*,
November 8, 2019, www.nytimes.com/2019/11/08/opinion/warren-
biden-trump.html.

11. Andrea Vacchiano, "Colleges Pay Diversity Officers More Than Professors, Staff," *Daily Signal*, July 14, 2017, www.dailysignal.com/2017/07/14/
colleges-pay-diversity-officers-more-than-professors-staff/.

12. Alex_TARGETjobs, "Equality and Diversity Officer: Job Description."
TARGETjobs, July 30, 2019, targetjobs.co.uk/careers-advice/job-
descriptions/278257-equality-and-diversity-officer-job-description.

13. Jeffrey Aaron Snyder and Amna Khalid, "The Rise of 'Bias Response Teams' on Campus," *New Republic*, March 30, 2016, newrepublic.com/article/132195/rise-bias-response-teams-campus (accessed August 20, 2019).

14. Ryan Miller et al., "Bias Response Teams: Fact vs. Fiction," *Inside Higher Ed*, June 17, 2019, www.insidehighered.com/views/2019/06/17/truth-about-bias-response-teams-more-complex-often-thought-opinion.

15. Snyder and Khalid, "The Rise of 'Bias Response Teams'."

16. Tom Slater, "No, Campus Censorship Is Not a Myth," *Spiked*, April 2, 2019, www.spiked-online.com/2019/02/04/campus-censorship-is-not-a-myth/.

17. Slater, "Campus Censorship."

18. "Hypatia Editorial Office," archive.is, June 9, 2017, archive.is/kVrLb.

19. Jerry Coyne, "Journal Hypatia's Editors Resign, and Directors Suspend Associate Editors over Their Apology for the 'Transracialism' Article," *Why Evolution Is True*, July 22, 2017, whyevolutionistrue.wordpress.com/2017/07/22/journal-hypatias-editors-resign-and-directors-suspend-associate-editors-over-their-apology-for-the-transracialism-article/.

20. Jesse Singal, "This Is What a Modern-Day Witch Hunt Looks Like," Intelligencer, *New York Magazine*, May 2, 2017, nymag.com/intelligencer/2017/05/transracialism-article-controversy.html.

21. Kelly Oliver, "If This Is Feminism . . ." *Philosophical Salon*, May 9, 2017, thephilosophicalsalon.com/if-this-is-feminism-its-been-hijacked-by-the-thought-police/.

22. Adam Lusher, "Professor's 'Bring Back Colonialism' Call Sparks Fury and Academic Freedom Debate," *Independent*, October 12, 2017, www.independent.co.uk/news/world/americas/colonialism-academic-article-bruce-gilley-threats-violence-published-withdrawn-third-world-quarterly-a7996371.html.

23. Peter Wood, "The Article That Made 16,000 Ideologues Go Wild," *Minding the Campus*, October 18, 2017, www.mindingthecampus.org/2017/10/04/the-article-that-made-16000-profs-go-wild/.

24. Ben Cohen, "The Rise of Engineering's Social Justice Warriors," *James G. Martin Center for Academic Renewal*, January 3, 2019, www.jamesgmartin.center/2018/11/the-rise-of-engineerings-social-justice-warriors/.

25. Donna Riley, *Engineering and Social Justice* (San Rafael, CA: Morgan & Claypool Publishers, 2008), 109.

26. Enrique Galindo and Jill Newton, eds. *Proceedings of the 39th Annual Meeting of the North American Chapter of the International Group for the Psychology of*

Mathematics Education (Indianapolis, IN: Hoosier Association of Mathematics Teacher Educators, 2017).

27. Catherine Gewertz, "Seattle Schools Lead Controversial Push to 'Rehumanize' Math," *Education Week*, October 22, 2019, www.edweek.org/ew/articles/2019/10/11/seattle-schools-lead-controversial-push-to-rehumanize.html.

28. *Seriously* . . . "Seven Things You Need to Know about Antifa," BBC Radio 4, n.d., www.bbc.co.uk/programmes/articles/X56rQkDgd0qq-B7R68t6t7C/seven-things-you-need-to-know-about-antifa.

29. Peter Beinart, "Left Wing Protests Are Crossing the Line," *Atlantic*, November 16, 2018, www.theatlantic.com/ideas/archive/2018/11/protests-tucker-carlsons-home-crossed-line/576001/.

30. Yasmeen Serhan, "Why Protesters Keep Hurling Milkshakes at British Politicians," *Atlantic*, May 21, 2019, www.theatlantic.com/international/archive/2019/05/milkshaking-britain-political-trend-right-wing/589876/.

31. Shaun O'Dwyer, "Of Kimono and Cultural Appropriation," *Japan Times*, August 4, 2015, www.japantimes.co.jp/opinion/2015/08/04/commentary/japan-commentary/kimono-cultural-appropriation/#.XUdyw5NKj_Q.

32. Ade Onibada, "Macy's Admits It 'Missed the Mark' for Selling a Portion-Sized Plate That Some People Online Aren't Happy About," *BuzzFeed*, July 24, 2019, www.buzzfeed.com/adeonibada/macys-pull-portion-control-plate-mom-jeans.

33. Crystal Tai, "Noodle-Maker Nissin Yanks 'Whitewashed' Anime of Tennis Star Naomi Osaka," *South China Morning Post*, January 24, 2019, www.scmp.com/news/asia/east-asia/article/2183391/noodle-maker-nissin-withdraws-whitewashed-anime-ad-campaign.

34. Sarah Young, "Gucci Apologises for Selling Jumper That 'Resembles Blackface,'" *Independent*, February 13, 2019, www.independent.co.uk/life-style/fashion/gucci-blackface-sweater-balaclava-apology-reaction-twitter-controversy-a8767101.html.

35. Ben Beaumont-Thomas, "Katy Perry Shoes Removed from Stores over Blackface Design," *Guardian*, February 12, 2019, www.theguardian.com/music/2019/feb/12/katy-perry-shoes-removed-from-stores-over-black-face-design.

36. Julia Alexander, "The Yellow $: A Comprehensive History of Demonetization and YouTube's War with Creators," *Polygon*, May 10, 2018, www.polygon.com/2018/5/10/17268102/youtube-demonetization-pewdie-pie-logan-paul-casey-neistat-philip-defranco.

37. Benjamin Goggin, "A Top Patreon Creator Deleted His Account, Accusing the Crowdfunding Membership Platform of 'Political Bias' after It Purged Conservative Accounts It Said Were Associated with Hate Groups," *Business Insider*, December 17, 2018, www.businessinsider.com/sam-harris-deletes-patreon-account-after-platform-boots-conservatives-2018-12?r=US&IR=T.

38. Kari Paul and Jim Waterson, "Facebook Bans Alex Jones, Milo Yiannopoulos and Other Far-Right Figures," *Guardian*, May 2, 2019, www.theguardian.com/technology/2019/may/02/facebook-ban-alex-jones-milo-yiannopoulos.

39. BBC News, "Twitter Bans Religious Insults Calling Groups Rats or Maggots," *BBC News*, July 9, 2019, www.bbc.co.uk/news/technology-48922546; Julia Manchester, "Self-Described Feminist Banned from Twitter Says Platform Is Setting 'Dangerous' Precedent," *Hill*, December 6, 2018, thehill.com/hilltv/rising/420033-self-described-feminist-banned-from-twitter-says-platform-is-setting-a.

40. Jose Paglieri, "Sexist Tweets Cost Business Insider Executive His Job," *CNN.com*, September 10, 2013, money.cnn.com/2013/09/10/technology/business-insider-cto/index.html; Emily Alford, "Denise Is Fired," *Jezebel*, April 1, 2019, jezebel.com/denise-is-fired-1833701621; Shamira Ibrahim, "In Defense of Cancel Culture," *Vice*, April 4, 2019, www.vice.com/en_us/article/vbw9pa/what-is-cancel-culture-twitter-extremely-online.

41. Alex Culbertson, "Oscars to Have No Host after Kevin Hart Homophobic Tweets," *Sky News*, January 10, 2019, news.sky.com/story/oscars-to-have-no-host-after-kevin-hart-homophobic-tweets-11603296.

42. CNN, "Ellen's Usain Bolt Tweet Deemed Racist," *CNN.com*, August 17, 2016, edition.cnn.com/2016/08/16/entertainment/ellen-degeneres-usain-bolt-tweet/index.html.

43. Hannah Jane Parkinson, "Matt Damon, Stop #Damonsplaining. You Don't Understand Sexual Harassment," *Guardian*, December 19, 2017, www.theguardian.com/commentisfree/2017/dec/19/matt-damon-sexual-harassment.

44. Brendan O'Neill, "Why Is Mario Lopez Apologising for Telling the Truth?" *Spiked*, August 1, 2019, www.spiked-online.com/2019/08/01/why-is-mario-lopez-apologising-for-telling-the-truth/.

45. Frances Perraudin, "Martina Navratilova Criticised over 'Cheating' Trans Women Comments," *Guardian*, February 17, 2019, www.theguardian.com/sport/2019/feb/17/martina-navratilova-criticised-over-cheating-trans-women-comments.

46. "John McEnroe Says He Regrets Comments on Serena Williams and Is 'Surprised' by Reaction," *Telegraph*, June 29, 2017, www.telegraph.co.uk/tennis/2017/06/29/johnmcenroe-says-regrets-comments-serena-williams-surprised.

47. Stefania Sarrubba, "After Trans Protests, Scarlett Johansson Still Says She Should Play Everyone," *Gay Star News*, July 14, 2019, www.gaystarnews.com/article/scarlett-johansson-casting-controversy/#gs.y12axx.

48. Louis Staples, "JK Rowling's Late Attempts to Make Harry Potter More Diverse Help No-One," *Metro*, March 18, 2019, metro.co.uk/2019/03/18/jk-rowlings-late-attempts-make-harry-potter-diverse-nothing-lgbt-fans-like-8930864/.

49. Alison Flood, "JK Rowling under Fire for Writing about 'Native American Wizards,'" *Guardian*, March 9, 2016, www.theguardian.com/books/2016/mar/09/jk-rowling-under-fire-for-appropriating-navajo-tradition-history-of-magic-in-north-america-pottermore.

50. Nadra Kareem Nittle, "Cultural Appropriation in Music: From Madonna to Miley Cyrus," *ThoughtCo*, February 24, 2019, www.thoughtco.com/cultural-appropriation-in-music-2834650.

51. Nittle, "Cultural Appropriation."

52. Helena Horton, "Beyoncé Criticised for 'Cultural Appropriation' in New Music Video with Coldplay and Sonam Kapoor," *Telegraph*, January 29, 2016, www.telegraph.co.uk/music/news/beyonc-criticised-for-cultural-appropriation-in-new-music-video/.

53. Sam Gillette, "Dr. Seuss Books Like Horton Hears a Who! Branded Racist and Problematic in New Study," *People.com*, February 28, 2019, people.com/books/dr-seuss-books-racist-problematic/.

54. "6 Racist TV Stereotypes White People Still Don't Notice," *Digital Spy*, February 16, 2019, www.digitalspy.com/tv/a863844/racism-movie-tv-stereotypes/.

55. Amber Thomas, "Women Only Said 27% of the Words in 2016's Biggest Movies," *Developer News*, January 10, 2017, www.freecodecamp.org/news/women-only-said-27-of-the-words-in-2016s-biggest-movies-955cb480c3c4/.

56. WatchMojo, "Top 10 Needlessly Sexualized Female Movie Characters," *Viva*, October 18, 2018, viva.media/top-10-needlessly-sexualized-female-movie-characters.

57. Chris Gardner, "Rose McGowan Calls Out 'X-Men' Billboard That Shows Mystique Being Strangled," *Hollywood Reporter*, June 2, 2016, www.hollywoodreporter.com/rambling-reporter/rose-mcgowan-calls-x-men-898538.

58. Randall Colburn, "Jessica Chastain Blasts *Game of Thrones*: 'Rape Is Not a Tool to Make a Character Stronger,'" *AV Club*, May 7, 2019, news.avclub. com/jessica-chastain-blasts-game-of-thrones-rape-is-not-a-1834581011.

59. Katherine Cross, "*Doctor Who* Has Given Us a Doctor without Inner Conflict," *Polygon*, January 1, 2019, www.polygon.com/2019/1/1/18152028/ doctor-who-whitaker-season-review.

60. Simon Baron-Cohen and Michael V. Lombardo, "Autism and Talent: The Cognitive and Neural Basis of Systemizing," *Dialogues in Clinical Neuroscience* 19, no. 4 (2017).

61. Thomas Clements, "The Problem with the Neurodiversity Movement," *Quillette*, October 15, 2017, quillette.com/2017/10/15/problem-neurodiversity-movement/.

62. Geoffrey Miller, "The Neurodiversity Case for Free Speech," *Quillette*, August 23, 2018, quillette.com/2017/07/18/neurodiversity-case-free-speech/.

63. Caroline Praderio, "Why Some People Turned Down a 'Medical Miracle' and Decided to Stay Deaf," *Insider*, January 3, 2017, www.insider.com/ why-deaf-people-turn-down-cochlear-implants-2016-12.

64. Danielle Moores, "Obesity: Causes, Complications, and Diagnosis," Healthline, July 16, 2018, www.healthline.com/health/obesity (accessed August 25, 2019).

65. Sarah Knapton, "Cancer Research UK Accused of 'Fat Shaming' over Obesity Smoking Campaign," *Telegraph*, July 5, 2019, www.telegraph. co.uk/science/2019/07/04/cancer-research-uk-accused-fat-shaming-obesity-smoking-campaign/.

66. Caroline Davies, "'Beach Body Ready' Tube Advert Protests Planned for Hyde Park," *Guardian*, April 28, 2015, www.theguardian.com/media/2015/apr/27/mass-demonstration-planned-over-beach-body-ready-tube-advert.

67. "Hidden Tribes of America," Hidden Tribes, hiddentribes.us/ (accessed November 7, 2019).

68. Lukianoff and Haidt, *The Coddling of the American Mind*.

69. Bradley Campbell and Jason Manning, *The Rise of Victimhood Culture: Microaggressions, Safe Spaces, and the New Culture Wars* (New York: Palgrave Macmillan, 2018).

70. See the chapter "False Accusations, Moral Panics and the Manufacture of Victimhood" in Campbell and Manning, *The Rise of Victimhood Culture*.

71. Lukianoff and Haidt, *The Coddling of the American Mind*, 176.

72. Ibid., 24.

73. Ibid., 24.

74. Campbell and Manning, *The Rise of Victimhood Culture*, 2.

75. Mike Nayna, "PART TWO: Teaching to Transgress," YouTube video, March 6, 2019, www.youtube.com/watch?v=A0W9QbkX8Cs&t=6s.

76. Bruce, DiAngelo, Swaney, and Thurber, "Between Principles and Practice."

77. Kathrine Jebsen Moore, "Knitting's Infinity War, Part III: Showdown at Yarningham," *Quillette*, July 28, 2019, quillette.com/2019/07/28/knittings-infinity-war-part-iii-showdown-at-yarningham/.

78. Amanda Marcotte, "Atheism's Shocking Woman Problem: What's behind the Misogyny of Richard Dawkins and Sam Harris?" *Salon*, October 3, 2014, www.salon.com/2014/10/03/new_atheisms_troubling_misogyny_the_pompous_sexism_of_richard_dawkins_and_sam_harris_partner/.

79. Southern Baptist Convention, "On Critical Race Theory and Intersectionality" (resolution, Southern Baptist Convention, Birmingham, AL, 2019), www.sbc.net/resolutions/2308/resolution-9--on-critical-race-theory-and-intersectionality.

10 *An Alternative to the Ideology of Social Justice*

1. John Stuart Mill, *On Liberty and Other Essays* (Oxford: Oxford University Press, 1998), 21.

2. Ibid, 21.

3. Ibid, 21.

4. Ibid, 26.

5. The observation in this paragraph is taken from Jean Bricmont, *La République des censeurs* (Paris, L'Herne, 2014), 24n25.

6. Pinker, *Enlightenment Now*.

7. Edmund Fawcett, *Liberalism: The Life of an Idea* (Princeton, NJ: Princeton University Press, 2015), xii–xiii.

8. Ibid., xiii.

9. Ibid., xiii.

10. Adam Gopnik, *A Thousand Small Sanities: The Moral Adventure of Liberalism* (London: Riverrun, 2019), 24.

11. Gopnik, *Thousand Small Sanities*, 24.

12. Gopnik, *Thousand Small Sanities,* 42.

13. Steven Pinker, *The Better Angels of Our Nature: The Decline of Violence in History and Its Causes* (London: Allen Lane, 2011).

14. Pinker, *Enlightenment Now,* 228.

15. Jonathan Rauch, *Kindly Inquisitors: The New Attacks on Free Thought* (Chicago: University of Chicago Press, 2014), 4.

16. Ibid., 38.

17. Ibid., 48–49.

18. Ibid., 48–49. Readers will notice that here Rauch is echoing the practical argument for the free exchange of ideas as posited by John Stuart Mill in 1859. See Mill, *On Liberty and Other Essays.*

19. Rauch, *Kindly Inquisitors,* 48.

20. Ibid., 49.

21. Ibid., 49.

22. Ibid., 6.

23. Ibid., 6.

24. Ibid., 6.

25. Ibid., 6.

26. Ibid., 6.

27. Ibid., 13.

28. Jonathan Haidt, *The Righteous Mind: Why Good People Are Divided by Politics and Religion* (New York: Penguin Books, 2013).

29. Nicholas Christakis looks at the way humans from vastly different cultures and times have commonly structured their societies in his book *Blueprint.* He asks,

> How can people be so different from—even go to war with—one another and yet also be so similar? The fundamental reason is that we each carry within us an evolutionary blueprint for making a good society. Genes do amazing things inside our bodies, but even more amazing to me is what they do outside of them. Genes affect not only the structure and function of our bodies; not only the structure and function of our minds and, hence, our behaviors; but also the structure and function of our societies. This is what we recognize when we look at people around the world. This is the source of our common humanity. (pp. xx–xxi)

Christakis identifies a "social suite" of evolved social features that humans possess and, by looking at different communities that have formed deliberately, like communes, and by accident, like shipwrecks, and their success and failure convincingly argues that no successful society can diverge too far from a structure that supports them. They are "(1) The capacity to have and recognize individual identity (2) Love for partners and offspring (3) Friendship (4) Social networks (5) Cooperation (6) Preference for one's own group (that is, "in-group bias") (7) Mild hierarchy (that is, relative egalitarianism) (8) Social learning and teaching" (p. 13). Nicholas A. Christakis, *Blueprint: The Evolutionary Origins of a Good Society* (New York: Little, Brown, Spark, 2019).

30. Haidt, *Righteous Mind*.

31. Pinker, *The Blank Slate*.

32. Martin Luther King, Jr., "'I Have a Dream" (address delivered at the March on Washington for Jobs and Freedom, 1963), available through the Martin Luther King, Jr., Research and Education Institute, Jkinginstitute. stanford.edu/king-papers/documents/i-have-dream-address-delivered-march-washington-jobs-and-freedom.

33. Of note, critical race Theorists sometimes consider this quote as a cherry-picked example of King's thought that white people use to control black people who espouse critical race Theory or who criticize "whiteness."

34. Michael Lee, "'Whiteness Studies' Professor to White People: You're Racist If You Don't Judge by Skin Color," *Pluralist*, May 29, 2019, pluralist.com/robin-diangelo-colorblindness-dangerous/.

35. "The desire for revenge is most easily modulated when the perpetrator falls within our natural circle of empathy. We are apt to forgive our kin and close friends for trespasses that would be unforgivable in others. And when our circle of empathy expands . . . our circle of forgivability expands with it" (Pinker, *Better Angels*, 541).

36. Elizabeth Redden, "Hungary Officially Ends Gender Studies Programs," *Inside Higher Ed*, October 17, 2018, www.insidehighered.com/quicktakes/2018/10/17/hungary-officially-ends-gender-studies-programs.

SELECT BIBLIOGRAPHY

Abelson, Miriam J. "Dangerous Privilege: Trans Men, Masculinities, and Changing Perceptions of Safety." *Sociological Forum* 29, no. 3 (2014): 549–70.

Allen, Amy. "Power/Knowledge/Resistance: Foucault and Epistemic Injustice." In *The Routledge Handbook of Epistemic Injustice*, edited by Ian James Kidd, José Medina, and Gaile Pohlhaus, Jr., 187–194. New York: Routledge, 2017.

Amoore, Louise. *The Global Resistance Reader*. London: Routledge, 2005.

Anderson, Elizabeth. "Epistemic Justice as a Virtue of Social Institutions." *Social Epistemology* 26, no. 2 (2012): 163–173.

Anderson, Eric. *Inclusive Masculinity: The Changing Nature of Masculinities*. London: Routledge, 2012.

Anderson, Walter Truett. *The Fontana Postmodernism Reader*. London: Fontana Press, 1996.

Andrews, Kehinde. "Preface." In *Rhodes Must Fall: The Struggle to Decolonise the Racist Heart of Empire*, edited by Roseanne Chantiluke, Brian Kwoba, and Athinangamso Nkopo. London: Zed Books, 2018.

Aphramor, Lucy and Jacqui Gringas. "Disappeared Feminist Discourses on Fat in Dietetic Theory and Practice." In *The Fat Studies Reader*, edited by Esther D Rothblum and Sondra Solovay, 97–105. New York: New York University Press, 2009.

Applebaum, Barbara. *Being White, Being Good: White Complicity, White Moral Responsibility, and Social Justice Pedagogy*. Lanham: Lexington Books, 2010.

Babbit, Susan E. "Epistemic and Political Freedom." In *The Routledge Handbook of Epistemic Injustice*, edited by Ian James Kidd, José Medina, and Gaile Pohlhaus, Jr., 261–269. London: Routledge, 2017.

Bacon, Linda. *Health at Every Size: The Surprising Truth about Your Weight*. Dallas, TX: BenBella Books, 2010.

Bailey, Alison. "The Unlevel Knowing Field: An Engagement with Dotson's Third-Order Epistemic Oppression." *Social Epistemology Review and Reply Collective* 3, no. 10 (2014): 62–68. ssrn.com/abstract=2798934.

Bailey, Alison. "Tracking Privilege-Preserving Epistemic Pushback in Feminist and Critical Race Philosophy Classes." *Hypatia* 32, no. 4 (2017): 876–92.

Barthes, Roland. "The Death of the Author." *Aspen* no. 5 6, item 3: Three Essays. Accessed November 9, 2019. www.ubu.com/aspen/aspen5and6/threeEssays.html.

Baron-Cohen, Simon, and Michael V. Lombardo. "Autism and Talent: The Cognitive and Neural Basis of Systemizing." *Dialogues in Clinical Neuroscience* 19, no. 4 (2017): 345–353.

Baudrillard, Jean. *Symbolic Exchange and Death*. Translated by Iain Hamilton Grant. London: SAGE Publications, 2017.

———. *Simulacra and Simulation*. Translated by Sheila Faria Glaser. Ann Arbor: University of Michigan Press, 2018.

Bell, Derrick A. "Brown v. Board of Education and the Interest-Convergence Dilemma." *Harvard Law Review* 93, No. 3 (1980): 518–533.

———. *Race, Racism, and American Law*. Boston: Little, Brown, and Co., 1984.

———. "Racial Realism." *Connecticut Law Review* 24, no. 2 (1992): 363–379.

———. *And We Are Not Saved: The Elusive Quest for Racial Justice*. New York: Basic Books, 2008.

Berenstain, Nora. "Epistemic Exploitation." *Ergo, an Open Access Journal of Philosophy* 3, no. 22 (2016): 569–590.

Beauvoir, Simone de. *The Second Sex*. Translated by H. M. Parshley. New York: Vintage Books, 1974.

Bhabha, Homi K. *The Location of Culture*. London: Routledge, 1994.

Bhambra, Gurminder K., Dalia Gebrial, and Kerem Nişancıoğlu, eds. *Decolonising the University*. London: Pluto Press, 2018.

Bishop, Alan J. "Western Mathematics: The Secret Weapon of Cultural Imperialism." *Race & Class* 32, no. 2 (1990): 51–65.

Bleier, Ruth. *Science and Gender: A Critique of Biology and Its Theories on Women*. New York: Pergamon Press, 1984.

Bohman, James. "Critical Theory." In *Stanford Encyclopedia of Philosophy*, edited by Edward N. Zalta (Winter 2019 Edition). plato.stanford.edu/archives/win2019/entries/critical-theory/.

Boyd, Brian. *Evolution, Literature and Film: A Reader.* New York: Columbia University Press, 2010.

Bricmont, Jean. *La République des censeurs.* Paris, L'Herne, 2014.

Butler, Judith. *Bodies That Matter: On the Discursive Limits of "Sex."* New York: Routledge, 1993.

———. "Contingent Foundations: Feminism and the Question of 'Postmodernism'." In *The Postmodern Turn: New Perspectives on Social Theory*, edited by Steven Seidman, 153–70. Cambridge: Cambridge University Press, 1994.

———. *Gender Trouble.* London: Routledge, 2006.

Campbell, Bradley, and Jason Manning. *The Rise of Victimhood Culture: Microaggressions, Safe Spaces, and the New Culture Wars.* New York: Palgrave Macmillan, 2018.

Campbell, Fiona Kumari. *Contours of Ableism: The Production of Disability and Abledness.* New York: Palgrave Macmillan, 2012.

Chantiluke, Roseanne, Brian Kwoba, and Athinangamso Nkopo, eds. *Rhodes Must Fall: The Struggle to Decolonise the Racist Heart of Empire.* London: Zed Books, 2018.

Chen, Mel Y. *Animacies: Biopolitics, Racial Mattering, and Queer Affect.* Durham, NC: Duke University Press, 2012.

Cho, Sumi, Kimberlé Williams Crenshaw, and Leslie McCall. "Toward a Field of Intersectionality Studies: Theory, Applications, and Praxis." *Signs: Journal of Women in Culture and Society* 38, no. 4 (2013): 785–810.

Christakis, Nicholas A. *Blueprint: The Evolutionary Origins of a Good Society.* New York: Little, Brown, Spark, 2019.

Code, Lorraine. "Epistemic Responsibility." In *The Routledge Handbook of Epistemic Injustice*, edited by Ian James Kidd, José Medina, and Gaile Pohlhaus, Jr., 89–99. London: Routledge, 2017.

Collins, Patricia Hill. "Toward a New Vision: Race, Class, and Gender as Categories of Analysis and Connection." *Race, Sex & Class* 1, no. 1 (1993): 25–45.

———. *Black Feminist Thought: Knowledge, Consciousness, and the Politics of Empowerment.* New York: Routledge, 2015.

———. "Intersectionality and Epistemic Injustice." In *The Routledge Handbook of Epistemic Injustice*, edited by Ian James Kidd, José Medina, and Gaile Pohlhaus, Jr., 115–24. London: Routledge, 2017.

Collins, Patricia Hill, and Sirma Bilge. *Intersectionality*. Cambridge: Polity Press, 2016.

Connell, Catherine. "Doing, Undoing, or Redoing Gender?" *Gender & Society* 24, no. 1 (2010): 31–55.

Connell, Raewyn. *Masculinities*. Vancouver: Langara College, 2018.

Conrad, Joseph. *Heart of Darkness: and Other Stories*. New York: Barnes & Noble, 2019.

Cooper, Charlotte. *Fat Activism: A Radical Social Movement*. Bristol, England: HammerOn Press, 2016.

Courville, Mathieu E. "Genealogies of Postcolonialism: A Slight Return from Said and Foucault Back to Fanon and Sartre." *Studies in Religion/Sciences Religieuses* 36, no. 2 (2007): 215–40.

Coveney, John, and Sue Booth. *Critical Dietetics and Critical Nutrition Studies*. Cham, Switzerland: Springer, 2019.

Crenshaw, Kimberlé. "Mapping the Margins: Intersectionality, Identity Politics, and Violence against Women of Color." *Stanford Law Review* 43, no. 6 (1991): 1241–1299.

———. "Demarginalizing the Intersection of Race and Sex: A Black Feminist Critique of Antidiscrimination Doctrine, Feminist Theory, and Antiracist Politics." *Feminist Legal Theory* (2018): 57–80.

Deleuze, Gilles and Felix Guattari. *Anti-Oedipus: Capitalism and Schizophrenia*. Translated by Robert J. Hurley. London: Bloomsbury Academic, 2016.

Delgado, Richard, and Jean Stefancic. *Critical Race Theory: An Introduction*. New York: New York University Press, 2017.

Derrida, Jacques. *Of Grammatology*. Translated by Gayatri Chakravorty Spivak. Baltimore: John Hopkins University Press, 1976.

———. *Speech and Phenomena: And Other Essays on Husserl's Theory of Signs*. Translated by David B. Allison. Evanston, IN: Northwestern University Press, 1984.

———. *Writing and Difference*. Translated by Alan Bass. London: Routledge, 2001.

Descartes René. *Discourse on the Method: The Original Text with English Translation*. Erebus Society, 2017.

Detmer, David. *Challenging Postmodernism: Philosophy and the Politics of Truth*. Amherst, NY: Humanity Books, 2003.

DiAngelo, Robin J. "White Fragility." *International Journal of Critical Pedagogy* 3, no. 3 (2011): 54–70.

———. *White Fragility: Why It's So Hard for White People to Talk about Racism*. London: Allen Lane, 2019.

Donaldson, Laura E. "Writing the Talking Stick: Alphabetic Literacy as Colonial Technology and Postcolonial Appropriation." *American Indian Quarterly* 22, no. 1/2 (1998): 46–62.

Dotson, Kristie. "Tracking Epistemic Violence: Tracking Practices of Silencing." *Hypatia* 26, no. 2 (2011): 236–57.

———. "How Is This Paper Philosophy?" *Comparative Philosophy: An International Journal of Constructive Engagement of Distinct Approaches toward World Philosophy* 3, no. 1 (2012): Article 5.

———. "Conceptualizing Epistemic Oppression." *Social Epistemology* 28, no. 2 (2014): 115–38.

Douglass, Frederick. *Narrative of the Life Frederick Douglass*. Lexington, KY: CreateSpace, 2013.

Dowd, Nancy E. *The Man Question: Male Subordination and Privilege*. New York University Press, 2016.

Du Bois, W. E. B. *The Souls of Black Folk: The Unabridged Classic*. New York: Clydesdale, 2019.

Fahs, Breanne, and Michael Karger. "Women's Studies as Virus: Institutional Feminism, Affect, and the Projection of Danger." *Multidisciplinary Journal of Gender Studies* 5, no. 1 (2016): 929–957.

Falk, Armin, and Johannes Hermle. "Relationship of Gender Differences in Preferences to Economic Development and Gender Equality." *Science* 362, no. 6412 (2018): eaas9899.

Fanon, Frantz, *The Wretched of the Earth*. Translated by Constance Farrington. Harmondsworth: Penguin, 1967.

———. *A Dying Colonialism*. Translated by Haakon Chevalier. Harmondsworth, Middlesex: Penguin Books, 1970.

———. *Black Skin, White Masks*. Translated by Richard Philcox. New York: Penguin Books, 2019.

Farrell, Amy Erdman. *Fat Shame: Stigma and the Fat Body in American Culture*. New York University Press, 2011.

Fawcett, Edmund. *Liberalism: The Life of an Idea*. Princeton, NJ: Princeton University Press, 2015.

Festinger, Leon, Henry W. Riecken, and Stanley Schachter. *When Prophecy Fails: A Social and Psychological Study of a Modern Group That Predicted the Destruction of the World*. New York: Harper Torchbooks, 1956.

Foucault, Michael. *The Archaeology of Knowledge: And the Discourse on Language.* Translated by A. M. Sheridan Smith London: Tavistock, 1972.

———. *Birth of the Clinic: An Archaeology of Medical Perception.* Translated by A. M. Sheridan Smith. London: Tavistock, 1975.

———. "On the Genealogy of Ethics: An Overview of Work in Progress." Afterword to *Michel Foucault: Beyond Structuralism and Hermeneutics*, 2nd ed., by Hubert L. Dreyfus and Paul Rabinow. Chicago: University of Chicago Press, 1983.

———. *The History of Sexuality: Volume 1, an Introduction.* Translated by Robert J. Hurley. New York: Penguin, 1990.

———. *Madness and Civilization: A History of Insanity in the Age of Reason.* Translated by Richard Howard and Jean Kafka. New York: Routledge, 2001.

———. *The Order of Things: An Archaeology of the Human Sciences.* London: Routledge, 2002.

Freeman, Alan David. "Legitimizing Racial Discrimination Through Antidiscrimination Law: A Critical Review of Supreme Court Doctrine." *Minnesota Law Review* 62, no. 1049 (1978): 1049–1119. scholarship.law.umn.edu/mlr/804.

Freeman, Elizabeth. *Time Binds: Queer Temporalities, Queer Histories.* Durham, NC: Duke University Press, 2010.

Fricker, Miranda. *Epistemic Injustice: Power and the Ethics of Knowing.* Oxford: Oxford University Press, 2007.

Friedan, Betty. *The Feminine Mystique.* New York: W. W. Norton & Company, 2013.

Gikandi, Simon "Poststructuralism and Postcolonial Discourse." In *Cambridge Companion to Postcolonial Studies.* Edited by Neil Lazarus. Cambridge: Cambridge University Press, 2004.

Gebrial, Dalia. "Rhodes Must Fall: Oxford and Movements for Change." In *Decolonising the University*, edited by Gurminder K. Bhambra, Dalia Gebrial, and Kerem Nişancıoğlu, 19–36. London: Pluto Press, 2018.

Gillborn, David. "Intersectionality, Critical Race Theory, and the Primacy of Racism." *Qualitative Inquiry* 21, no. 3 (2015): 277–87.

Goodley, Dan. *Dis/ability Studies: Theorising Disablism and Ableism.* New York: Routledge, 2014.

Gopnik, Adam. *A Thousand Small Sanities: the Moral Adventure of Liberalism.* London: Riverrun, 2019.

Gordon, Linda. "'Intersectionality,' Socialist Feminism and Contemporary Activism: Musings by a Second-Wave Socialist Feminist." *Gender & History* 28, no. 2 (2016): 340–57.

Gossett, Thomas F. *Race: The History of an Idea in America.* Oxford: Oxford University Press, 1997.

Gottschall, Jonathan. *Literature, Science and a New Humanities.* New York: Palgrave Macmillan, 2008.

Grasswick, Heidi. "Epistemic Injustice in Science." In *The Routledge Handbook of Epistemic Injustice,* edited by Ian James Kidd, José Medina, and Gaile Pohlhaus, Jr., 313–23. London: Routledge, 2017.

Greer, Germaine. *The Female Eunuch.* London: Fourth Estate, 2012.

Grey, Sandra J. "Activist Academics: What Future?" *Policy Futures in Education* 11, no. 6 (2013): 700–11.

Haidt, Jonathan. *The Righteous Mind: Why Good People Are Divided by Politics and Religion.* New York: Penguin Books, 2013.

Halberstam, Judith. *In a Queer Time and Place: Transgender Bodies, Subcultural Lives.* New York: New York University Press, 2005.

Halperin, David M. *One Hundred Years of Homosexuality: And Other Essays on Greek Love.* London: Routledge, 1990.

———. *Saint Foucault: Towards a Gay Hagiography.* New York: Oxford University Press, 1997.

———. "The Normalization of Queer Theory." *Journal of Homosexuality* 45, no. 2–4 (2003): 339–43.

Hancock, Ange-Marie. *Intersectionality: An Intellectual History.* New York: Oxford University Press, 2016.

Haraway, Donna, "Situated Knowledges: The Science Question in Feminism and the Privilege of Partial Perspective." *Feminist Studies* 14, no. 3 (1988): 575–99.

Harding, Sandra. "Rethinking Standpoint Epistemology: What Is 'Strong Objectivity'?" *Centennial Review* 36, no. 3 (1992): 437–70.

Harding, Sandra. *Whose Science/Whose Knowledge?* Ithica, NY: Cornell University Press, 1991.

———. *The Science Question in Feminism.* Ithaca, NY: Cornell University Press, 1993.

———. *Feminism and Methodology: Social Science Issues.* Bloomington, IN: Indiana University Press, 1996.

———. "Gender, Development, and Post-Enlightenment Philosophies of Science." *Hypatia* 13, no. 3 (1998): 146–67.

Harris, Angela P. "Race and Essentialism in Feminist Legal Theory." *Stanford Law Review* 42, no. 3 (1990): 581–616.

Harvey, David. *The Condition of Postmodernity.* Cambridge, MA: Blackwell, 2000.

Hawking, Stephen, and Leonard Mlodinow. *The Grand Design.* New York: Bantam Books, 2010.

Hegel, Georg W. F. *The Phenomenology of Spirit.* 1807.

Hicks, Stephen R. C. *Explaining Postmodernism: Skepticism and Socialism from Rousseau to Foucault.* Tempe, AZ: Scholargy Publishing, 2004.

Hiraldo, Payne. "The Role of Critical Race Theory in Higher Education." *Vermont Connection* 31, no. 7 (2010): Article 7. scholarworks.uvm.edu/tvc/vol31/iss1/7.

Hirschmann, Nancy J. "Choosing Betrayal." *Perspectives on Politics* 8, no. 1 (2010): 271–78.

hooks, bell. "Postmodern Blackness." In *The Fontana Postmodernism Reader,* edited by Walter Truett Anderson, 113–120. London: Fontana Press, 1996.

———. "Racism and Feminism: The Issue of Accountability." In *Making Sense of Women's Lives: An Introduction to Women's Studies,* edited by Lauri Umansky, Paul K. Longmore, and Michele Plott, 388–411. Lanham, MD: Rowman & Littlefield, 2000.

Horowitz, Mark, Anthony Haynor, and Kenneth Kickham. "Sociology's Sacred Victims and the Politics of Knowledge: Moral Foundations Theory and Disciplinary Controversies." *American Sociologist* 49, no. 4 (2018): 459–95.

Hutcheon, Linda. "'Circling the Downspout of Empire'." In *Past the Last Post: Theorizing Post-Colonialism and Post-Modernism,* edited by Ian Adam and Helen Tiffin, 167–89. London: Harvester/Wheatsheaf, 1991.

Jackson, Stevi. "Why a Materialist Feminism Is (Still) Possible—and Necessary." *Women's Studies International Forum* 24, no. 3–4 (2001): 283–93.

Jagose, Annamarie. *Queer Theory: An Introduction.* New York University Press, 2010.

Jameson, Fredric. *Postmodernism: Or, the Cultural Logic of Late Capitalism.* New York: Verso Books, 2019.

Jolivétte, Andrew. *Research Justice: Methodologies for Social Change.* Bristol, UK: Policy Press, 2015.

Jordan, Winthrop D. *White over Black American Attitudes toward the Negro, 1550–1812.* Chapel Hill, NC: University of North Carolina Press, 2012.

Kid, Ian James, José Medina, and Gaile Polhaus. "Introduction." In *The Rout-ledge Handbook of Epistemic Injustice*, edited by Ian James Kid, José Medina, and Gaile Pohlhaus, Jr., 1–9. London: Routledge, 2017.

Kimmel, Michael S. *The Politics of Manhood: Profeminist Men Respond to the Mythopoetic Men's Movement (and the Mythopoetic Leaders Answer)*. Philadelphia: Temple University Press, 1995.

Kramer, Caroline K., Bernard Zinman, and Ravi Retnakaran. "Are Metaboli-cally Healthy Overweight and Obesity Benign Conditions?: A Systematic Review and Meta-analysis." *Annals of Internal Medicine* 159, no. 11 (December 3, 2013). annals.org/aim/article-abstract/1784291/metabolically-healthy-overweight-obesity-benign-conditions-systematic-review-meta-ana lysis?doi=10.7326/0003-4819-159-11-201312030-00008.

Koehler, Daniel. "Violence and Terrorism from the Far-Right: Policy Options to Counter an Elusive Threat." *Terrorism and Counter-Terrorism Studies* (February 2019). doi.org/10.19165/2019.2.02.

Kupers, Terry A. "Toxic Masculinity as a Barrier to Mental Health Treatment in Prison." *Journal of Clinical Psychology* 61, no. 6 (2005): 713–24.

Kvale, Steinar, "Themes of Postmodernity." In *The Fontana Postmodernism Reader*, edited by Walter Truett Anderson, 18–25. London: Fontana Press, 1996.

Landén, Mikael, and Sune Innala. "The Effect of a Biological Explanation on Attitudes towards Homosexual Persons. A Swedish National Sample Study." *Nordic Journal of Psychiatry* 56, no. 3 (2002): 181–86.

Langton, Rae. "Epistemic Injustice: Power and the Ethics of Knowing by Miranda Fricker." Book review. *Hypatia* 25, no. 2 (2010): 459–464.

Lauretis, Teresa De. *Queer Theory: Lesbian and Gay Sexualities*. Providence, RI: Brown University Press, 1991.

LeBesco, Kathleen. "Prescription for Harm: Diet Industry Influence, Public Health Policy, and the 'Obesity Epidemic'." In *The Fat Studies Reader*, edited by Esther D. Rothblum and Sondra Solovay, 65–74. New York: New York University Press, 2009.

Lind, Rebecca Ann. "A Note From the Guest Editor." *Journal of Broadcasting & Electronic Media* 54 (2010): 3–5.

Lorber, Judith. "Shifting Paradigms and Challenging Categories." *Social Problems* 53, no. 4 (2006): 448–53.

Lorde, Audre. *Sister Outsider: Essays and Speeches*. Berkeley, CA: Crossing Press, 2007.

Lukianoff, Greg and Jonathan Haidt. *The Coddling of the American Mind: How Good Intentions and Bad Ideas Are Setting Up a Generation for Failure*. New York: Penguin Books, 2019.

Lyotard, Jean François. *The Postmodern Condition: A Report on Knowledge*. Manchester: Manchester UP, 1991.

Maldonado-Torres, Nelson, Rafael Vizcaíno, Jasmine Wallace, and Jeong Eun Annabel. "Decolonizing Philosophy." In *Decolonising the University*, edited by Gurminder K. Bhambra, Dalia Gebrial, and Kerem Nişancıoğlu. 64–89. London: Pluto Press, 2018.

Manne, Kate. *Down Girl: The Logic of Misogyny*. New York: Oxford University Press, 2018.

McLeod, John, ed. *The Routledge Companion to Postcolonial Studies*. London: Routledge, 2007.

McHale, Brian. *The Cambridge Introduction to Postmodernism*. Cambridge: Cambridge University Press, 2015.

McIntosh, Peggy. *On Privilege, Fraudulence, and Teaching As Learning: Selected Essays 1981–2019*. New York: Taylor & Francis, 2019.

McRuer, Robert, and Michael Bérubé. *Crip Theory: Cultural Signs of Queerness and Disability*. New York University Press, 2006.

Medina, José. *The Epistemology of Resistance: Gender and Racial Oppression, Epistemic Injustice, and Resistant Imaginations*. New York: Oxford University Press, 2013.

———. "Varieties of Hermeneutical Injustice." In *The Routledge Handbook of Epistemic Injustice*, edited by Ian James Kidd, José Medina, and Gaile Pohlhaus, Jr., 41–52. London: Routledge, 2017.

Mill, John Stuart. *On Liberty and Other Essays*. Oxford: Oxford University Press, 1998.

Millett, Kate, Catharine A. MacKinnon, and Rebecca Mead. *Sexual Politics*. New York: Columbia University Press, 2016.

Mills, Charles. "Ideology." In *The Routledge Handbook of Epistemic Injustice*, edited by Ian James Kidd, José Medina, and Gaile Pohlhaus, Jr., 100–11. London: Routledge, 2017.

Mitchell, Allyson. "Sedentary Lifestyle: Fat Queer Craft." *Fat Studies* 7, no. 2 (2017): 147–58.

Morton, Stephen. "Poststructuralist Formulations." In *The Routledge Companion to Postcolonial Studies*, edited by John McCleod, 161–72. London: Routledge, 2007.

Mutua, Kagendo, and Beth Blue Swadener. *Decolonizing Research in Cross-cultural Contexts: Critical Personal Narratives*. Albany, NY: SUNY Press, 2011.

Nanda, Meera. "We Are All Hybrids Now: The Dangerous Epistemology of Post-colonial Populism." *Journal of Peasant Studies* 28, no. 2 (2001): 162–86.

Neill, Michael. "'Mulattos,' 'Blacks,' and 'Indian Moors': Othello and Early Modern Constructions of Human Difference." *Shakespeare Quarterly* 49, no. 4 (1998): 361–374.

Norwood, Carolette R. "Decolonizing My Hair, Unshackling My Curls: An Autoethnography on What Makes My Natural Hair Journey a Black Feminist Statement." *International Feminist Journal of Politics* 20, no. 1 (2017): 69–84.

Oliver, Michael, Bob Sapey, and Pam Thomas. *Social Work with Disabled People.* Basingstoke: Palgrave Macmillan, 2012.

Ortner, Sherry B. "Is Female to Male as Nature Is to Culture?" In *Woman, Culture, and Society,* edited by Michelle Zimbalist Rosaldo and Louise Lamphere, 67–88. Palo Alto, CA: Stanford University Press, 1974.

Perna, Laura W. *Taking It to the Streets: The Role of Scholarship in Advocacy and Advocacy in Scholarship.* Baltimore: Johns Hopkins University Press, 2018.

Pilcher, Jane, and Imelda Whelehan. *Key Concepts in Gender Studies.* Los Angeles: Sage, 2017.

Pinker, Steven. *The Blank Slate: The Modern Denial of Human Nature.* London: Penguin, 2002.

———. *The Better Angels of Our Nature: The Decline of Violence in History and Its Causes.* London: Allen Lane, 2011.

———. *Enlightenment Now. The Case for Reason, Science, Humanism and Progress.* Penguin Books, 2019.

Poovey, Mary. "Feminism and Deconstruction." *Feminist Studies* 14, no. 1 (1988): 51–65.

Rauch, Jonathan. *Kindly Inquisitors The New Attacks on Free Thought.* Chicago: University of Chicago Press, 2014.

Rawls, John. *A Theory of Justice.* Oxford: Oxford University Press, 1999.

Rich, Adrienne. *Compulsory Heterosexuality and Lesbian Existence.* Denver, CO: Antelope Publications, 1982.

Riley, Donna. *Engineering and Social Justice.* San Rafael, CA: Morgan & Claypool Publishers, 2008.

Roberson, Lara L., et al. "Beyond BMI: The 'Metabolically Healthy Obese' Phenotype and Its Association with Clinical/Subclinical Cardiovascular Disease and All-Cause Mortality—A Systematic Review." *BMC Public Health* 14, no. 1 (2014): Article 14.

Rorty, Richard. *Philosophy and the Mirror of Nature.* Princeton, NJ: Princeton University Press, 1979.

———. *Contingency, Irony, and Solidarity*. Cambridge: Cambridge University Press, 2009.

Rothblum, Esther D., and Sondra Solovay, eds. *The Fat Studies Reader*. New York Unviersity Press, 2009.

Rubin, Gayle. "Thinking Sex: Notes for a Radical Theory of the Politics of Sexuality." In *The Lesbian and Gay Studies Reader*, edited by Henry Abelove, Michèle Aina Barale, and David M. Halperin, 3–44. Abingdon: Taylor & Frencis, 1993.

Said, Edward. *Orientalism*. London: Penguin, 2003.

Scuro, Jennifer. *Addressing Ableism: Philosophical Questions via Disability Studies*. Lanham, MD: Lexington Books, 2019.

Seidman, Steven. *The Postmodern Turn: New Perspectives on Social Theory*. Cambridge: Cambridge University Press, 1998.

Sedgwick, Eve Kosofsky. *Epistemology of the Closet*. Berkeley, CA: University of California Press, 2008.

Shapiro, Joseph P. *No Pity: People with Disabilities Forging a New Civil Rights Movement*. New York: Times Books, 1994.

Shotwell, Alexis. "Forms of Knowing and Epistemic Resources." In *The Routledge Handbook of Epistemic Injustice*, edited by Ian James Kidd, José Medina, and Gaile Pohlhaus, Jr., 79–88. London: Routledge, 2017.

Sleeter, Christine E. "Critical Race Theory and Education." In *Encyclopedia of Diversity in Education*, edited by James A. Banks, 491–95. Thousand Oaks, CA: SAGE, 2012.

Smith, Linda Tuhiwai. *Decolonizing Methodologies: Research and Indigenous Peoples*. London: Zed Books, 1999.

Sokal, Alan, and Jean Bricmont. *Fashionable Nonsense: Postmodern Intellectuals Abuse of Science*. New York: St. Martin's Press, 1999.

Soueif, Ahdaf. "The Function of Narrative in the War on Terror." In *War on Terror*, edited by Chris Miller, 28–42. Manchester: Manchester University Press, 2009.

Spivak, Gayatri Chakravorty. "Can the Subaltern Speak?" In *Marxism and the Interpretation of Culture*, edited by Cary Nelson and Lawrence Grossberg, 271–313. Chicago: University of Illinois Press, 1988.

———. "Subaltern Studies: Deconstructing Historiography." In *Selected Subaltern Studies*, edited by Ranajit Guha and Gayatri Chakravorty Spivak, 3–32. New York: Oxford University Press, 1988.

Stern, Mark, and Khuram Hussain. "On the Charter Question: Black Marxism and Black Nationalism." *Race Ethnicity and Education* 18, no. 1 (2014): 61–88.

Toth, Lucille. "Praising Twerk: Why Aren't We All Shaking Our Butt?" *French Cultural Studies* 28, no. 3 (2017): 291–302.

Tovar, Virgie. *You Have the Right to Remain Fat.* New York: Feminist Press, 2018.

Truth, Sojourner. "The Narrative of Sojourner Truth." In *A Celebration of Women Writers*, edited by Olive Gilbert. www.digital.library.upenn.edu/women/truth/1850/1850.html.

Tuana, Nancy. "Feminist Epistemology: The Subject of Knowledge." In *The Routledge Handbook of Epistemic Injustice*, edited by Ian James Kidd, José Medina, and Gaile Pohlhaus, Jr., 125–138. London: Routledge, 2017.

Wanderer, Jeremy. "Varieties of Testimonial Injustice." In *The Routledge Handbook of Epistemic Injustice*, edited by Ian James Kidd, José Medina, and Gaile Pohlhaus, Jr., 27–40. London: Routledge, 2017.

Wann, Marilyn. "Foreword." In *The Fat Studies Reader*, edited by Esther D. Rothblum and Sondra Solovay. New York: New York University Press, 2009.

West, Candace, and Sarah Fenstermaker. "Doing Difference." *Gender and Society* 9, no. 1 (1995): 8–37.

West, Candace, and Don H. Zimmerman. "Doing Gender." *Gender and Society* 1, no. 2 (1987): 125–51.

Williams, Patricia J. *The Alchemy of Race and Rights.* Cambridge, MA: Harvard University Press, 1991.

Wilson. E. O. "From Sociobiology to Sociology." In *Evolution, Literature, and Film: A Reader*, edited by in Brian Boyd, Joseph Carroll, and Jonathan Gottschall, 135–143. New York: Columbia University Press, 2010.

Wolf, Allison B. "'Tell Me How That Makes You Feel': Philosophys Reason/Emotion Divide and Epistemic Pushback in Philosophy Classrooms." *Hypatia* 32, no. 4 (2017): 893–910. doi.org/10.1111/hypa.12378.

INDEX

ABOUT THE AUTHORS

Helen Pluckrose is a liberal political and cultural writer and speaker. She is the editor of *Areo Magazine* and the author of many popular essays on postmodernism, critical theory, liberalism, secularism, and feminism. A participant in the Grievance Studies Affair probe, which highlighted problems in social justice scholarship, she is today an exile from the humanities, where she researched late medieval and early modern religious writing by and for women. She lives in England and can be found on Twitter @HPluckrose.

James Lindsay is a mathematician with a background in physics and founder of New Discourses (newdiscourses.com). He is interested in the psychology of religion, authoritarianism, and extremism. His books include *Everybody Is Wrong about God*, *Life in Light of Death*, and *How to Have Impossible Conversations*. His essays have appeared in the *Wall Street Journal*, *Los Angeles Times*, *Philosophers' Magazine*, *Scientific American*, and *Time*. He led the Grievance Studies Affair probe that made international headlines in 2018, including the front page of the *New York Times*. He lives in Tennessee and can be found on Twitter @ConceptualJames.